Kenneth Burns

Strengthening the Retention of Child Protection Workers

Career Preferences, Exchange Relationships and Employment Mobility

EHV)

Kenneth Burns

Strengthening the Retention of Child Protection Workers

Studies in Comparative Social Pedagogies and International Social Work and Social Policy, Vol. XXIII

EHV)

www.eh-verlag.de

Burns, Kenneth

Strengthening the Retention of Child Protection Workers
Career Preferences, Exchange Relationships and Employment Mobility

Studies in Comparative Social Pedagogies and International Social Work and Social Policy, Vol. XXIII

Editor of the series: Peter Herrmann

www.socialcomparison.org

1. Edition 2012
ISBN: 978-3-86741-829-4
© Europäischer Hochschulverlag GmbH & Co. KG, Bremen, 2012.
www.eh-verlag.de

EHV)

For
Ella and Leah

Notes

The genesis for this text is a PhD completed at the School of Applied Social Studies, University College Cork, Ireland. This text is a somewhat revised version of that document. Professor Alastair Christie was the academic supervisor for the research study.

Parts of this text were previously published in revised formats in the following publications:

Burns, K. (2012) "Moving beyond 'case-management' supervision: Social workers' perspectives on professional supervision in child protection", in Lynch, D. and Burns, K. (eds.), *Children's Rights and Child Protection: Critical Times, Critical Issues in Ireland*, Manchester, Manchester University Press.

Burns, K., & MacCarthy, J. (2012). "An impossible task? Implementing the recommendations of child abuse inquiry reports in a context of high workloads in child protection and welfare". *Irish Journal of Applied Social Studies, 12* (1), 4-17.

Burns, K. (2011) "'Career preference', 'transients' and 'convert': A study of social workers' retention in child protection and welfare", *British Journal of Social Work*, 41, pp. 520-538.

Lynch, D. and Burns, K. (2008) "Contexts, themes and future directions in Irish child protection and welfare social work", in Burns, K. and Lynch, D. (eds.), *Child Protection and Welfare Social Work: Contemporary Themes and Practice Perspectives*, Dublin, A. & A. Farmar.

Burns, K. (2008) "Making a difference: Exploring job retention issues in child protection and welfare social work", in Burns, K. and Lynch, D. (eds.), *Child Protection and Welfare Social Work: Contemporary Themes and Practice Perspectives*, Dublin, A. & A. Farmar.

Table of Contents

Chapter 3
Researching social workers' decisions to stay or leave child protection and welfare

List of Tables

List of Figures

Chapter 1
When are you leaving? Retaining social workers in statutory child protection and welfare in the Republic of Ireland

1.1 Introduction

Both nationally and internationally, retaining social workers in statutory child protection and welfare work has been identified as a problem. In Ireland, the present Minister for Children and Youth Affairs has commented on this issue (RTÉ, 2008a, b), it has been frequently raised in Dáil Éireann debates (see, for example, Houses of the Oireachtas, 1996, 2003a, 2008), policy and government reports have identified it as a concern (see, for example, Social Services Inspectorate, 2003; Ombudsman for Children, 2006b). In addition, an Irish child abuse inquiry implicated it as a factor in one Health Board's failure to protect a child at risk (McGuinness, 1993), critical commentaries in Irish social work periodicals have raised it as a matter for the profession to address(McGrath, 2001) and service users have reported that it impacts upon the quality of services they receive (Ombudsman for Children, 2006a; Buckley et al., 2008). However, there is no research that examines the factors influencing child protection and welfare social workers' retention in the Republic of Ireland[1].

The international literature also reports similar concerns to the Irish experience, with reports of problems retaining workers in child protection and welfare in other countries including the United Kingdom, Sweden, the United States of America, Australia and Canada (Gibbs, 2001; Audit Commission, 2002; Mor Barak et al., 2006; Stalker et al., 2007b; Tham, 2007; Lee et al., 2011). This book examines this issue in the context of the Health Service Executive (HSE), which is the major employer of social workers engaged in child protection and welfare work in Ireland.

As early as 1980, an unpublished report by Inbucon Management Consultants (cited in Skehill, 2004), which examined the operation of the Community Care system, recorded a high turnover rate for social work staff. Unfortunately, the HSE has no data on staff turnover and employment movements in child protection and welfare for any period[2].

---

[1] Hereafter, Ireland will be used to denote the 26 counties of the Republic of Ireland.

[2] The HSE human resource department directed me to the NSWQB (2000, 2002,

1

This is particularly interesting as retaining child protection and welfare social workers was identified as a labour force planning issue by a senior HSE manager with overall responsibility for child and family services (RTÉ, 2006) and by the Minister for Children and Youth Affairs. A report undertaken by the Social Service Inspectorate (2003) into the implementation of *Children First: National Guidelines for the Protection and Welfare of Children* guidelines (Department of Health and Children, 1999) indicated that Health Boards (HSEs) were having difficulties with the recruitment and retention of social workers in child protection and welfare. Barry Andrews, Minister for Children and Youth Affairs, in a debate with Alan Shatter TD on RTÉ's *Prime Time* current affairs television programme regarding the statutory child protection and welfare system in Ireland, acknowledged that:

> ... social workers work very hard under sometimes very challenging and difficult situations ... huge benefit would derive from trying to improve morale for social workers ... one of the aspects is that you have a huge turnover of staff (RTÉ, 2008b).

Over three decades after the Inbucon report first highlighted high staff turnover in child protection and welfare, retaining social workers appears to continue to be problematic for employers and the social work profession. Furthermore, Minister Andrews clearly links the retention of social workers to low morale of staff which is likely to impact on the quality of child protection and welfare services. In a report by the Ombudsman for Children in Ireland, service users were critical of a lack of adequate and appropriate services post-disclosure [of child abuse], and social workers' turnover was explicitly linked with problems with service quality in this area:

> Many complainants referred to difficulties encountered with regard to the turnover of social workers. Children and families felt the onus was placed on them to rebuild an understanding of the case with each new social worker assigned to the case (Ombudsman for Children, 2006a, p. 11).

During my period of employment in child protection and welfare, I recognised how the work negatively affected some of my colleagues and a number of them ended up leaving child protection and welfare social work prematurely or taking extended sick leave periods to recover emotionally and physically from stress and demands of the work. Others

---

2006) labour force studies for data on turnover in social work.

seemed to deal with the challenging nature of child protection and welfare social work by passing through on their way to some other social work practice context. On the positive side, there were also colleagues who thrived in child protection and welfare and wanted to stay; they enjoyed amongst other factors the variety of the work and its challenges, they experienced a good degree of autonomy in their work, they liked the fast pace of child protection and welfare social work, and working with children. A quotation from Roisin, one of the social workers that participated in the study, highlights both the positive and negative elements as follows:

> I did some time in there [child protection and welfare] and I have seen maybe both sides of it, people who were under enormous pressure in there and then I have seen people who have got on really well and are still in it years later and wouldn't work in…you know, wouldn't work anywhere else (Roisin).

While the above reports and commentaries (for example, McGrath, 2001; Social Services Inspectorate, 2003; RTÉ, 2008a) state that turnover is problematic, they do not provide data on the extent of the issue, explore why they thought it was an issue, or consider the implications beyond the recruitment of replacement staff. It is the contention of this book that high employee turnover rates in this type of work should be of concern to policy makers, employers, the general community and the social work profession, as it may have negative implications for potential service users, current service users, social workers, the social work profession and the wider community. Service users are affected by a loss of continuity of workers through repeatedly working with new and sometimes inexperienced newly-qualified graduates who are learning the job, all of which fundamentally impacts upon the important work of relationship and trust-building in effective social work practice (Thompson, 2002; Buckley, 2008). Turnover in staff results in the organisation losing skills and expertise, which can affect the quality of service, replacing staff can be costly, and retention issues can affect the atmosphere in teams. Individual social workers who leave face a disruption in social networks, stress associated with deciding whether leaving is the right choice, and transition adjustments affect both those who leave and those who stay (Holtom et al., 2006).

The development of Irish child protection and welfare systems, policies and practices and its impact on the lives of children and families has received significant attention from Government and researchers (see, for example, Government of Ireland, 1970; Buckley et al., 1997; Ferguson and O'Reilly, 2001; Office of the Minister for Children, 2006; Oireachtas, 2006). Research that specifically focuses on child protection and welfare employees has received less attention, and in particular, there is an absence of research that examines how their professional experiences in child protection and welfare influences their decisions to stay or leave.

My professional experience in child protection and welfare and subsequent decision to leave this work, conversations with social work educators, practitioners and past students about their experiences of this work, and the realisation that there was a significant gap in research on this topic, led me to explore this issue for this study. The initial aims and objectives of the study were:

- to establish a turnover rate for child protection and welfare social workers in one Health Service Executive area;

- to establish social workers' views on retention and turnover in child protection and welfare, and to explore whether social workers wanted to stay in or leave this work;

- to identify the factors influencing social workers' decisions to stay or leave this work;

- to develop recommendations from the findings for policy, practice and social work education to reduce the impact of this work on social workers' health and welfare, to improve the quality of their experience of working as a social worker in this practice context, and to potentially reduce the turnover of social workers.

A set of research questions grew out of these initial aims, and were refined during the literature review and research design phase, and are presented in Chapter Four. The kind of questions I was interested in asking are set within the qualitative research tradition. The study seeks to explain how social workers understand, interpret and construct their experiences of working in child protection and welfare and how these constructions, and the meanings which they ascribe to these experiences, shape their decisions to stay in or leave their work. The epistemological orientation of the study is broadly interpretivist, which Bryman (1999, p. 264) defines as 'an understanding of the social world through an interpretation of that world by its participants'. The ontological orientation of the study is constructivist 'which implies that social properties are outcomes of the interactions between individuals, rather than phenomena 'out there' and separate from those involved in its construction' (p. 266). The study's research methodology is examined in greater depth in Chapter Four.

This introductory chapter sets the background for the study by addressing three contextual topics. First, the organisational context in which social work services are delivered in Ireland is described; I identify the location of child protection and welfare social work services within the Health Service Executive, and I present an overview of the research setting in which this study was undertaken. Second, I place the discussion of child protection and welfare work in a wider context of the changing nature of work in contemporary Irish society. Third, I explore the social and political practice context of child protection and welfare in Ireland. The chapter concludes with an outline of the chapters in this book and some of the potential limitations of this study.

1.2 Setting the context

1.2.1 The Health Service Executive

The Health Service Executive (HSE) coordinates the provision of personal, health and social services in Ireland. The HSE was established on 1st January 2005, replacing the existing 11 Health Boards, most of which were established under Section 4 of the Health Act 1970. It employs 100,000 staff making it the largest employer in the state, and had a current operating budget of €12 billion (Health Service Executive, 2008b). The HSE is divided into 4 administrative areas (see figure 1.1): HSE South, HSE West, HSE Dublin Mid-Leinster, and the HSE Dublin North East:

Figure 1.1: Map of HSE administrative areas and local health offices (Health Service Executive, 2008c):

The organisational structure of the HSE is divided into three sections: health and personal social services, support services, and reform and innovation. Health and personal social services is further sub-divided into three 'service delivery units' which are: population health; the national hospitals office (NHO), and primary, community and continuing care (PCCC) (Health Service Executive, 2007a). PCCC services include: 'primary care, mental health, disability, children, youth and families, community hospital, continuing care services and social inclusion services' (Health Service Executive, 2007a, p. 19). Child protection and welfare social work teams are part of the PCCC services and there are 32 Local Health Offices (LHOs) in the PCCC services. Each LHO has a child protection and welfare social work team[3]. The research for this book was undertaken in five of the ten child protection and welfare social work teams based in the LHO areas of the Health Service Executive 'Area A'. The physical size of the combined five LHO areas that are the focus of this study is 4,727 square kilometres. The breakdown of the size of each LHO in square miles is provided in table 1.1:

Table 1.1: Area of five LHO's in square miles

	Total	Team 1	Team 2	Team 3	Team 4	Team 5
Area in Sq Miles	4,727	663.17	879.77	985.62	390.46	1,828

Source: (Health Service Executive, 2003).

Figure 1.2 helps to clarify this somewhat complex organisational structure[4]:

---

[3] A list of all 32 child protection and welfare teams can be found in *Parents Who Listen, Protect* (Health Service Executive, 2007b).

[4] This organisational chart is based on a HSE document called *An Introduction to the HSE*(Health Service Executive, 2007a). Other units such as Reform and Innovation, Support Services and the Office of the CEO, are excluded for the purposes of clarity and can be found in the *Corporate Safety Statement – October 2006* (Health Service Executive, 2006a).

Figure 1.2: HSE organisational structure and the 'location' of child protection and welfare teams

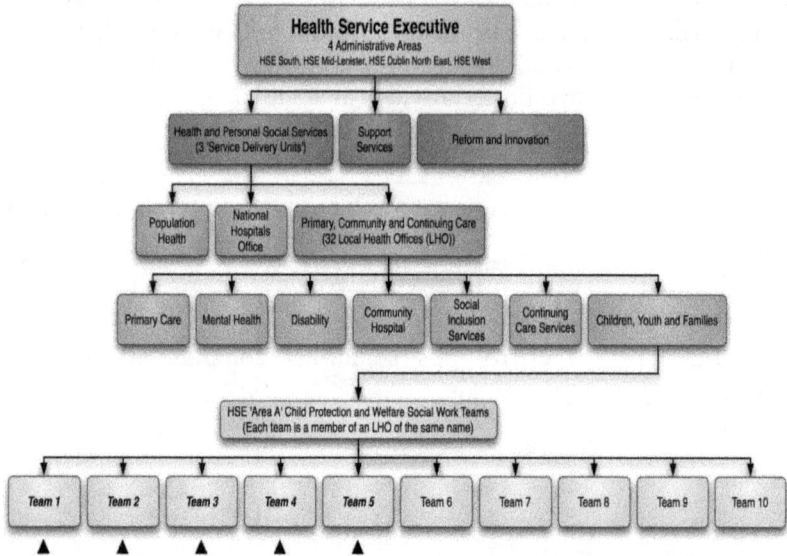

The present location of child protection teams within the HSE has been much criticised (Burns and Lynch, 2012), and at the time of writing, the Minister for Children and Youth Affairs announced that child protection and welfare teams and other ancillary children's services, by 2013, would be removed from the HSE and established in a new body called the Child and Family Support Services Agency with its own dedicated line management and budget.

At the time of the data collection for this study, nearly 15% (147,943) of all children aged 17 and under in Ireland lived in the two counties served by these five teams[5](Health Service Executive, 2008a). The five community care teams that are the focus of this study employ 140[6] staff in direct service provision[7], the vast majority of which are social workers

---

5   Total children aged 17 and under living in Ireland = 1,013,031.

6   Figure does not include administrators. See table 3.1 in Chapter Three for comprehensive breakdown of 140 posts by grade and profession.

7   'Direct service provision' staff refers to staff who provide care, assessment, therapeutic and intervention services to children and families in child protection and welfare the majority of which are social workers and senior social work practitioners. This term is used in preference to 'front-line' staff, which is the more commonly used term in the literature (see, for example, Office of the

(104). A comprehensive breakdown of staffing levels and the demographic background of social workers is provided in the methodology chapter.

Since the establishment of the HSE in 2005, the organisation undertook a radical reorganisation and restructuring, a process which was scheduled to be completed by 2010 (Health Service Executive, 2006b). However, reform appeared to be perpetual and there was growing dissatisfaction amongst the public, staff and politicians with the organisation. The government now plans to dismantle the HSE and replace it with new smaller directorates. The ever-changing HSE organisational structure has caused considerable confusion for staff. In conversations with social work managers they explained that many of the decision-making responsibilities that had been devolved locally under the Health Board structures, were recentralised. In addition to a focus on the reorganisation of health and personal social services in Ireland, there has also been a focus on the growing centrality of work in Irish society and the relationship between work and employees' health and welfare.

1.2.2 Work in contemporary Irish society

There has been a significant research and public debate on the changing nature of work in society. A range of factors, including work-related stress, changing patterns of employment, increased job insecurity, labour market flexibility, the globalisation of economies, growing diversity of employees[8], and the use of information and communication technologies, are reshaping the workplace and redrawing traditional boundaries between work and the private sphere (Beck, 2000; Stiglitz, 2003; European Foundation for the Improvement of Living and Working Conditions, 2005). In contemporary western societies, work has become one of the key measures of human activities and one's contribution to society is measured primarily in economic terms. This theme was reflected in public consultation fora on the Irish 'family', wherein one participant asked: 'When was the last time we heard the Government refer to Ireland as a society and not an economy – Ireland Inc.?' (Daly, 2004, p. 56).

The above transformations have led to discernible changes in our relationship with work and a renewed critical reflection upon the influence of work environments on key 'quality of life' indicators for

---

Minister for Children, 2007).

[8] Increased participation by women and older age adults, plus labour migration.

workers. The *Fourth European Survey on Working Conditions 2005* (Parent-Thirion *et al.*, 2007), undertaken in 31 countries[9], found that fatigue and stress were the second and third most common work-related health problems after back-ache and muscular pains.

Economic theory proposed that material affluence would result in higher satisfaction levels and well-being (Karasek and Theorell, 1990). At the time of the study, Ireland was the second wealthiest country in the Organisation for Economic Co-operation and Development (OECD), yet there is significant evidence to show that we are no happier than when we were less well-off (Oswald, 2002). Job-insecurity is increasing in some western industrialised democracies, particularly the USA (Blanchflower and Oswald, 1999) and the increase in job insecurity and the deterioration of working conditions is also evident in some employment sectors in Ireland[10]. 'Work stress', 'burnout' and 'work-life balance' have become prominent in public and political debates. Workers in Ireland are reporting increasing levels of stress (O'Connell *et al.*, 2004), they are increasingly time-poor when it comes to leisure and quality time with family and friends, and more explicit links are now being made between physical and mental health 'problems' and workplace environments (Davies, 1998; European Foundation for the Improvement of Living and Working Conditions, 2005).

The rapid period of economic growth in Ireland since the end of the 1990s, commonly referred to as the *Celtic Tiger,* heralded an increase in labour force participation and resulted in Ireland moving up the *United Nations Development Programme* ranking of the richest countries in the world. In the *Human Development Report*(United Nations Development Programme, 2005), using Gross Domestic Product (GDP) as a measure of wealth, Ireland moved to second in a list of the world's wealthiest nations[11]. However, the global economic crisis hit Ireland particularly hard and Ireland lost its fiscal sovereignty to the troika (EU, ECB and IMF) in return for a financial bailout of €67 billion. This development

---

[9] EU 25 countries plus Bulgaria, Croatia, Norway, Romania, Turkey and Switzerland.

[10] See Begg (2005) for a case study on the *Irish Ferries* labour 'displacement' policy.

[11] It has been argued that Ireland's GDP figure should be regarded with care due to the amount of multi-national companies trading in Ireland. Gross National Product (GNP) or Gross National Income (GNI) would be a better measure of actual wealth, as it differentiates income from foreign investments and excludes repatriated profits and income (OECD Observer, 2005).

resulted from the collapse of Irish banks due to property speculation and the worldwide economic recession. Ireland's unemployment rate rose to 14% in 2012.

Prior to the *Celtic Tiger* period, an international study on well-being, insecurity and job satisfaction found that Ireland had one of the highest levels of job satisfaction, despite being 'one of poorest countries in our sample' (Blanchflower and Oswald, 1999, p. 9). This finding is consistent with a subsequent piece of research on Irish workers' experience (O'Connell *et al.*, 2004) of the changing workplace undertaken by the *Economic and Social Research Institute*, towards the height of the *Celtic Tiger* period of economic development. This study examined the determinants of job satisfaction and work stress, work attitudes and experiences, and workplace practices, along with a number of other indicators that provided information on employees' views and experiences. This study found that while 90% of Irish workers were happy with their job, 47% of the workers in the study found work stressful, 44% said that they come home from work exhausted and 36% were too tired to enjoy home life after work. These findings are not only relevant to workers' experiences of the changing workplace, but are also relevant to their opportunities and engagement with family, friends and civil society. Economic imperatives such as capital accumulation, productivity and international competitiveness appear to be the primary consideration for employers, whereas the needs and conditions of workers are secondary. This is despite international evidence that improved working conditions 'enhance worker productivity, and lower overall costs – or at least do not raise costs very much' (Stiglitz, 2003, p. 69). The social and political factors that shape the practice context and working conditions of social workers in child protection and welfare are examined in the next section.

1.2.3 The social and political practice context of child protection and welfare in Ireland

In 2005[12], the four Health Service Executive's (HSE) received 21,783 new reports under the categories of 'child abuse' and 'child welfare' and were looking after over 5,200 children in care (Health Service Executive, 2008a, d, e, f). 21 years earlier, only 479 reports were received by the Health Boards, representing a 45-fold increase in reports received in the intervening period. The extraordinary increase in the number of children

---

[12] Most up-to-date published statistical datasets.

11

and families coming to the attention of the HSE and the subsequent growth of child protection and welfare services are the result of Irish society's changing knowledge, values and attitudes towards children's welfare, primarily stimulated by a series of child abuse inquires and scandals in the 1990s (see, for example, McGuinness, 1993; Moore, 1995; Department of Health, 1996; Western Health Board, 1996).

The recommendations of the *Kilkenny Incest Investigation* (McGuinness, 1993), in particular, shaped the development of the Irish child protection system and public awareness and attitudes towards child (sexual) abuse (Ferguson, 2004). The impetus to reform what were considered antiquated child care policies and legislation, and an underdeveloped child protection system, came from criticisms contained in child abuse inquiry reports (Ferguson, 2004), media pressure (see, for example, Raferty and O'Sullivan, 1999, 'States of Fear' documentary), professional representative bodies such as the *Irish Association of Social Workers* (Kearney and Skehill, 2005)and international reports (Committee on the Rights of the Child, 1998, 2006). A comprehensive examination of the historical development and functioning of the Irish child protection system is beyond the scope of this review and has been addressed in detail elsewhere (see, for example, Ferguson and O'Reilly, 2001; Buckley, 2002; Skehill, 2004).

The previously politically neglected area of child care and child protection received considerable investment and attention with the publication and enactment of an extensive range of policy documents and legislation, procedures, and the expansion of services and bureaucratic structures. These changes co-occurred with a crisis in public confidence in the Catholic Church as a result of child sexual abuse by priests (see, for example, The Ferns Report, Murphy *et al.*, 2005). Public and media reactions to these scandals resulted in a loosening of the bonds between Church and State and contributed to the dissolution of the 'subsidiarity' principle as a guiding standard underpinning public policy with children and families (Richardson, 2004). Employment in statutory child protection and welfare increased to deal with the widening scope of responsibilities and the ever-increasing number of children at risk being identified. 'Child and family (statutory)' continues to be the largest area of social work employment in Ireland with 33 per cent of all posts[13](National Social Work Qualifications Board, 2006) and social

---

[13] In 2005, 'Child and Family (Statutory)' as an area of social work practice comprised 737.9 posts out of a total of 2237 social work posts in the Republic of

12

work continues to occupy the central role in the Irish child protection system (Skehill, 1999).

Buckley (2002) argues that the growth of the child protection and welfare system led to a more defensive and narrow type of social work practice, with less emphasis on preventative/therapeutic work and a 'naive optimism' that the application of rational measures could alleviate childhood adversity. This decreased focus on preventative/therapeutic work, together with an increased focus on legal mandates to intervene in families and an ever increasing amount of policy guidelines, is referred to as the 'bureaucratisation of social work' (Howe, 1992; Lawrence, 2004). This bureaucratisation of social work, where social work 'retreats' from 'front-line' practice with a defensive and narrow practice focus situated deep within a large bureaucracy, leads to less 'face-to-face' time with service users. Jordan and Jordan (2000, p. 8) argue that in the United Kingdom an instrumental and technical rationality guide social work assessments and planning, where social work practice in the public sector has become 'legalistic, formal, procedural and [at] arm's length'. They further argue that the human engagement aspect of practice, which is a core of social work practice, is becoming less prevalent as the 'face-to-face' work is contracted out to other organisations. Social workers often perceive that their skills and abilities are under-utilised and that social work practice within their organisation has a primarily investigative, defensive and abuse orientation. The Victoria Climbié inquiry report in the United Kingdom noted a concern at social workers' diminished levels of direct face-to-face contact and home visits, which, they argued, are of seminal importance in the identification and protection of children at risk (Lord Laming, 2003). The focus on investigative and adversarial functions over more preventative/therapeutic 'helping' roles, which are usually associated with social workers' motivations for entering the field, are linked in the research with burnout and turnover (Stalker *et al.*, 2007a). Similar arguments can be made for the way child protection and welfare social work has developed in Ireland.

Ireland (33%). In related areas of work with children and families in the statutory sector, there were 178.2 posts in Fostering (8%) and 90.2 posts in Adoption (4%). There were 13 posts in 'Child and Family Work (Non-statutory). Skehill (2004) quoting from the unpublished *Manpower Report on Social Work* noted that in 1980 there were 242 social work posts in the Health Boards, most of which were within the community care programme. This represented 35% of all filled social work posts (800 posts total, with 100 vacant posts).

The reform of the child protection system in Ireland has led to a fundamental reorganisation of the State's relationship with 'the family' and a prominent statutory role for social work in the identification, assessment and management of child abuse (Skehill, 1999; Ferguson and O'Reilly, 2001; Buckley, 2002). While the Irish State nominally took over responsibility for 'child and family welfare' from the voluntary sector in 1970, this role was only legislated for with the publication and enactment of the Child Care Act, 1991,andin practice, the State only began to take its responsibilities seriously when pressured by public reaction to child abuse inquiries in the 1990s. Despite the investment in and modernisation of the Irish child protection and welfare system, there are significant areas that require further investment and development, and criticisms persist regarding the functioning of the system (see, for example, Social Services Inspectorate, 2003; Ombudsman for Children, 2006a; Social Services Inspectorate, 2006; Buckley et al., 2008). Examples of areas for further development include the inadequate resourcing of alternative care services and therapeutic services for children, legal and policy gaps which still permit the physical punishment of children, the subordination of children's rights to those of their parents under the Irish Constitution (see baby 'Ann' adoption case in the Supreme Court, Murray, 2006; O'Mahony et al., 2012) and the need to strengthen laws associated with the legal age of sexual consent and child sexual abuse (see 'CC case', Oireachtas, 2006). While the State is now more proactive in protecting and promoting the welfare of children, these identified gaps raise questions about the State's full commitment to protecting and safeguarding Irish children, and the provision of adequate resources to support those who undertake this work. These are issues which are shared with other countries (Morris, 2005), but in Ireland, the Irish Constitution further complicates matters.

The Irish Constitution expressly protects the family from unnecessary State intrusions and does not contain a provision for a separate set of rights for children, independent of their parents. Child protection and welfare social workers often find themselves in an invidious position between contradictory childcare policy objectives and the values of the Irish Constitution. Since 1993, reports from child abuse inquiry panels, non-governmental organisations, international bodies and Government committees (McGuinness, 1993; All Party Oireachtas Committee on the Constitution, 1996; Committee on the Rights of the Child, 1998; Murphy et al., 2005; Committee on the Rights of the Child, 2006; Ombudsman for Children, 2006b) have all recommended Constitutional reform on the issue of children's rights as a specific measure to facilitate the safeguarding and promotion of children's welfare. Irish child abuse inquiries have repeatedly identified this Constitutional omission as a contributing factor in the abuse of children, but it was only in 2006, following pressure arising from another crisis associated with children, this time in the area of the legal age of sexual consent (Oireachtas, 2006), that the Government committed to a referendum on the issue and there are yearly commitments to hold this referendum with the most recent commitment to hold a referendum in Autumn 2012. This reform process repeats previous patterns of development in the Irish child protection system where developments happen in an *ad hoc* manner rather than as a result of a systematic, planned and resourced child care strategy which articulates the values, beliefs and standards for child care and welfare in Ireland. On the one hand, new child care policy and legislative measures shifted practice away from *laissez faire* principles and tasked social workers with intervening in the 'private' and 'protected domain' of the family to assess families' child-rearing practices, while on the other hand, this role is accorded only qualified support by the State.

Esposito and Fine (1985, cited in Stalker *et al.*, 2007b, p. 8) argue that burnout and turnover in 'child welfare' are a result of the systemic issues in child protection systems identified above and that burnout is an ideology that camouflages such paradoxes inherent in these systems. Social workers are employed to 'manage basic contradictions in our society': 1) they are expected to prevent children from abuse and neglect, yet they should not interfere in the private sphere of the family, and 2) they are 'expected to police families and [at the same time] provide caring, compassionate and skilful intervention to alleviate very complex problems' (p. 8). The process of trying to 'manage' these paradoxes and contradictions contributes to job stress and 'burnout' for child protection social workers, which may explain some of the job retention issues in this setting.

The link between 'burnout' and the stresses associated with undertaking this work, is well documented in the literature (see, for example, Stanley and Goddard, 2002; Lonne, 2003). Carrying the statutory responsibility for the care and protection of children and families can place social workers in an onerous position. Ferguson (2004, pp. 115-117) argues that social workers and other child protection professionals now undertake their work in the 'full glare of public attention' in a context of a 'greatly increased sense of risk and danger in child protection'. Social services' role as a container for societies' anxieties about abuse, death, sickness and violence (Obholzer, 1994), leads to these anxieties being managed by the professionals who undertake these roles within the public sector, anxieties which Morrison (1996, p. 131) describes as 'like a vein which runs through the child protection process'. Ferguson (2004, p. 117) illustrates these anxieties by highlighting the language used by social workers to describe their work and how these anxieties seep into and affect their personal lives. He describes how:

> ... there is no escape even in sleep ... practitioners' language illustrates that underlying the anxiety is the 'explosive' nature of the work. Every referral is a 'potential minefield'. Cases 'blow up', 'explode', workers 'burn out'.

Social workers are only too aware that no child protection system can protect and safeguard every child at risk, yet this is juxtaposed with public and political expectations to the contrary. Ferguson (2004, p. 120), employing Beck's work on the Risk Society (1992), argues that social workers in late-modern child protection are acutely aware of risk:

> At the core of risk anxiety in late-modern child protection are two primal fears: of being blamed with and by the organization and society for failing to protect; and of being responsible for prolonging children's suffering.

These anxieties are exacerbated as social problems for these children and families are often complex and intractable, child protection is under-resourced, social workers' working conditions are poor and violence and threats are habitual (Ferguson and O'Reilly, 2001; Ferguson, 2004). This under-resourcing of the sector was pointed out in a media report which highlighted how staff shortages and the HSE/public sector recruitment moratorium has resulted in long waiting lists for child protection assessment and support services in some areas, leading to the professional social work representative body (IASW) raising doubts about the sector's ability to protect and promote the welfare of children (O'Brien, 2007). In a wider social context where child protection and welfare social workers are continually subject to scrutiny and critique from the media, academia and statutory bodies (see, for example, Buckley, 2005; Ombudsman for Children, 2006a; Waters, 2007), it is essential that they are supported by their employing organisation and profession. Perceptions of support from one's employing organisation and recognition of one's work, in particular, are linked with the retention of child protection workers (Audit Commission, 2002; Ellet, 2007). Social workers' perceptions of support for their work is discussed in the section on 'perceived organisational support theory' in the next chapter.

The stresses associated with undertaking child protection and welfare social work are likely to be exacerbated when workers feel unsupported. There is ample evidence from research and inquiries that the quality of care to children is affected when staff are under-resourced and feel unsupported (Reder *et al.*, 1993; Stanley and Goddard, 2002). These feelings are exacerbated as opportunities for positive feedback and feelings of success can be limited as child protection and welfare clients are often 'involuntary', a factor which increases conflict levels and strain for workers and is linked to employee turnover in child protection (Barber, 1991; Ferguson, 2005). The cost to children and families who receive services from burnt-out workers is highlighted in the burnout literature: burnt-out workers who are emotionally exhausted and have feelings of reduced personal accomplishment can have a cynical attitude towards and de-personalise service users, (Maslach *et al.*, 2001). The under-resourcing of social work led Bourdieu (1998, p. 3) to remark:

> All that is somewhat shocking, especially for those who are sent into the front line to perform so-called 'social' work to compensate for the most flagrant inadequacies of the logic of the market, without being given the means to really to do their job. How could they not have the sense of being constantly undermined or betrayed?

1.3 Discussion and analysis

While there is evidence in the literature of job stress and employee turnover in the sector, there are also studies which show that child protection social workers can enjoy high levels of job satisfaction, even though they may experience high levels of job strain (Lonne, 2003; Stalker *et al.*, 2007b). This point is supported by the findings of a study of occupational job satisfaction in the UK which found that social workers scored well on job satisfaction; lower than child care workers, but significantly higher than non-partner solicitors who had the lowest job satisfaction (Rose, 2003). However, Lonne (2003) argues that too much attention has been focused on a relatively small number of social workers who are burnt out, to the exclusion of a larger majority who enjoy the work and find it professionally satisfying. While there are reports of high turnover rates, high levels of job stress and low morale in the child protection and welfare social work (Loughran, 2000; McGrath, 2001; Burns and Murray, 2003; Ferguson, 2003; RTÉ, 2008b), there is no research that specifically examines child protection and welfare social workers' retention.

While there is consensus in the international literature that retaining committed employees in child protection is problematic (Landsman, 2001), caution should be observed in uncritically applying the above findings to social work in Ireland. There is some evidence that child protection policies and practices may be different in Ireland in at least two aspects. Firstly, a major study of child protection services by Ferguson and O'Reilly (2001) found that social workers were still able to find time for welfare (preventative) cases as well as more serious child abuse and reactive work. Secondly, the strict proceduralisation and bureaucratisation of child protection may not be as extensive in Ireland as reported elsewhere (Kemp, 2008). Research on Irish child protection services has tended to focus on the operation of services, or when children have died or were severely abused (see, for example, Western Health Board, 1996; Buckley et al., 1997; Ferguson and O'Reilly, 2001; Horwath and Bishop, 2001; Buckley, 2002).

Outside of the National Social Work Qualifications Board (2000, 2002, 2006) labour force surveys[14] which examine the turnover rate for all social workers in Ireland, very little is known about the actual rates of turnover in child protection and welfare social work, whether social workers want to stay or leave their jobs in statutory child protection and welfare and the factors that contribute to these decisions[15]. The underpinning of this study is not about keeping social workers at all costs, but one based in a quality of working life model which seeks to improve the working conditions of those that do this work (Watson, 2003).

1.4 Overview of chapters and research limitations

While there is little Irish literature on retention and turnover in statutory child protection and welfare, there is an international literature that specifically examines this issue. In Chapter Two, this literature is

---

[14] Composite data on turnover rates for social workers in Ireland. No breakdown provided by work type. A more comprehensive analysis of these documents is presented in Chapter Five.

[15] Recruitment and retention are usually presented as symbiotic themes in the literature. This research study does not explicitly focus on recruitment as concerns about recruiting social workers to work in child protection and welfare reported earlier in the decade (Houses of the Oireachtas, 2000; National Social Work Qualifications Board, 2002) appear to have abated. On the 1st September 2005, only 2.8% of posts in child protection and welfare were vacant (National Social Work Qualifications Board, 2006).

explored to establish the extent of job turnover and retention issues in child protection in an international context. I go on to examine the impact and implications of high job turnover on service users, social workers, employing organisations and the profession of social work. I examine the main theoretical models of job retention and turnover, and conceptual/definitional issues are explained. The findings of key studies are compared and contrasted to identify key factors that are influential in child protection workers' decisions to stay or leave this work. I argue that a focus only on those who leave because of stress and burnout is less helpful than research on those who are presently working in the system, their experiences and their decisions to want to stay or leave this work, as well as analysing the experiences of those who left. In this research I also argue that it would be erroneous to apply uncritically the international literature to Ireland as some of the organisational, political and professional conditions present in other countries are not readily comparable or applicable to child protection and welfare in Ireland.

In Chapter Three, I describe the methodology and research design used to research social workers' retention in statutory child protection and welfare in Ireland. The literature review chapter noted the predominance of quantitative methodologies in the international research, but also identified a growing trend towards employing qualitative or mixed-method methodologies to examine job retention and turnover in child protection and welfare. In the first part of the chapter, I examine the under-utilisation of qualitative methods in research on organisations and argue for the merits of utilising qualitative methods in this research study. The chapter then presents a set of research questions which were based on a revision of the original aims of the study and an analysis of the literature review. I go on to present my research design which outlines the sampling strategy and profile of research participants, choices made regarding the selection of data collection methods and my decision to use semi-structured interviews as the main data collection method. The chapter concludes with an examination of the ethical considerations associated with undertaking this research.

In Chapter Four, the first of four findings chapters, I analyse the quantitative data collected on child protection and welfare social workers' turnover and employment movements in the HSE 'Area A' over a 22-month period. This analysis examines the turnover and employment mobility of this staff, and compares the findings with international studies. This provides a basis to interrogate assumptions that turnover in this sector is high and that employment growth is static.

In Chapter Five, I present the findings from qualitative data collected during interviews with 35 social workers and senior social work practitioners in direct service provision in child protection and welfare in the HSE 'Area A'. These interviews explored social workers' experiences of 'doing' child protection and welfare work, and the factors that they understand are important in shaping their decisions to want to stay or leave. This chapter examines a common perception within the profession that all social workers want to leave this work and identifies the core factors which social workers see as contributing to their decisions to stay or leave this work. Social workers' accounts of doing this work will also facilitate a secondary analysis of the 'state' of the child protection and welfare system in Ireland and the HSE's support for and recognition of this work. The analysis in this chapter utilises the key findings from the literature review as a framework to structure the chapter under three main headings: individual factors, supervisory and social supports, and organisational factors that influence social workers' retention.

In Chapter Six, I extend the analysis of how social workers make decisions to stay and leave by focusing on social workers' understanding of a career in social work. I argue that social workers' choices to stay in or leave child protection and welfare needs to be placed within a broader understanding of a career in the profession. This analysis led to the identification of three 'types' of social worker, each with a specific approach to making decisions regarding their employment and retention in child protection and welfare.

In Chapter Seven, the fourth and final findings chapter, I analyse the accounts of social workers and senior social work practitioners who left their employment in child protection and welfare in the HSE 'Area A'. This analysis explores their professional experiences in this sector and identifies the factors which social workers described as contributing to their decisions to leave this work. The data from these exploratory interviews with a small sample of social workers will provide a contrast with the data from Chapters Five and Six.

In the concluding chapter, the research findings are discussed in terms of their implications for users of child protection and welfare services, social work practitioners, the social work profession, social work employers and social work education. As this study is the first undertaken in Ireland to examine this issue and is therefore exploratory in nature, the concluding chapter identifies avenues for further research. This chapter also examines wider issues connected with child protection and welfare in Ireland that were raised during this study and links are made between the study's findings and national and international developments in this field such as the issues raised in the 'In Harm's Way' documentary (RTÉ, 2008c) and the report into the death of 'Baby P' in the United Kingdom (Ofsted, 2008).

There are some potential limitations of this research. Given the wide scope of potential participants that could have contributed to the study, I chose to focus on the experiences of social workers and senior social work practitioners in direct service provision in child protection and welfare in one Health Service Executive area. This strategy excluded the participation of groups such as: social work managers, service users, policy makers, other professions and administrators working in child protection and welfare; staff in related areas such as fostering, adoption, and family centres, and social workers on other related teams (case conference department, training department, and so on), who would have made important contributions to the study. While recognising the limitations of this selection strategy, I will argue in Chapter Three that my sampling strategy contributes to a richer and more focused study of one specific group's experience of doing this work and their decisions to stay or leave child protection and welfare. A second limitation of the study is its focus on only one HSE area. HSE areas vary but social work services are provided within a common framework of national legislation, policy and practice guidelines. The decision to focus on one HSE area was based on the limited resources available for the research and on the belief that the specific contexts of this HSE area would be significant in the analysis of social workers' experiences. While recognising that it may have been advantageous to have generated a larger sample population of social workers from the four HSE areas to interview, I believe that the smaller geographical focus was practical and that the research findings will be generalisable to child protection and welfare social work in the other three HSE areas. A third limitation was that the sample of social workers in this HSE did not have much diversity when it comes to race and disability.

I begin the next chapter by clarifying conceptual and definitional issues arising in the literature before going on to examine international research and theories on turnover and retention in child protection and welfare.

Chapter 2
Job retention and turnover in statutory child protection and welfare agencies

2.1 Introduction

This chapter reviews the literature and research findings on the factors that are significant in social workers' decisions to stay or leave child protection and welfare. Firstly, the chapter outlines the conceptual and definitional issues concerning retention and turnover. Secondly, the chapter examines literature on the extent of job turnover in child protection in the international context. Thirdly, the chapter explores the consequences and implications of high job turnover in the areas of service quality, financial and organisational costs, on individual social workers, the social work profession and the mix of skilled and novice staff in direct service provision will be discussed. Fourthly, I discuss the main theoretical models of job retention and turnover from the disciplines of economics, psychology and sociology. Fifth, I consider the key individual, supervisory and social support, and organisational factors implicated in the turnover and retention of child protection and welfare workers. The chapter highlights the often contradictory nature of the findings in this literature and concludes by identifying gaps in the literature. The key themes identified in this chapter contributed to the development of the research questions, the methodological approach chosen for this study and the analysis of the research data.

2.2 Conceptual underpinnings and definitions

Prior to analysing the available international data on job turnover and retention, it is important to examine and clarify distinctions between different but related concepts found in the literature. *Retention* refers to the number of employees who stay in an organisation and the organisation's capacity to keep them and *Turnover* is the percentage of employees who leave the organisation irrespective of their reason for leaving (Phillips and O'Connell, 2003). While high levels of staff retention are desirable for most jobs, there are both costs and benefits from having some degree of staff turnover. In research on recruitment and retention, Eborall and Garmeson (2001, p. 17) reported the findings of a National Health Service (NHS) report in the United Kingdom (UK) that outlined both the costs and benefits of high and low staff turnover:

Table 2.1: Costs and benefits of high and low staff turnover (NHS, UK)

	High Staff Turnover	Low Staff Turnover
Benefits	*Permits rapid restructuring*	*Stable workforce*
	Enables quick wage bill reductions	*Better continuity of care*
	Brings in new blood	*Low cost of recruitment, induction and temporary cover*
	Provides opportunities for internal promotion	*Retention of expertise*
Costs	*Loss of skills and local knowledge*	*High wage bill*
	Less continuity of care	*Career blockages*
	High cost of recruitment and induction + temporary cover	*Stagnation*
	Undermines morale	*Difficult to implement change*
	Difficult to establish culture	*Lack of fresh ideas*
	Can lead to service reductions and closures	*Danger of out-dated approaches*
	Cannot choose who leaves: good staff often leave first	

Turnover is usually calculated as a percentage of the number of employees who leave the organisation each month, or over a 12-month period, divided by the total number of employees. It is possible to further define turnover into *avoidableturnover* where employees leave for better pay, better working conditions, because they have problems with managers or because their work is not being recognised, and *unavoidable turnover* where an employee leave because of death, retirement, geographical move, or does not return to work after the birth of child. The American Public Human Service Association (2001, p. 4) found that 60% of the turnover rate for 'public child welfare workers' was preventable, where *preventable turnover* was defined as 'workers who leave the agency for reasons other than retirement, death, marriage/parenting, returning to school, or spousal job move'. The avoidable/unavoidable turnover definitions do not account for employee performance, where some organisations contribute to turnover rates by 'moving on' what are considered to be poor-performing employees which is known as *functional turnover*, and turnover which is *dysfunctional* when valued and high-performing employees leave the organisation (Gibbs and Keating, 1999; Phillips and O'Connell, 2003, pp. 42-43).

A turnover rate of 10% or below is considered a low turnover rate that is achieved by very few organisations. A rate of 18% is considered the turnover rate at which employers should be prompted into significant action to reduce turnover (Phillips and O'Connell, 2003). A rate above 20% has been identified as being a significant threat to the human resources within an organisation and its effectiveness (Balfour and Neff, 1993). In Mor Barak *et al.'s* (2001) meta-analysis of 25 articles identifying antecedents to retention and turnover among child welfare, social work and other human service employees, some of the studies definitions of turnover included leaving the profession altogether. However, the term *attrition* is usually employed to described a situation where a person leaves the profession (National Social Work Qualifications Board, 2006).

Intentions to leave denotes a situation in which workers have seriously considered leaving their job (Mor Barak *et al.*, 2001; Jacquet *et al.*, 2007). While expressing an intention to leave is considered a predictor of turnover, it does not necessarily translate into actual turnover. A number of intermediate factors are suggested to explain why an expressed desire or attitude to leave does not result in a person actually leaving. These factors include the risks involved in quitting one's job, personality factors and the availability of alternative employment (Allen, 2004; Mor Barak *et al.*, 2006). Ellet *et al.*(2006) argue that *intentions to stay*, which denotes a worker's strong commitment to staying in the organisation, is an active process which is different to just not leaving. However, the difference between 'commitment to stay' and 'deciding to stay' may be hard to identify and assess.

Most of the studies examined in this chapter were located in the United States of America or Australia, where the practice setting is usually referred to as *child welfare* or *public child welfare*. Within the UK and Ireland, is has been the practice to use the label *child protection*, or in recent times in Ireland *child protection and welfare* (see, for example, Department of Health and Children, 1999; Buckley, 2002; Skehill, 2004). All of these terms are used interchangeably in the subsequent sections, but refer to statutory (public/state) work undertaken to protect and safeguard the welfare of children and families, usually by social workers, although this is not always the case. In studies where the work is undertaken by social workers as well as those with other professional qualifications, they are invariably described as *public child welfare workers* or *child welfare professionals* (see, for example, American Public Human Services Association, 2001, 2005; Ellet *et al.*, 2006).

2.3 International data on job retention and turnover in child protection and welfare

There is only limited published international research on job turnover and retention in child protection and welfare and there is some speculation that this data in some countries is not collected and/or not made available for political reasons (Lonne, 2003). There is data available for a number of countries: the United States of America (U.S.A.), Sweden, the U.K. and Australia. In the U.S.A. studies, the turnover rates for child welfare employees vary significantly between states, with the average length of employment being less than two years (Anderson, 2000; United States General Accounting Office, 2003; American Public Human Services Association, 2005). Estimations of turnover rates within the U.S.A. literature are inconsistent, which may suggest that the extent of the problem varies both across and within states, and/or different definitions of turnover are being used. However, overall this literature reports very high annual turnover rates: 30%-85% (Mor Barak *et al.*, 2006), 23%-85% (Smith, 2005), 6.2%-27.3% (National Council on Crime and Delinquency, 2006) and between 20%-40%, with some U.S.A. counties reporting 100% turnover rates (American Public Human Services Association, 2005; Ellet, 2007).

In a study of rural child welfare social workers in Australia, the mean time for social workers' length of stay in their post was 16.1 months, with 34% staying less than 12 months (Lonne, 2003). In the Victorian Child Protection Programme, a turnover rate of 30% was reported in mid-1990s and 55% of child welfare staff had less than two years' experience (Hodgkin, 2002). Another study of recruitment and retention in the same region also found issues with worker retention: at the level of direct service workers in child welfare, 46% of staff at the entry level of practice had less than six months' experience and 26% at the higher level also had less than six months' experience (Gibbs and Keating, 1999).

Research reports from other countries also report varying degrees of the same problem. A study of child protection workers in Sweden found that although 54% of social workers had been in their posts for less than 2 years, and 48% intended to leave their jobs (Tham, 2007). In the United Kingdom, however, there was a downward trend in turnover for 'field social workers (children)' from 15.3% in 2000 to 11% in 2005 (Eborall and Garmeson, 2001; Local Authority Workforce Intelligence Group, 2006). A study in Wales reported a 15% turnover rate across all social care services, with children's services having the highest rate of 19% (Colton and Roberts, 2007).

Returning to Ireland, Seamus Mannion, HSE National Care Group Manager for Children and Family Services, in an interview on RTÉ Radio1's *News at One,* acknowledged that: '... there have been problems; there is no doubt about it, with the turnover of social work employees [statutory child protection and welfare social workers]' (RTÉ, 2006). Mannion's statement does not clarify whether these problems are continuing. In Ireland, unpublished figures provided by the National Social Work Qualifications Board (2007, personal correspondence) indicated that the turnover rate of *permanent* statutory child protection and welfare social workers in Ireland was 11.9% in 2005. This figure is likely to be an underestimation of actual turnover as it only includes permanent staff and refers to a human resource climate in the HSE during which a 'recruitment embargo' was in place. Since 2005 there has been a reduction in new posts and an increased supply of social work graduates. This has eased staffing difficulties in child protection and welfare that were experienced at the end of the last and the start of this decade, when the HSE actively recruited social workers from other countries to fill vacant posts (National Social Work Qualifications Board, 2000, 2002). This would suggest that challenges posed in recruiting new employees into child protection and welfare experienced in other countries (Harlow, 2003; Ellet *et al.*, 2006; Westbrook *et al.*, 2006) are currently less of an issue in Ireland. The vacancy rate of child protection and welfare posts in 2005 was only 2.8% (National Social Work Qualifications Board, 2006). Up-to-date data on these posts is unavailable for 2011 and anecdotal accounts for practice are that all posts are filled except for some maternity leave posts. The reason for such an exceptionally low vacancy rate in 2012 is due to a government commitment to fill existing posts in this sector outside of the employment control framework, a shortage of public sector posts, and a large the supply of graduates and experienced staff seeking work.

It is difficult to draw definitive conclusions from this data. Figures for turnover and intentions to leave are not readily comparable as they refer to countries where child welfare practices, cultural and organisational supports, professional qualifications and employment contract standards are quite diverse. The reports do not always clearly explain how the data was collected and analysed, or what definition of turnover was used. What one can draw from these studies is that the difficulties of retaining social workers in child protection and welfare posts appears to be a recurring theme across the identified countries. Another recurring theme was the number of young, newly-qualified, and therefore inexperienced workers employed in this setting and the short length of time they stay in this type of work.

Difficulties in retaining social workers inevitably raise questions regarding the quality of service provided and the impact of the working conditions on social workers. If the average length of stay is less than two years (United States General Accounting Office, 2003; American Public Human Services Association, 2005) and it takes approximately two years to develop the practice knowledge base and skills to work independently (Louisiana Office of Community Services Job Task Force, 2000 cited in Ellet *et al.*, 2006), this means that a large cohort of the workforce is likely to remain at the 'novice' phase and are unlikely to develop into 'expert' child protection and welfare practitioners (Healy *et al.*, 2009). Social workers are employed to safeguard and protect children and families in need, work that requires a high degree of professional skills and knowledge, yet it is work primarily undertaken by newly-qualified staff. The next section identifies literature that focuses on the potential consequences of these high turnover rates, and on the experience levels and working conditions for those associated with these services.

2.4 Consequences of retention and staff turnover problems

While the previous section identified extensive variations in the extent of employee turnover and intentions to leave child protection and welfare, what is clear is that it is a significant problem, and one that is likely to have consequences for those associated with the sector. As already stated in Table 2.1, employee turnover may not always be a negative phenomenon: low staff turnover can have positive benefits by contributing to more stable teams where skills, knowledge and expertise are retained. However, according to Healy *et al.* (2009, pp. 2-3), high staff turnover in child protection and welfare can be problematic for the following reasons: (1) service quality, (2) financial and organisational costs, (3) 'suffering' to individual social workers, (4) costs to the social work profession, and (5) a lack of experienced practitioners at the direct service provision. These issues will be further examined in the following five sub-sections.

2.4.1 Service quality

Service quality can be affected when organisations are unable to retain a cohort of experienced and skilled staff. In Chapter One, I outlined the complex and demanding nature of child protection and welfare social work. However, the international literature highlights the fact that this work appears to be primarily undertaken by newly-qualified (novice) workers, workers who do not stay long enough to learn the job thoroughly, which leads to a workforce with insufficient numbers of 'expert' workers (Healy *et al.*, 2009). Studies have also concluded that high turnover in the sector can affect the quality and consistency of service. Research studies with children in foster care (Sinclair *et al.*, 2003; Sinclair *et al.*, 2005; McEvoy and Smith, 2011), residential care inspection inquiry reports (Social Services Inspectorate, 2001) and the representative body for foster carers in Ireland (Wayman, 2008), attribute some of the problems associated with service quality for children in care to employment instabilities in child protection and welfare teams. Unpublished HSE statistics quoted by *The Irish Times* identified that 13% of Irish children in foster care had no allocated social worker, where Louth had the lowest rate with 58% of children in state care not having an allocated social worker (Wayman, 2008; O'Brien, 2009b). This is contrary to national care standards and given the centrality of social workers in promoting these children's well-being (Gilligan, 2000), these figures are particularly troubling. The Irish Foster Care Association directly link this resource issue with a shortage of child protection and welfare social workers, a problem which they feel is exacerbated by the HSE recruitment 'embargo' (Wayman, 2008). For example, children who require consistency of care-giving may end up with multiple changes of social workers due to staff turnover. This point was further evidenced in a study of service users' perceptions of child protection and welfare social work services in Ireland, where

> The turnover of workers and the necessity of form new relationships was considered to be a major deficit in current service provision, often construed by the services users as indifference to their situations (Buckley *et al.*, 2008, p. 67).

High employee turnover can also lead to a reduction in confidence amongst users of the service (Mor Barak *et al.*, 2001). Child abuse inquiry reports in the UK and Ireland have also linked staff turnover with negative effects on service delivery and the welfare of service users. In the *Kilkenny Incest Investigation* (McGuinness, 1993), the report noted that the response of the community care services to protect 'Mary' was hampered by the turnover of senior social workers in the team. In the Laming report (2003), there are repeated references to recruitment and retention issues in the child protection social work department. This report recommended that the high turnover of these staff should be addressed as a 'prerequisite to improving performance' (p. 357). In the United States General Accounting Office (2003, p. 20) study, they found links between recruitment and retention challenges and the protection of children. They reported that the actual magnitude of this effect was unknown, although a recurring theme in the study was evidence that high caseloads impacted on workers' ability to 'make well-supported and timely decisions regarding children's safety'. The Child Welfare League of America (2008, p. 10) summed up this concern succinctly when it observed that:

> ... no issue has greater effect on the capacity of the child welfare system to effectively serve vulnerable children and families than the shortage of a competent and stable workforce.

With this level of concern it is perhaps surprising that more research is not undertaken on how to maintain a competent and stable social work workforce.

2.4.2 Financial and organisational costs

Financial and organisational costs associated with high employee turnover for employing organisations include frequent recruitment drives, the almost continuous provision of staff induction and training, and increased pressure on existing staff who have to cover the caseloads of vacant posts. While financial costs can be considerable, there are also harder to quantify human capital costs in terms of staff morale and the reputation of the service (Eborall and Garmeson, 2001; Smith, 2005). Service delivery can be affected as cases may remain unallocated due to vacancies, and existing staff may be under extra pressure to cover high priority cases or unallocated caseloads. Organisations may not even have enough staff to ensure that they meet their statutory obligations to safeguard and protect children (Healy et al., 2009), as experienced by Irish children in care without a social worker and the reported 1,500 children 'at risk' in the community who are on waiting lists for a child protection assessment because of social workers' heavy caseloads (O'Brien, 2009a). There is also a loss of productivity while new employees take time to gain the requisite knowledge, skills and experience required to achieve 'mastery of the job' (Mor Barak et al., 2001, p. 627), a loss of capacity which is exacerbated if this is a perpetual process with a significant percentage of the staff group. Expertise and knowledge gained from attaining mastery of the job is lost to the organisation and its service users if experienced staff cannot be retained. These losses affect the transmission of expertise and knowledge through supervision, mentoring and peer-support networks (Westbrook *et al.*, 2006). A text on retention indicated that the cost of health care workers' turnover is twice an employee's salary and benefits (Phillips and O'Connell, 2003).

2.4.3 Consequences for social work staff

The costs for social workers and other professionals who undertake this work have received significant coverage in the literature (see, for example, Dickinson and Perry, 2002; Nissly *et al.*, 2005; Strolin *et al.*, 2007). Furthermore, Healy *et al.* (2007) describe the 'suffering' that high turnover causes individual social workers who bear the emotional stresses of transitions. This experience may lead some to leave the profession, although Healy *et al.* (2007) do not provide evidence to support the latter outcome. Gilligan (2000, p. 270) argues that the ever increasing expectations of social workers' practice in child protection versus what is possible for them to do given the available resources and supports, may lead to 'anxiety and cognitive dissonance on the part of workers. In an understandable attempt to protect themselves from such stress, some social workers may withdraw from the work'.

Outcomes associated with working in child protection such as burnout, high job stress and low job satisfaction have been a particular focus of the literature (see, for example, Drake and Yadama, 1996; Anderson, 2000; Mor Barak *et al.*, 2006). The effects on individual employees, the employing organisation, professional bodies and service users can lead to a range of adverse factors and negative outcomes such as high employee turnover, increased rates of intention to quit, dissatisfaction, decreased work performance and increased absenteeism (Lonne, 2003). The emotional labour aspect of child protection work places social workers at particular risk of job strain, strain that should be contained and ameliorated through effective and supportive supervision (Morrison, 1993). Studies have consistently shown that quality professional supervision and support can ameliorate the personal and professional impact of this work (Rushton and Nathan, 1996; Gibbs, 2001). Supervision and support are two of the strongest factors associated with retention, yet supervision is not always available or adequate (Jacquet *et al.*, 2007). This can further compound the impact of, and contribute to, job stress and may lead to a perception that the employing organisation is unsupportive of child protection workers (Lonne, 2003).

2.4.4 Consequences for the social work profession

The cost for the social work profession may be experienced indirectly as reports of high turnover, for example, reduce the number of candidates willing to come into the profession. The relative neglect of this theme within the profession may lead social workers to believe that the professional and qualification bodies and universities are uninterested in staff turnover. The reputation of the profession can also be affected as the high turnover of staff contributes to a lack of skills and experience in the sector, which may affect the quality of work and subsequent perceptions of standards. Also, some social workers may perceive that their professional training did not adequately prepare them for the realities of practice in this challenging work context (Healy and Meagher, 2007). This may lead to disillusionment with their professional career choice. However, this latter view is inconsistent within the literature, as academic training has also been found to be insignificant in decisions to leave by Samantrai (1992).

2.4.5 Lack of experienced practitioners in direct service provision

The fifth dimension identified by Healy and Meagher (2007) concerns the impact of having a lack of expertise at the level of direct service provision. They argue that 'many workers are simply not in the role long enough to develop the strong body of context-based knowledge and skills required for expert child protection practice' (p. 3). They point out using research on professional development models (see, for example, Rønnestad and Skovholt, 2003) that 'novice professionals' benefit from the support and supervision of experienced supervisors, which is less likely without a stable workforce as staff get promoted into supervisory positions before they achieve advanced levels of professional expertise. This issue will be examined further in Chapter Five.

This section has explored the scope of employee retention and turnover in child protection and its consequences for those associated with the setting. While employee retention and turnover is identified in the literature as a significant issue, there is also some optimism expressed that there are specific organisational changes that could be made to improve the situation. The next section examines theories of employee turnover and retention which indicate some of these areas for change which could influence social workers' retention.

2.5 Theories of employee turnover and retention

The literature which deals with employee turnover and retention in child protection and welfare highlights the complex nature of this issue and the fact that there is no single explanation or potential solution (Audit Commission, 2002). Studies have identified a broad range of factors (see section 2.6 below), which they believe are significant in employee turnover and retention, although there is little agreement on which factors are most significant. Some of the factors implicated in the retention of social work and other child welfare staff in child protection include: professional supervision and managerial supports (Gibbs, 2001; Smith, 2005; Jacquet *et al.*, 2007); organisational commitment (Strolin *et al.*, 2007); organisational climate and working conditions (Tham, 2007; Healy *et al.*, 2009); social supports (Nissly *et al.*, 2005; Stalker *et al.*, 2007a), and making a difference with clients (Samantrai, 1992; Rycraft, 1994; Ellet *et al.*, 2006), amongst others. In reaching these conclusions, researchers have employed a diverse range of theoretical underpinnings to support their research. It has been suggested that much of the research in job retention and turnover is relatively atheoretical, with the focus of research being on the development and testing of multivariate predictive models (Weaver and Chang, 2004). While this may be an over-statement, what is evident is that there is no grand unifying theory that explains job turnover and retention. Job turnover research has employed theories from the disciplines of economics, psychology and sociology (Mor Barak *et al.*, 2001; Weaver and Chang, 2004), and theories from these three disciplines will be explored in further depth in the following sub-sections.

2.5.1 Economic theory

Economic explanations of turnover consider the role of the labour market in employee turnover. Economic explanations focus on the supply and demand of labour, 'job search, subjective expected utility and rational economic choice, availability of job opportunities or perceived alternatives, reward and investments or 'sunk' costs' (Morrel *et al.*, 2001, p. 227). Economic accounts of turnover focus on factors that are generally external to the organisation. Steel (2004) observes that the available evidence on the impact of labour markets on individual decisions such as turnover is limited. Over-simplified constructions of labour markets in turnover models and a lack of information about how individuals use information about labour markets lead to questions regarding the comprehensiveness of these explanations. Steel also argues that it is not labour markets *per se,* but personally relevant labour markets based upon occupational and experiential skill sets.

Job search theory highlights the imperfect nature of workers' knowledge of geographical and occupational markets; job searches generate alternatives for employees, and while some are related to leaving, other alternatives are related to staying, for example by confirming one's current value and salary. Criticisms of economic explanations of job turnover include a reliance on economic variables to the exclusion of affective factors and intrinsic satisfactions in the work. It is simplistic to account for what appears to be a complex process in which a person decides to stay in or leave their job in purely economic terms where job opportunities, labour markets and pay and reward conditions are the sole or primary drivers of turnover. However, it would also be unwise to reject their value in an overall inclusive understanding of job retention and turnover. Economic explanations and variables are often incorporated into psychological and sociological accounts of job retention and turnover.

2.5.2 Psychological theories

Psychological theories which attempt to explain and predict turnover include stress theories such as burnout (Maslach, 1982; Maslach *et al.,* 2001) and secondary traumatic stress (Figley, 1995, 2002), voluntary turnover models such as Lee and Mitchell's unfolding model of voluntary turnover (Lee and Mitchell, 1994), Price/Mueller's causal model of voluntary turnover, job embeddedness (Holtom *et al.,* 2006), attribution theory, and personality and dispositional theories such as locus of control (Weaver and Chang, 2004). Psychological models examine how personal characteristics, perceptions and attitudes towards work shape employees' responses to the workplace, leading to certain behavioural outcomes (performance, turnover, absenteeism, and so on). Job design theories (see, for example, Hackman and Oldham, 1980; Karasek and Theorell, 1990; Hackman *et al.,* 2000) also explain how work characteristics affect job satisfaction and subsequent behavioural outcomes such as performance and turnover. The following sections will examine the specific theories used in this study: Lee and Mitchell's unfolding model of voluntary turnover, job embeddedness theory, and job design theory. The concept of 'burnout' is often used in discussion of social workers' retention and turnover. It is described and criticised at the end of this section; however, it was not used in the analysis of this study's data.

Unfolding model of voluntary turnover

The model of voluntary turnover developed by Lee and Mitchell contributes to our understanding of psychological decision-making processes used by workers in deciding to stay in or leave a job. Traditional models of voluntary turnover such as March and Simons (1958) sought to explain turnover as being a result of two key factors: (1) 'perceived desirability of movement' – influenced by job satisfaction; (2) 'perceived ease of movement' – influenced by a worker's assessment of perceived or actual job alternatives, which proved to be the basis of subsequent theories of turnover, including Price/Mueller's causal model and Mobley and colleagues' expanded model (Morrel *et al.*, 2001; Yao *et al.*, 2004).

Lee and Mitchell's model extended traditional models of voluntary turnover by identifying the psychological decision-making processes used by workers in deciding to stay in or leave their job and moving the analysis beyond job dissatisfaction. In this model, thinking about leaving one's job arises from a 'shock' event, either inside or outside of the organisation, which can be either a positive or a negative event (for example, an industrial dispute, birth of a child, death or loss, being head-hunted, dispute with manager/colleague). The model proposes that the 'unfolding process of leaving' happens as a result of a 'shock' rather than as a result of job dissatisfaction (Holtom *et al.*, 2002). The 'shock' event leads a worker to take one of four decision paths to process and interpret the shock, to evaluate the shock in relation to the work environment, and identify and evaluate decisions, all of which lead to a response (for example, a decision to stay or leave). According to Lee and Mitchell, the merit of this theory is its ability to facilitate managers in identifying which decision path an employee may take as a result of the shock, and to respond by taking corrective actions which may assist in retaining the worker in the organisation. Criticisms of Lee and Mitchell's model include a lack of emphasis on the economic consequences of quitting, an empirical focus on 'quitters' rather than 'stayers' and the role of gender in choosing decision paths (Donnelly and Quirin, 2006). This theory does not specifically fit this study's design that primarily focuses on those who are presently employed and why they stay, therefore it was not used to structure the data collection. However, as will be discussed in Chapter Three, a small sample of social workers who quit/left child protection and welfare were also interviewed. In the analysis of the data from this smaller sample of social workers, two of the social workers accounts appeared to 'fit' with this theory and it is used to analyse data from these interviews.

The unfolding model of voluntary turnoverled to the development of another theory of job turnover called job embeddedness, a theory which focuses on why people stay.

Job embeddedness theory

Job embeddedness theory employs the metaphor of a spider's web to conceptualise the diverse strands that make up a person's social connections – those with more roles, relationships and connections are considered to have more complex webs. This metaphor is used to explain how workers make decisions to stay in or leave their job – those with more complex webs face greater disruption if they leave. Workers with good inter-personal networks and friendships in the job and local community, whose children are in good childcare either locally or within the organisation, and who perceive that they have a good job with responsibilities and tasks to which they are committed, are likely to face more disruption to their web if they leave than a person with less complicated webs (fewer friends, fewer links in the community and so on). The person's 'embeddedness' in a job is a function of three key dimensions (Holtom *et al.*, 2002, pp. 319-320):

> *Fit*: an employee's personal values, career goals, and plans for the future must "fit" with the larger corporate culture and the demands of his or her immediate job (e.g. job knowledge, skills and abilities) ... [and] how well he or she fits with the community and surrounding environment.
>
> *Links* are formal and informal connections between an employee and institutions or people.
>
> *Sacrifice* represents the perceived cost of material or psychological benefits that are forfeited by organisational departure. For example, leaving an organisation may induce personal losses (losing contact with friends, personally relevant projects or perks).

Those who are more 'embedded' and 'bound' to an organisation (good fit with organisation and local community, large number of links in a person's web, and the higher loss or sacrifice associated with leaving) are less likely to leave the organisation. In this sense, it is not a purely psychological theory of employee retention as it employs an ecological analysis to understand reasons why workers stay. The theory directs that organisations take a proactive role in helping employees to manage the complexities of modern living, and when workers perceive that organisations value them and help them to manage these complexities, they are more likely to stay (Holtom *et al.*, 2006). This theory was used to structure part of the data analysis.

Job design theory

Job design theories (see, for example, Hackman and Oldham, 1980; Karasek and Theorell, 1990) explain how job characteristics (characteristics that also appear in various forms across theories and factors examined in this chapter) affect outcomes such as job performance, job satisfaction, absenteeism and turnover (Morgeson and Campion, 2003). Job design theories such as job characteristics theory (JCT) (Hackman and Oldham, 1980; Campion *et al.*, 2005) are not specific theories of turnover, but are over-arching psychological theories of work that define the optimal constituent parts of a job. Job design is concerned with the 'nature of the work itself' - the tasks and activities undertaken within an organisation by employees (Oldham, 1996, p. 33). Job design theories have been employed as one part of the research design in two studies examining child protection and welfare workers' retention and turnover (Lonne, 2003; Healy *et al.*, 2009).

JCT emphasises job design enhancements (job enrichment) that reversed the job design trends under Taylorism and scientific management, which incorporated job simplification, removing employee discretion over how tasks were completed and a 'technical division of labour' that created jobs where employees only did one specialised task (Parker and Wall, 1998; Watson, 2003). Watson argues that job redesign ideas consolidated as part of a social movement that aimed to improve the 'Quality of Working Life' of employees in industrial societies. Where my research diverges from 'traditional' job design proponents is that I am less concerned with the *financial cost* issues associated with job design and more with a *social concern* for the quality of employees' lives.

The JCT suggests that high levels of five core job characteristics can enhance employee' motivation, satisfaction and performance (Oldham, 1996). The five core job characteristics in the JCT are defined as follows:

Task significance

The degree to which the job has a substantial impact on the lives of other people, whether those people are in the immediate organisation or in the world at large.

Skill variety

The degree to which a job requires a variety of different activities in carrying out the work, involving the use of a number of different skills and talents of the person.

Autonomy

The extent to which the job provides substantial freedom, independence, and discretion to the individual in scheduling the work and in determining the procedures to be used in carrying it out.

Task identity

The degree to which a job requires completion of a 'whole' and identifiable piece of work, that is, doing a job from beginning to end with a visible outcome.

Job feedback

The degree to which carrying out the work activities required by the job provides the individual with direct and clear information about the effectiveness of his or her performance (Hackman and Oldham, 1980, pp. 76 - 80).

The model proposes that these five core characteristics lead to three critical psychological states - experienced meaningfulness, experienced responsibility for outcome of the work and knowledge of the actual results of the work activities - which in turn, influence a range of outcomes namely high internal work motivation, high growth satisfaction, high general job satisfaction and high work effectiveness. A range of moderators which are described in figure 2.1 influences the core job characteristics and critical psychological states:

Figure 2.1: Hackman and Oldham's Job Characteristics Theory (Oldham, 1996)

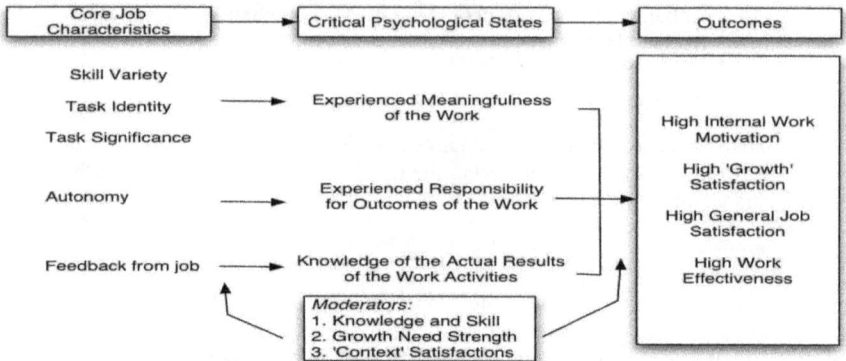

The model's analysis of jobs is structural; change the job, not the person. Research over the past two decades support the fundamental premise of the JCT; that job characteristics are important determinants of outcomes, although it has been found to be incorrect in its detail (Parker and Wall, 1998; Judge and Church, 2000; Parker, 2002). The mediating role of critical psychological states has been found to be unnecessary as a link to outcomes (Parker and Wall, 1998). Other limitations of the JCT include the neglect of other important characteristics of jobs such as 'time-pressure', 'dealing with others' (the degree to which the job requires employees to work closely with other people)and 'agent feed-back' (degree to which employees receive feedback from supervisors and co-workers) (Oldham, 1996). Research has indicated that increased job enrichment, as proposed by the JCT, can lead to employee's experiencing greater levels of self-efficacy (Campion *et al.*, 2005). The core job characteristics of the JCT will be used to structure the interview guide and data collection to generate data associated with the nature of work and working conditions in child protection and welfare, however the model's survey instrument will not used in this study as it is inconsistent with the study's methodological approach. Following a review of the literature, particular attention will be paid to the collection of data in three of the core job characteristics which were also present in other research as important factors in social workers' decisions to stay or leave: autonomy, task significance (making a difference) and skill variety.

Burnout theory

Burnout theory has been used extensively in studies to examine turnover in child protection and welfare and human service organisations (see, for example, Jayaratne and Chess, 1984; Söderfeldt *et al.*, 1995; Drake and Yadama, 1996). 'Burnout', as described by Maslach and colleagues (1982, 1993; 2001, p. 399), refers to 'a psychological syndrome in response to chronic interpersonal stressors on the job'. Burnout research began within the field of human service occupations, including social work, but has since expanded to include other work contexts such as education, military, management and clerical contexts (Maslach *et al.*, 2001). Burnout is a negative affective response (over time, rather than an immediate response) by the employee to work stresses and demands such as workloads, role conflict and unsupportive environments, leading to occupational stress (Koeske and Koeske, 1989; Lonne, 2003). Burnout refers to three key dimensions (Maslach *et al.*, 2001):

1. *emotional exhaustion*, which is the depletion of a worker's physical and emotional resources as a result of interpersonal contact

2. *cynicism* (depersonalisation), which is the negative, callous or cynical attitudes towards service users, and

3. *a sense of inefficacy*, which is a reduced sense of personal accomplishment and a negative attitude towards one's work.

Researchers have argued that emotional exhaustion is *the* central component of burnout (Stalker *et al.*, 2007b) and studies on child protection and welfare workers using the Maslach Burnout Inventory (MBI) have found that they scored high on emotional exhaustion (Drake and Yadama, 1996; Anderson, 2000; Stalker *et al.*, 2007b). Drake and Yamada (1996) found that emotional exhaustion was linked with 'job exit' in their study, however Anderson (2000) who also found high levels of emotional exhaustion amongst child welfare workers (62% in the higher range), noted that less than 7% were planning to leave their jobs in the subsequent 9 months. Canadian research (Stalker *et al.*, 2007a), after undertaking a 'confirmatory factor analysis' of the MBI, recommended that researchers discontinue their reliance on the MBI to assess burnout due to doubts about the conceptualisation on which it is based and reliability issues with the MBI scales. Thus, this recommendation raises some doubt about the findings and reliability of previous burnout research. Earlier criticisms of the burnout concept discussed in Chapter One questioned the 'existence' of this concept (Esposito and Fine, 1985, cited in Stalker *et al.*, 2007b, p. 8), sentiments echoed by others who have speculated that it 'may be a misnomer and proxy attestation for a set of organisational and individual factors that contribute to turnover among child welfare staff' (Westbrook *et al.*, 2006, p. 41). This study does not employ theories of burnout or stress as it is a concern of the researcher that their use may lead to a deficit approach where it is assumed, either explicitly or implicitly, that social workers are stressed or burnt out. However, it is possible that in their interviews, participants may use burnout in its colloquial meaning, and therefore this section is included to clarify its use in the literature.

2.5.3 Sociological theories

Sociological theories focus less on personal factors and more on the structural conditions of work and their relationships with retention and turnover. Sociological theories used to examine and explain turnover include social exchange theory and the related perceived organisational support theory.

Social exchange theory

The disciplinary origins of social exchange theory are in sociology, anthropology, and social psychology. Social exchange theory describes how 'individuals build relationships by trading resources they own for those they need or want through formal and informal transactions' (Miller, 1996, p. 17). This theory examines the social relationships formed between two partners - workers and employing organisation; workers and supervisors; workers and co-workers - and has been used to understand human workplace behaviour in areas such as social power, networks, organisational justice, and in the field of management research outcomes such as turnover. Social exchange theorists generally agree that it 'involves a series of interactions that generate obligations ... and relationships evolve over time into trusting, loyal, and mutual commitments' (Cropanzano and Mitchell, 2005, pp. 874-875).

Miller (1996) outlines a number of core assumptions about exchange relationships contained in this literature. Firstly, that those involved in exchange relationships make rational decisions about the content of transactions, and these do not occur when a person is unhappy with the content or does not get the expected benefit of the exchanges. Secondly, the benefits you get out of the interaction depends on what you provide in exchange. Thirdly, 'mutually beneficial transaction can produce long-term exchange relations' (Blau, 1964 cited in Miller, 1996, p. 17). How a worker values their interactions, or exchanges with their employer, supervisor or colleagues, influences how they value their work conditions. He goes on to argue that the value of these exchanges resources is best accessed through employees' subjective interpretations and evaluations, which in the context of this research, will be through semi-structured interviews (see section 3.4.2 in Chapter Three). Contextual factors such as where the exchanges occur (the HSE 'Area A' and the nature of work in child protection and welfare - see sections 1.2.1 and 1.2.3), and personal factors specific to individuals (for example, family circumstances), are important in workers' evaluations of exchange resources.

Social exchange theory contributes to our understanding of the exchange resources that influence workers' retention beyond the factors suggest by economic theory in an earlier section. Exchanges between the two parties can be viewed in terms of economic resources such as wages, promotions, goods and services, but also social resources defined in more symbolic terms; examples include love, status, approval, praise and information (Miller, 1996; Cropanzano and Mitchell, 2005). Social exchange theory helps to explain why workers stay or leave their jobs, as employment is 'the exchange of effort and loyalty ... for material or social rewards' (Miller, 1996, p. 17), rewards which include support, salary and recognition (Van Knippenberg and Sleebos, 2006).

Social workers in this study are involved in exchange relationships with supervisors, co-workers and the HSE 'Area A'; exchange relationships that provide reinforcement for their practice endeavours. According to social exchange theory, social workers will decide to leave when they perceive that 'staying with their current employment relationship (i.e. working conditions) costs more than switching to another employment relationship' (Miller, 1996, pp. 20-21). Costs in this sense are more than just economic costs, and includes a broad range of social exchange resources.

The importance of workplace relationships has been a particular focus within social exchange theory and organisational research, and social exchange relationships are seen to 'evolve when employers 'take care of employees" (Cropanzano and Mitchell, 2005, p. 882). While this sentiment recurs in the job retention literature (see, for example, Audit Commission, 2002; Tham, 2007) it is usually not explicitly based on social exchange theory, rather an independent variable or significant theme, although there are research studies which clearly explicate their SET underpinnings (see Smith, 2005). In the forthcoming data analysis chapters, social workers describe how their exchange relationships with colleagues which focus on the exchange of resources such as support, mentoring and praise; exchange relationships with supervisors which focus on the exchange of resources such as supervisor support and supervision (quality and frequency of supervision, praise, affirmation, containment); and exchange relationships with the HSE 'Area A' including the exchange of resources such as salary/benefits and employment conditions, influence their decisions to want to stay or leave child protection and welfare.

Social exchange theory was employed in this study to structure the collection and analysis of data from interviews with social workers. The theory was chosen as it is a specific theory of turnover, and it provides a useful framework to focus on key themes and relationships at a range of levels - including colleagues, supervisors and the employing organisation - that are identified as significant in the broader research literature and which are examined in greater depth in section 2.6. To further structure the collection of data connected with the employing organisation (HSE 'Area A') and to explore how exchange relationships between social workers and their employer influence social workers' retention, perceived organizational support theory, which is based on social exchange theory, also contributed to the research design.

Perceived organisational support theory

Perceived organisational support theory refers to employees' 'perceptions of the extent to which the organisation values their contributions and cares about their well-being' (Eisenberger *et al.*, 2004, p. 206). In this theory organisations are important sources of 'socio-economic' resources such as respect and caring, as well as the more traditional material benefits of wages and medical benefits (Eisenberger *et al.*, 2004). Eisenberger's concept of perceived organizational support (POS) reflects workers' perceptions of the extent to which employers/organisations meet their part of the exchange relationship (Van Knippenberg and Sleebos, 2006). Employees who perceive that their employer is supportive are likely to reciprocate in their performance, commitment and attachment to the organisation, thereby increasing the likelihood of retention. Eisenberger *et al.*(2002) in a large scale study found that employees' perceptions of supervisor support contributes to perceptions that the organisation is supportive, and ultimately, to their retention. The study suggested that as direct supervisors have most direct daily contact with employees than senior management, they are more readily positioned to 'convey positive valuations and caring' (p. 572).

In her review of the literature, Smith (2005) noted that when workers perceived that their supervisor was supportive, their commitment to the supervisor, and perhaps the organisation, increased. The role of supportive supervision in child protection and welfare is well documented in the literature (see section 2.6.2 below) and has been shown to impact on job retention, with supportive supervisors facilitating the retention of staff, and less supportive supervisors being linked with turnover. Smith (2005) found that perceptions of supervisor support affect turnover independently of organisational supports (for example, work-life balance initiatives), due to the seminal role of supervision in child protection and welfare. Perceived organisational support theory was employed in this study to structure the collection and analysis of data from interviews with social workers regarding their perceptions of the extent to which the HSE 'Area A' meets its part of the exchange relationship.

In summary, Mor Barak *et al.*(2001) argue that theoretical aspects of all three aforementioned disciplines are necessary to explain the turnover process. Empirical support for the prevailing model of turnover, summarised in the introduction to this section, has been shown to be relatively weak, with questions raised about the analysis of variables and turnover relationships (Morrel *et al.*, 2001; Holtom *et al.*, 2006). These relationships include the satisfaction-turnover relationship or commitment-turnover relationship within the sociological and psychological traditions, and opportunity-turnover and pay-turnover relationships within the economic tradition (Morrel *et al.*, 2001). It has also been noted that there has been less research focus on staying, which for some people is merely the opposite of leaving, but for others it is conceptually different from leaving and in need of further study (Holtom *et al.*, 2006; Ellet, 2007). Despite these critiques of existing theory, studies continue to examine the relationships between various factors and job retention and turnover, while acknowledging that there is a need for additional theory development in this area. The next section examines the key themes identified in research studies which are important in affecting employee turnover and retention which the literature typically organises into three key dimensions: individual, supervisory/social supports, and organisational factors.

2.6 Factors implicated in job turnover and retention in child protection and welfare

Workers' attitudes towards their jobs and the availability of employment alternatives are identified as the key antecedents to turnover. Two major factors recur in turnover research: first, those who are satisfied with their jobs (salary, supervision, opportunities for promotion, work environment and tasks) are more likely to stay, and second, 'given the same level of job dissatisfaction, people with more alternatives are more likely to leave than those with fewer alternatives' (Holtom *et al.*, 2006, p. 318). Studies which explore job retention and turnover in child protection and welfare generally categorise the factors implicated in job retention and turnover into three main areas: individual, supervision and social supports, and organisational factors (Strolin *et al.*, 2007). The following sections examine the research findings in these three areas and the final section concludes with a brief summary of the least cited factors.

2.6.1 Individual factors

Individual factors which are identified in the literature as being significant in the retention and turnover of child welfare and other human service professionals include: making a difference with children and families; professional commitment to child protection and welfare work; burnout; educational background, and age.

Making a difference with children and families

The potential of a job to 'engage, enable and support staff to make a positive difference to service users and communities' (Audit Commission, 2002, p. 59) was found in research studies to be important in workers' turnover and intentions to leave (Reagh, 1994; Rycraft, 1994; Ellet *et al.*, 2006; Mor Barak *et al.*, 2006; Ellet, 2007). Those who work in this sector want to support and protect children and families: when they perceive that their job conditions do not facilitate them in meeting these professional goals, particularly if their stressful work conditions contribute to actually endangering children, their job satisfaction suffers (Eborall and Garmeson, 2001; Mor Barak *et al.*, 2006). Pryce *et al.* (2007, p. 49), in their review of the literature, identify the rewards that social workers feel when 'individual lives are transformed due to the efforts of the child welfare worker' as one of the most important reasons why social workers stay. This theme of making a difference is synonymous with the task significance core job characteristic in the job characteristics theory described in section 2.5 above.

Two qualitative studies undertaken in the 1990s in the United States that examined why social workers stay in their jobs found that the desire to improve the living conditions or circumstances of children, something which they perceived can be done despite the challenges of working in a bureaucracy, was important (Reagh, 1994; Rycraft, 1994). Of note in the Reagh study, was social workers' acceptance that small changes in the lives of their clients can occur, even if they occur incrementally over years. This acceptance contributes to workers feeling that they are making a difference, even if these changes are on a small scale or are not even visible to the wider community. Many of the social workers in Reagh's study had experienced burnout at some stage and keeping sight of the meaning and significance of their work meant the difference between leaving and staying.

The seminal role played by supervisors in facilitating staff to develop competence in this work, and supervisors who support and invest time in their supervisees' self-efficacy beliefs 'are likely to strengthen employee retention, and thus the quality of services provided to clients that caseworkers serve' (Ellet, 2007, p. 58). The role of social work education in developing students' confidence and competence for work in child protection, increasing the likelihood of increased feelings of success and accomplishment with clients and job satisfaction, is also highlighted. Ellet's study found a clear link between child protection workers' beliefs regarding their self-efficacy and intentions to remain employed, although while the relationship was found to be moderately significant, once again it was only one of a large range of other factors including geographical location, general levels of satisfaction, organisational culture and so on, which shape a worker's decision to stay in their job. Lonne (2003, p. 288) observes that while some studies have shown that one of the strongest factors implicated in burnout is 'a lack of therapeutic success', others did not support the link, although there appears to be agreement that a '... practitioner's self-efficacy is inversely related to burnout and job dissatisfaction'.

The role of female gender socialisation in social workers' perceptions of making a difference and its influence on staying in one's job, despite the negative impact on women's health and identities, was highlighted in two studies (Morris, 2005; Stalker et al., 2007b). Studies from all countries in this and the previous chapter indicate that women comprise the majority of the direct service provision workforce in child protection and welfare.

Morris's study, which employed a life history narrative and feminist inquiry methodology, argues that women's socialisation as nurturers, which creates an orientation for 'pleasing' and 'serving others', may appear as anathema to the control function of child protection work and the undertaking of the 'dirty work' of society. Dressel's research on 'service work' as 'dirty work' refers to social workers (and others) having the task of implementing policies that regulate the intimate lives of service users and performing a 'buffer' role between society and service users. These roles, she argues, inevitably leads to criticisms towards those associated with implementing these policies and 'negative consequences' for the individuals who perform these roles. She argues that women are attracted to child protection work as female socialisation can fit comfortably into the care of children, but once they are employed in this setting, they then realise that they are society's 'dirty workers'. This may help explain why social workers leave their posts. Morris's study suggests that

> ... this group of women make sense of their work lives by constructing a counterstory to replace the power they lose by doing "dirty work" in society. Their explanation is that they are actually saving society from itself, in spite of the obstacles put before them (p. 144).

For the social workers in this study to perceive that they are making a difference and to stay in this work, they must believe that their counterstory (their work contributes to the greater good – 'for the children') is true and that it is powerful. This belief, Morris argues, helps them to tolerate the contradictions inherent in the job (examined in Chapter One), to repair or protect their identities and to cope with the challenges of working in and improving the 'broken' system. The authors of a Canadian study (Stalker *et al.*, 2007b, p. 7), which unexpectedly found a coexistence between a high level of emotional exhaustion and high levels of job satisfaction among child welfare workers, argued that the 'ability to find reward in helping others', which may be more prevalent in women due to their 'induction into gendered social and economic roles', helps them to sustain the tensions between these high levels of emotional exhaustion and job satisfaction. The ability to find reward in helping others moderates the effects of job overload and job satisfaction ensues, and similar to the Morris study, a strong belief that one's labour is helping children and making a positive difference in their lives is important (this is a significant theme in the findings of my study which will be presented in Chapter Five). They also argue that access to social supports (co-worker and supervisor supports), a theme I will address in a later section, is particularly important. Staying in these challenging jobs where working conditions are less than optimal and where this is significant job strain, appears to be linked to an 'ethic of care'. Stalker and colleagues (2007a, p. 6) sum up this theme in their observation that a sizeable number of workers in care-giving occupations,

> seem willing to accept the fatigue and exhaustion that often accompany this work as long as they believe that they are helping others, or that their labour makes a positive difference in their clients' lives.

Professional commitment to child protection and welfare work

Employees' commitment to the work of child protection and welfare is recognised as a significant factor in retention. A variety of labels are used to describe this commitment: mission, altruism and strength of service orientation (Reagh, 1994; Rycraft, 1994; Landsman, 2001), although there is some variation in whom or what the worker is supposed to be committed to. Studies identify workers' commitments to children and families, commitment to the employing organisation and commitment to the profession as significant. Landsman (2001), in her study of commitment in child welfare, found that the single most important factor in a worker's commitment to child welfare was the strength of their service orientation: a worker's belief in the importance of social work positively affected firstly their job satisfaction and secondly their attachment to the field of child welfare, leading to retention. The link between professional commitment to the field of child welfare and retention has also been found in other studies (Ellet and Ellet, 2003; Weaver and Chang, 2004; Ellet *et al.*, 2006). It has been hypothesised that organisational commitment, which is the 'the degree to which an employee identifies with, connects to, and supports the organisation' (Phillips and O'Connell, 2003, p. 55) is related to retention. Employees with lower levels of organisational commitment and who are dissatisfied are more likely to leave the organisation (Mor Barak *et al.*, 2001) or express an intention to leave (Mor Barak *et al.*, 2006). The latter study cautioned that there is an added element which may be unique to child protection, which is that these workers show a higher level of commitment and responsibility towards their clients than they do to the agency. Social workers with low organisational commitment due to issues such as supervision standards and working conditions may, nevertheless, stay due to their commitment to clients and professional practice expectations. The research further elaborates that such commitments lead workers to stay at the expense of their emotional health and places them at a higher risk of burnout.

Educational background

Due to the de-professionalisation of child welfare work in some countries (for example, the U.S.A.), the role of professional education, and a professional social work qualification, is considered a significant factor in the retention of child welfare workers (Freund, 2005). Child welfare staff with social work degrees (MSW and BSW) are more likely than staff with other degrees to be retained in child welfare (Jones, 2002; Robin and Hollister, 2002; Westbrook *et al.*, 2006). A large-scale study in the U.S.A. found that having a social work degree was second only to the quality of supervision in retaining child welfare employees (American Public Human Services Association, 2005). This finding has limited benefit to my research as a social work degree and professional qualification[16] are prerequisites for being a child protection and welfare worker in Ireland.

Age

Discussion of age as a demographic factor appears infrequently within the literature. A study based in America noted that older workers may express lower intentions to leave as they may see advantages in staying in their post and value their employment benefits (Mor Barak *et al.*, 2006). As previously discussed in sections 2.4.1 and 2.4.5, child protection and welfare teams in Ireland have a relatively young age profile, with few 'older' workers. This relatively low number of 'older' and experienced workers may however have a direct effect on the social supports available to younger 'novice' workers in the form of mentoring in their first year, which may influence their intentions to stay (Westbrook *et al.*, 2006; Healy *et al.*, 2009).

---

[16] In Ireland, the accreditation body for social work is the Health and Social Care Professionals Council (CORU). Upon completion of a Master of Social Work or a Bachelor of Social Work degree, students are awarded their degree and become eligible to apply to be placed on the register and use the title of 'social worker'. Prior to the establishment of CORU, social workers trained in Ireland were awarded a NQSW by the National Social Work Qualifications Board, and before that, a CQSW by an accreditation body in the United Kingdom.

2.6.2 Supervision and social supports

Of all of the themes identified in the literature as being significant in the retention of child protection and welfare workers, the importance of supervision and the role of supervisors and colleagues in providing social supports are the most consistent. The central role of supervision in reducing the stressful nature and emotional impact of social work has been written about extensively in the general social work and child protection literature (see, for example, Morrison, 1993; White and Harris, 2007). Its importance has been emphasised in child abuse inquires in Ireland (McGuinness, 1993; Western Health Board, 1996) and in the U.K. (Lord Laming, 2003), and in Irish child protection policy (Department of Health and Children, 1999). Supervision has been described as a '... worker's most essential professional relationship' (Morrison, 1993, p. 1), yet this important relationship has been under threat from the shift towards managerialism in the public sector, a model which seeks greater managerial control over workers, economy, efficiency and effectiveness, and a focus on setting and measuring outcomes (Peach and Horner, 2007). In social exchange theory, exchange relationships between workers and supervisors emphasise the exchange resources of supervision and support. Perceived organisational support theory emphasised the seminal role that direct line supervisors play because of their daily contact with employees, to convey through their actions and the exchange of these resources, that the organisation values social workers' contributions and cares about their well-being.

In my interviews with social workers, supervision as an exchange resource was considered one of the key factors in their decisions to stay or leave child protection and welfare social work. A typical aspect of these discussion was the unbalanced focus of supervision, where the administrative focus was prominent with little attention on the other foci of supervision. The administrative focus in supervision is only one of three main functions of supervision within social work practice, which are: educational, supportive and administrative (Hawkins and Shohet, 1989, p. 43). The primary foci of each are outlined in table 2.2:

Table 2.2: Primary foci of professional supervision

Purpose Focus	
To provide a regular space for the supervisees to reflect upon the content and process of their work	*Educational*
To develop understanding and skills within the work	*Educational*
To receive information and another perspective concerning one's work	*Educational/Supportive*
To receive both content and process feedback	*Educational/Supportive*
To be validated and supported both as a person and as a worker	*Supportive*
To ensure that as a person and as a worker one is not left to carry unnecessarily difficulties, problems and projections alone	*Supportive*
To have space to explore and express personal distress, re-stimulation, transference or counter-transference that may be brought up by the work	*Administrative*
To plan and utilise their personal and professional resources better	*Administrative*
To be proactive rather than reactive	*Administrative*
To ensure quality of work	*Administrative/Supportive*

It has been argued that the professional support and development functions of supervision within social work have been lacking, with too much focus on managerial surveillance (Gibbs, 2001; White and Harris, 2007). The shift towards managerialism may contribute to a greater distance and power imbalance between workers and managers, a shift which could further undermine the potential of professional supervision. This is a particular issue within social work, as professional supervision is primarily provided by social work line managers. This issue has led some within the literature to question whether direct-line managers can perform *both* the management supervision function (also known as the clinical governance or 'inquisitorial' function) and the practice supervision function ('empathic-containing') (Rushton and Nathan, 1996; Gibbs, 2001; Peach and Horner, 2007). A published study that examined the impact of stress on child welfare supervisors highlights how supervisors are also at risk of burnout and/or compassion fatigue, a situation which would severely undermine their capacity to provide support and supervision to their supervisees (Dill, 2007). If the focus of supervision is managerial and the supportive function does not attend to the expressive needs of workers to address issues such as work stress, it can contribute to a worker's decision to leave the job (Gibbs, 2001).

The high value placed by workers on good quality supervision is repeatedly highlighted (Morrison, 1996; Social Services Inspectorate, 2003) and while it is only one factor, it is *the* most consistent factor identified in deciding whether to stay in or leave a child protection job (Pryce *et al.*, 2007). Research studies in 'child welfare' which focused on workers' intentions to stay found that supportive supervision was especially significant (Rycraft, 1994; Gibbs and Keating, 1999; Landsman, 2001). Studies that focused on decisions to leave also found that a lack of supportive supervision was one of the main factors which contributed to workers expressing an intention to leave their job (Samantrai, 1992; United States General Accounting Office, 2003). These findings are contradicted by two studies: A Swedish study which addressed factors associated with intention to leave found no relationship between support and feedback from a supervisor with intention to leave (Tham, 2007), as did a much older study which looked at a sample of workers who had resigned (Powell and York, 1992). Despite these two studies, the overwhelming thrust of the literature is that if a child protection worker receives regular supportive supervision, which addresses all of the functions of supervision, from a supervisor whom they perceive to be competent and supportive (Smith, 2005), workers are less likely to express intention to leave or actually leave their job. The inter-personal relationship with one's supervisor contributes to the worker's experience of social supports within the organisation, an experience that is complemented by the support of colleagues.

Social supports provided by colleagues are usually presented in the literature as a related theme to the supportive role of supervision, as both contribute to a worker's assessment of social supports within their agency. Those who perceive that they are in receipt of good quality social supports are less likely to think about leaving (Jayaratne and Chess, 1984; Weaver and Chang, 2004; Nissly *et al.*, 2005; Stalker *et al.*, 2007b). Social supports, as exchange resources between colleagues, can take the form of formal mentoring systems, informal peer supports, helping with the work, listening to work-related issues, and case discussions. An ability to form relationships with colleagues and to get support from supervisors appears to 'buffer' social workers who stay in child protection from the 'difficulties and isolation – and exhaustion' (Dickinson and Perry, 2002, p. 101).

Low social support, particularly co-worker support, when present with demanding workloads, places child protection workers at greater risk of burnout (Koeske and Koeske, 1989). Research reported in the stress literature highlights the importance of social support from co-workers and supervisors as a buffer against negative outcomes (Morgeson and Campion, 2003). Landsman (2001) argues that the support from colleagues and supervisors is positively associated with job satisfaction and organisational commitment. A study undertaken in Northern Ireland found that for 80% of social workers in the study, colleagues were the most significant source of support, followed by support from professional organisations at 2% and one's employing organisation at 3% (Gibson *et al.*, 1989). The support from colleagues is particularly important in child protection work, as social workers work in team-based structures and they must often rely on their team to get the work done. In summary, Collins (2008) in his review of the literature, argues that research studies consistently note the importance of supports from colleagues as *the* key source of support, and as a one of the most important contributing factors in improving job satisfaction and mediating burnout.

2.6.3 Organisational factors

Organisational factors which are identified in the literature as being significant in the retention and turnover of child welfare and other human service professionals include organisational culture and climate, caseload size/workloads, salary and promotional opportunities and alternative employment opportunities. This section will now look at each of these four factors in more depth, and conclude with a short summary of some other factors that received a very limited coverage in the job retention and turnover literature: the preparation of new graduates by universities, the impact of court work and the legal ethic, and the impact of violence and threats.

Organisational climate and culture

An organisational climate and culture refers to the degree of perceived organisational support, administrative burdens, cultures of blame and poor reward, and the perception that workers feel that their work is valued by the organisation. The main conclusion of Tham's (2007, pp. 1

and 18) Swedish study was that the organisation's human resource orientation has the most important bearing on child welfare workers' intentions to leave the job, referring to the extent to which workers are 'rewarded for a job well done, feel well taken care of and where management is interested in their health and well-being', which broadly represents the theoretical focus of perceived organisational support theory. She places this recommendation in a broader social context where clients are 'involuntary' and social workers may be subject to repeated criticism from inquiries, the media and the community. In this context, it is even more important that the organisation is seen to support and contain the anxieties of the worker. Strategies which organisations can adopt include verbal and other acknowledgements, higher salary, a pleasant, safe and secure working environment, being listened to and being visible within the organisation, and sufficient and adequate job induction, particularly for newly qualified graduates. The latter recommendation is of particular significance given the large number of newly qualified and inexperienced graduates that work in this practice setting (National Social Work Qualifications Board, 2006).

The stressful characteristics of the work, as previously outlined, are compounded when the worker perceives that the organisational climate is unsupportive and is clearly linked in the literature with stronger intentions to leave (Audit Commission, 2002; Ellet, 2007). There is a specific role for organisations (and the profession) in demonstrating their support and reinforcing the value of the work, which is particularly significant in a context where workers receive negative messages and criticism from other domains (Gibbs and Keating, 1999; Gibbs, 2001). Other factors which contribute to organisational climate, perceptions of support and job retention include the degree of autonomy and control over decisions (Audit Commission, 2002; Stalker et al., 2007a), a culture of blame and poor rewards (Healy et al., 2009), arrangements that support work-life balance (Smith, 2005), bureaucracy and excessive paperwork (Audit Commission, 2002), and the quality of supervision. Professional supervision is central in addressing Tham's recommendations, many of which dove-tail with the foci of supervision outlined in a preceding section (for example: feedback, safety, concern for the welfare of employees, providing affirmation, and so on).

Caseload size/workloads

The term 'caseload' refers to the number of cases assigned to a worker. The size of a caseload gives limited insight into the amount of work undertaken, whereas workload 'takes into account the amount of time it takes to complete all tasks related to job functions ... including direct client contact, paperwork, supervision, court, interagency collaborations, etc.' (Strolin *et al.*, 2007, p. 38). The volume and scope of the work that Irish child protection and welfare social workers now undertake has grown significantly. Irish Government statistics do not count on-going work (caseloads) held by each social worker, therefore it was not possible to establish whether caseloads in Ireland are higher or lower than international standards[17]. It was possible to locate an unpublished Irish report which examined workloads in four social work sites in 2004, two of which were child protection teams (Social Information Systems, 2005). The report concludes that the number of cases was not the issue *per se*, but that the caseloads of 'many staff' were saturated[18], which meant that a small number of 'major' time-consuming cases dominated the work and that crisis work may be the norm on child protection social work caseloads. As a consequence, a number of children received no service at all as they were on 'substantial' waiting lists (Area 7, Ballymun/Santry) or because they represented a 'dormant case' that was not dealt with due to the amount of time spent on the 'major' cases. The report clearly identified the stressful impact of these situations on social workers. Judge Conal Gibbons (2007) writing in *The Irish Times* about the plight of children in care in Ireland, noted that child protection and welfare social workers had,

> impossibly large caseloads in a climate of scare resources and crisis management ... [without] the necessary technology and systems that any modern agency would require.

The Irish literature does note a 'crisis' in child protection due to unmanageable workload levels that increasingly lead to crisis work only being carried out, but exact details are not provided to support the claim that workload levels are unmanageable (see, for example, Lavan, 1998). Referring to the 1982 and 1983 period of interventions in the *Kilkenny*

---

[17] The researcher became aware from some Principal Social Workers that the HSE is presently undertaking a national audit of social workers' workloads, which includes child protection and welfare. This process was still on-going at the time of writing.

[18] "'Saturation' was calculated by identifying which the time-consuming cases were (any cases occupying 10% or more of client-*assigned* time) and what proportion of available time those clients saturated. The higher the saturation level for an individual worker, the more that a handful of cases dominated their work" (Social Information Systems, 2005, p. 22).

Incest Investigation, the report noted that 'there was pressure on resources including high caseloads' (McGuinness, 1993, p. 79), but unfortunately the report does not define what was meant by high caseloads.

American studies report a wide variation in caseload sizes; Strolin *et al.* (2007) recorded up to 100 cases per worker; the American Public Human Services Association study reported between 10 and 110 children, with an average of 24-31 children per worker (American Public Human Services Association, 2001); and workers in Smith's (2005) study had a mean of 22.8 cases per worker. However, it is not always clear if a case means one child or one family. The exact effect of high caseloads on retention is problematic in the literature. Caseload size and workloads have been linked with retention issues for child welfare staff, increasing the likelihood of turnover, expression of intentions to leave and a lowering of job satisfaction (Powell and York, 1992; Landsman, 2001; United States General Accounting Office, 2003; Ellet, 2007). Smith (2005) showed that as child protection caseload sizes increases, the probability of actual turnover also increases. While other studies acknowledge that while one might intuitively make the link between caseload size, workload and retention, the empirical evidence does not support such a relationship (Lonne, 2003; National Council on Crime and Delinquency, 2006; Jacquet *et al.*, 2007; Tham, 2007). However, one study (Weaver and Chang, 2004) did note that the pace at which new workers are brought up to a full caseload may be an important factor in their decision to stay. The inconclusive relationship between caseloads and retention should not lead to a premature dismissal of this theme, as the link between caseload levels and quality of service is both important for outcomes for children and social workers' job satisfaction (Landsman, 2001; United States General Accounting Office, 2003; Strolin *et al.*, 2007). High workloads may lead to negative outcomes for individuals and organisations when 'translated to high job demands, in conjunction with low control, low autonomy, inadequate resources and low support' (Lonne, 2003, p. 287) and this issue will be explored with social workers in their interviews and this data will be presented in Chapter Five (section 5.4.1).

Salary and promotional opportunities

Salaries and promotional opportunities are exchange resources between workers and their employing organisation in social exchange theory. Research findings are inconsistent in relation to the merits of higher salaries: some researchers felt that it had a role to play as a predictor of turnover or intention to leave (Powell and York, 1992; Audit Commission, 2002; National Council on Crime and Delinquency, 2006), while others found it inconsistently related to turnover (Landsman, 2001; Smith, 2005; Strolin et al., 2007). Findings regarding salary should be approached cautiously as salaries and the cost of living vary significantly across countries, and in the U.S.A, where child welfare was de-professionalised, salaries would be lower than other social work jobs (United States General Accounting Office, 2003). However, promotional opportunities, and consequently higher salaries, did find some support within the literature as a factor which could aid retention and improve job satisfaction. Koeske and Kirk (1995) found that the opportunities for promotion were a predictor of actual employee turnover in child welfare. Healy et al.(2009) argued for the introduction of a senior practitioner level to retain skilled practitioners who do not want to become managers, and Landsman (2001) found that the availability of a career ladder to promote continuing professional development was a strong element in improving job satisfaction. The senior social work practitioner level argued for by Healy and colleagues (2007) is already in place in Ireland as it was introduced in the mid-2000s as a progression pathway for experienced social work practitioners who did not want to become managers. However, this will not form part of the analysis as the HSE 'Area A' was still rolling out these posts during the fieldwork period of this study.

Alternative employment options

Perceptions of the availability of alternative job opportunities, both within and external to the organisation, are also associated with intentions to leave one's job (Samantrai, 1992; Mor Barak et al., 2001; Audit Commission, 2002; Smith, 2005). Even if workers are happy in their jobs, those who perceive that there are better local jobs are more likely to express an intention to leave (Weaver and Chang, 2004). This finding may have a particular resonance for child protection teams in more rural areas where there is a very limited supply of alternative local employment opportunities. It is also important to acknowledge that some workers stay, not because they enjoy the work and want to stay, but because they 'feel trapped' (Smith, 2005, p. 167) because they would have difficulty finding, or were unaware of, other job alternatives. This may be a particular concern in Ireland as during the fieldwork period the HSE operated a 'recruitment embargo', which considerably reduced opportunities to leave child protection work for other jobs within the HSE, and there also were few non-HSE social work posts available.

Some other factors which received limited coverage in the job retention literature in child protection include: the preparation of new graduates by universities for the realities of practice, which was found to be insignificant by Samantrai (1992) and to be important by others (Healy and Meagher, 2007; Healy *et al.*, 2009); the impact of court work and the legal ethic on turnover in child welfare (Vandervort *et al.*, 2007), and the impact of violence and threats, which was considered significant by some authors (Stanley and Goddard, 2002; Ferguson, 2005), but was found to have a weak relationship with intention to leave by another (Tham, 2007). While the factors in this paragraph were occasionally raised in my interviews with social workers, they were not significant in social workers' decisions to stay or leave.

2.7 Discussion and analysis

In summary, studies which examined job retention and turnover in child protection and welfare emphasise the scale of retention problems in the sector and categorise the individual, supervision and social supports, and organisational factors which contribute to workers' decisions to stay or leave. While it was possible to discern a clear body of literature, with a particular surge of published studies since 2003, this area has received limited attention from researchers, particularly outside of the United States of America and Australia.

Earlier studies tended to focus on turnover and examined why social workers leave, with research focusing on factors associated with social workers' intentions to leave. There have also been a small number of studies that conceptualise intention to stay as a different construct from intention to leave. While most of the research studies focused on job turnover, few have specifically examined why social workers stay in their jobs despite stressful work conditions and challenging organisational systems. The sample of participants in some studies have tended to highlight exclusively staff who had stayed beyond normative expectations for tenure in this sector (Reagh, 1994; Rycraft, 1994; Ellet, 2007), whereas other studies '... have extrapolated why employees stayed from the variables that had low or negative relationships' (Mor Barak *et al.*, 2006, p. 567).

Overall, the research discussed in this chapter suggests that retention and turnover are best understood as outcomes of complex interactions between a variety of socio-cultural, organisational, supervisory and personal factors. Firstly, the broader external socio-cultural context in which child protection and welfare work operates contributes to job stress and influences retention in a negative way through the low level of government support, the under-resourcing of this work, and the low social status of this 'dirty work' (Dressel, 1984; Thompson, 2000). Secondly, organisational environments should support and resource those who undertake this work to enable workers to feel that they can make a positive difference in the lives of children and families. Thirdly, social work supervisors play an essential role in staff retention through the provision of regular safe and supportive supervision which values the worker and their work, and equally addresses all of the supervisory functions. Fourthly, in conjunction with the quality of supervision, the quality of inter-personal relationships with colleagues and supervisors is consistently linked with job retention in the literature (social supports). Fifthly, a commitment to the field of child protection and its clients contributes to workers' intentions to stay. Sixthly, the over-representation of young and inexperienced workers in child protection and their relatively short tenure may contribute to a 'turnover culture' in which the low level of skills and experience mix contribute to instability in teams, making it harder for others to stay. The reason why so many young and inexperienced workers work in child protection was implied rather than explicitly addressed in the literature. This issue will be explored further in Chapter Six.

To examine these range of factors, the following theoretical and conceptual frameworks were chosen to structure the data collection and analysis. No one turnover theory seemed adequate to support the study as each had specific limitations, none were comprehensive enough, and the choice of one specific theory would have restricted the type of data collected and the subsequent analysis.

Social Exchange Theory will be used to examine the social exchanges relationships between social workers and the HSE (exchange resources such as salary, benefits, recognition for their work), social workers and their supervisors (exchange resources such as supervision, praise, affirmation, support), and social workers and their co-workers (exchange resources such supports, peer-mentoring, praise, affirmation). As described in section 2.5, given their daily contact with workers, supervisors play a seminal role in conveying whether the organisation is supportive (for example, through the provision of supervision and supports). Hawkins and Shohet's (1989) framework will be employed to structure social workers' analysis of the quality and key facets of their supervision. Perceived Organisational Support Theory (Eisenberger *et al.*, 2004) will be used as a framework to collect and analyse data to examine the extent to which social workers describe the HSE as being supportive and whether social workers feel the HSE values their contributions and is concerned about their welfare.

While not exclusively a theory of retention, job design theory when used in the redesign of work, have been shown to increase job satisfaction and retention (Morgeson and Campion, 2003). Therefore, this theory can make a contribution to structuring the interviews to collect data associated with the nature of work and working conditions in child protection and welfare, and their influence on social workers' retention. While all of the five concepts in this model will be used to structure the interviews, this research is specifically interested in three of the concepts due to their importance in the literature: task significance, skill variety and autonomy.

The study will also consider economic explanations for turnover (Steel, 2004) by specifically exploring social workers' perceptions of the availability of alternative employment opportunities, pay, conditions, benefits, and rewards, and examines whether social workers describe these factors as important in their retention.

This study will employ the concepts of retention and 'avoidable' turnover as defined in section 2.2 (Phillips and O'Connell, 2003). While it is one of the objectives of the study to capture a turnover rate for these social workers, a mere statistic does not provide insight into why social workers left their work and whether their turnover was avoidable. Therefore, the qualitative analysis explores whether social workers describe their decision to want to leave or their actual turnover, as being avoidable. A description of how turnover is to be calculated in this study will be examined in Chapter Four.

While the unfolding model of voluntary turnover (Lee and Mitchell, 1994) was not used to design the interview guide, it was drawn upon in parts of the data analysis as aspects of this theory helped to understand the reasons why some social workers in the study had left child protection and welfare in the HSE 'Area A'.

The research interviews will also collect data on social workers' caseloads, violence and threats towards social workers, and social workers' health to examine their influence on social workers' decisions to stay or leave. The use of grounded theory will also allow for other understandings, explanations and concepts to emerge during the data collection and analysis, which are not part of this analytical framework.

The literature review also illustrated the dominance of large-scale quantitative surveys employing causal modelling to identify key variables in job retention and turnover (see, for example, Mor Barak *et al.*, 2001; Smith, 2005). It also identified a limited use of qualitative research methods in the 1990s (Reagh, 1994; Rycraft, 1994), and these qualitative studies played an influential role in shaping subsequent research in the field and are frequently cited in the literature reviews. In recent years, there has been a renewed interest in the potential of qualitative research methods in job retention research (see, for example, Ellet and Ellet, 2003; Morris, 2005; Ellet *et al.*, 2006) and mixed method studies (see, for example, Mor Barak *et al.*, 2006; Jacquet *et al.*, 2007), although the majority of studies still employ quantitative methods. Qualitative methods can contribute to a deeper understanding of, and meanings associated with, job retention. This point was highlighted in Tham's (2007) study, where she identified the limitations of using questionnaires for data-collection as she was unable to elaborate or clarify what workers meant in their answers. The use of qualitative methods in this PhD research study will be described in Chapter Three.

2.8 Concluding comments

Despite the challenging organisational conditions, possible health effects and the perceived lack of support from employing organisations and the community, studies have found that some child protection and welfare social workers are committed to staying in their job (Lonne, 2003; Ellet *et al.*, 2006). While the Irish literature presented in Chapter One suggested that retaining social workers in this practice setting may be problematic, there are no published Irish studies which specifically examine this issue. The dearth of Irish research that specifically examines child protection and welfare social workers' working conditions and job retention, emphasises the contribution my research will make in addressing this gap. As there is an over-representation of U.S.A. based research on the retention of social workers, some caution is needed in drawing conclusions from practice contexts that are in many ways dissimilar to Ireland. Bearing this in mind and despite some inconsistencies in the research findings, it was possible to discern some key themes which consistently appear to influence turnover and retention in child protection and welfare. The research suggests that retention and turnover are best understood as outcomes of complex interactions between a variety of organisational, social support, supervisory and personal factors.

The analysis in this chapter raises important questions and provides a framework with which to examine these questions for child protection and welfare social work in Ireland. What are social workers' attitudes towards staying and leaving statutory child protection and welfare in the Ireland? What are child protection and welfare social workers' understandings of the individual, supervisory, and organisational factors that influence their decisions to want to stay in or leave their current employment? Taking into account the stressful working and organisational conditions in child protection and welfare, why do some social workers stay? Why do other social workers leave, and where do they go? The present study builds upon existing research on employee turnover and retention in child protection and welfare and it will contribute to this literature by firstly, focusing specifically on statutory child protection and welfare social workers in one Health Service Executive in Ireland; secondly employing a qualitative methodology to explore social workers' attitudes towards their retention in child protection and welfare, and thirdly grounding the study in the current literature on workforce retention. The next chapter examines how a qualitative methodology supports the aims of this study, and develops the questions identified in this chapter.

Chapter 3
Researching social workers' decisions to stay or leave child protection and welfare

3.1 Introduction

In the previous chapters, the context of child protection and welfare social work in Ireland and relevant theory and research on job retention and turnover was described. The literature review suggests that turnover in child protection and welfare appears to be high in the identified countries, but I argued that the literature on social work in Ireland offers little beyond the anecdotal in exploring this issue. This reveals a significant gap in the research. I also argued that it would be unhelpful to apply uncritically the international literature to Ireland as some of the organisational, political and professional conditions are not readily comparable with child protection and welfare here. In Chapter Two, I noted that there is an under-utilisation of qualitative research methods in this research literature, and while dominated by quantitative methods, research in this area can benefit from qualitative research design. There is some evidence of the use of both qualitative and mixed methods in some recent studies that examine job retention and turnover for child protection workers (see, for example, Dollard *et al.*, 2001; Ellet *et al.*, 2006; Mor Barak *et al.*, 2006).

This chapter describes the development of a qualitative research design to examine social workers' professional experiences in a child protection and welfare organisation and their reasons for wanting to stay in or leave their work. The chapter presents the objectives of the research study and a revised set of research questions to reflect the findings of the literature review. I outline a mixed-methods approach to data collection, and my use of grounded theory to analyse the qualitative data is examined. The chapter concludes by examining ethical considerations associated with undertaking this study.

3.2 Interpreting and giving meaning to professional experiences

Organisational culture and change management are significant emerging themes in qualitative social work research which has become 'pre-occupied with organisational and professional adaptation as a continuous feature of organisational life' (Shaw and Gould, 2001, p. 41). Ferguson and O'Reilly (2001), in their research on Irish child protection and welfare practices, argued that 'social abstractions' like 'child protection and welfare' are best understood by talking with, and trying to understand, the experiences of both social workers and service users. As yet, not enough is known about how social workers construct, interpret and give meaning to their professional experiences and how these experiences shape their on-going decisions to stay in or leave their job.

Reviews of the organisational research literature highlight the dominance of quantitative methods as a result of methodological biases in management and organisational psychology training (Cassell and Symon, 1994; Lee, 1999). Research methodology texts emphasise that *the* key debate within social research is between the use of quantitative and qualitative research. In this debate qualitative and quantitative methods are presented as polar opposites and perceived to be philosophically irreconcilable, with one tradition claiming superiority over the other (Lee, 1999; Bryman, 2004). However, each tradition comes from a different epistemological perspective and has its own unique perspective on the nature of knowledge and its construction. There has been some focus on the use of multi-method approaches to social research where each tradition should not be seen as competing and contradictory, but complementary strategies where each has some merit depending on the type of research questions or issues (Snape and Spence, 2003).

In the last chapter, I highlighted the dominance of quantitative approaches in job retention and turnover research, while also highlighting a move towards qualitative and mixed methods in recent research. Turnbull (2002, citing Symon and Cassell, 1997) suggests that quantitative researchers have down-played the complexities of organisational life in their attempts to establish reductionist causal relationships, which she suggests has led researchers to explore the merits of qualitative research. I believe that qualitative methods and research from an interpretivist paradigm underpinned by a social constructionist approach, is most appropriate to the kind of research questions I want to ask about child protection and welfare social work. Bryman (1999, p. 264) defines interpretivism as an epistemological position in contrast to the natural scientific method that stresses 'an understanding of the social world through an interpretation of that world by its participants'. The ontological orientation of qualitative research is constructivist which 'implies that social properties are outcomes of interaction between individuals, rather than a phenomena 'out there' and separate from those involved in its construction' (Bryman, 2001, p. 264). Constructionism is antithetical to positivism, by rejecting the modernist view there is a knowable objective reality and truth that can be measured.

Reality is contested, meanings are not fixed and researchers and research participants' accounts of the world are understood as social constructions. The complex nature of the social world is reflected in the way in which actors interpret events, experiences and process in different ways, thereby constructing multiple constructed realities.

By adopting a social constructionist approach, this study seeks to explain how social workers understand and interpret the meaning given to their experiences and how these meanings shape their decisions to stay in or leave their work. Causal explanations sought by quantitative researchers are not the focus of this study and the cause and effect argument is itself viewed as a social construction (Turnbull, 2002). Social constructionist research seeks to capture the individual's perspective through 'rich descriptions of the social world' by using data collection methods such as interviews and observation, rather than large-scale survey methods, and an 'explanation about how social experience is created and given meaning' (Turnbull, 2002, p. 320). The researcher's choice of data collection methods is described later in the chapter.

Within this tradition, and as emphasised by feminist methodologies (see Stanley and Wise, 1993), the researcher should acknowledge and make clear his or her own biases and assumptions. As discussed in Chapter One, I previously worked in child protection and welfare social work for five years before moving to an academic post at University College Cork. The researcher's own practice experience as the genesis of a research project is recognised as a potential advantage within the qualitative research tradition (Richards and Morse, 2007), while also recognising that it can also lead to bias. During my time in the Southern Health Board, the turnover of child protection and welfare social workers appeared to be excessively high. Some social workers 'thrived' in this 'turbulent environment' (Hughes and Pengelly, 1997), enjoyed the work and wanted to stay, whereas others were affected by the work (including, suffering from work related ill-health) and were planning to leave. As someone who left this social work setting, I was curious to explore with social workers their experiences and to understand how they made decisions to stay in or leave this work, and why some stayed longer than others. This experience also contributed to the selection of certain topics for the literature review, in particular social supports from co-workers and supervision. However, these were very strong and persistent themes in the literature anyway and would have been selected irrespective of my experience.

In summary, qualitative research is the most appropriate research approach to achieve the objectives of this research as it focuses upon individual experiences, meanings and understandings. The core objective of this study was to undertake an inquiry into the professional experiences of social workers working in child protection and welfare in Ireland, and how these experiences influence their choices to stay or leave. The next section introduces the research questions that guided the study, and subsequent sections outline the design of the research.

3.3 Research questions

The overall aim of the research is to examine the retention and turnover of child protection and welfare social workers. This aim is achieved by asking the following questions:

1. What are the turnover and employee mobility rates of child protection and welfare social workers, specifically in the Health Service Executive 'Area A', between March 2005 and December 2006?

2. What are child protection and welfare social workers' under-standings of the individual, supervisory, social support, and organisational factors that influence their decisions to want to stay in or leave their current employment?

3. What role is played by social exchanges between child protection and welfare social workers, their supervisors and colleagues, in the retention of the former?

4. Do child protection and welfare social workers perceive the HSE 'Area A' as a supportive organisation that values their contribu-tions and cares about their well-being, and what influence has these perceptions on their retention?

5. What specific factors do social workers who left their post in child protection and welfare in the Health Service Executive 'Area A' between March 2005 and December 2006 attribute to their decision to leave and was their turnover avoidable?

6. How useful are social exchange theory, perceived organisational support theory and job characteristics theory in helping to explain child protection and welfare social workers' retention?

7. How do child protection and welfare social workers' understandings of career pathways in social work influence their motivations to work in child protection and welfare and subsequent decisions to stay or leave?

8. What essential factors highlighted in this study could contribute to the development of a retention policy for social workers in child protection and welfare?

3.4 Research design

In this section, I examine and describe the sampling strategy and characteristics of interview participants, data collection methods used to answer the research questions, the use of Information and Communication Technologies in qualitative studies, and ethical considerations associated with undertaking this study.

3.4.1 Sampling strategy and characteristics of interview participants

A core aspect of research design is making decisions about whom to interview. Bryman (2004) argues that often in qualitative research studies, it is difficult to ascertain *why* and *how* participants were selected and how many were chosen. This study was based in one HSE area, the Health Service Executive 'Area A', which has ten child protection and welfare teams. For practical and financial reasons the research was limited to the HSE 'Area A' (all of the teams were within 80 miles of the university). The HSE 'Area A' child protection and welfare teams represent a good variety of urban/rural, large/small teams and include duty, intake, long-term, and generic teams. While this is not a national sample, the findings are likely to have implications for national HSE child protection and welfare teams.

Child protection and welfare teams are staffed by social workers, senior social work practitioners, administrators, social work team leaders, principal social workers, child care workers/leaders, and by a very small number of other professionals. Social workers are also employed in ancillary/supportive services such as family centres, neighbourhood youth projects, adoption and fostering. However, as the focus of this study is the provision of statutory child protection and welfare services, I restricted the selection of social workers to two grades: professionally qualified social workers and senior social work practitioners. The rationale for this decision was that the core tasks and responsibilities of other teams (for example, fostering), social work managers, administrators and other professionals in child protection and welfare are qualitatively different from the two social work grades selected for the study. Also, these two grades constitute the majority of employees in this practice setting (61% of all WTEs, see table 3.1).

The most recent social work labour force study (National Social Work Qualifications Board, 2006) indicated that there were 738 social workers employed in 'child and family work (statutory)' in 2005 (33% of a total social work workforce of 2237). Of the total workforce, there were 388 male social workers (16.8%) and male social workers were over-represented in management grades. For example, in the 'Health/General' category, women social workers represented 86% of the workforce while women occupied only 73.5% of management posts in this category. The majority of social workers in Ireland in 2005 were aged between 26-45 (1,432, 62%). Overall, 60% of social workers in child protection and welfare were under 35 years of age (58.6%). 699 social workers (33%) held 'non-national social work qualifications', and the majority (62%) of these practitioners were employed by the Health Service Executive.

The HSE 'Area A' does not publish this depth of data on its social work workforce in its 'section 8' reports[19], but I obtained some additional data for the HSE 'Area A' on its social work workforce. This facilitated a more in-depth analysis of the HSE 'Area A's' child protection and welfare workforce, which is presented in the following tables and figures. These datasets facilitated the construction of a population sample that was used to select the study sample using my sampling decisions. I will describe the broader workforce first and then focus on the numbers and profile of social workers and senior social work practitioners in the HSE 'Area A'. In September 2005, there were circa 140 staff[20] employed in the five child protection and welfare teams, where 79% of all Whole Time Equivalents (WTEs) were social work posts (see table 3.1). Team 1 was the largest team with 37% of all WTEs and Team 2 was the smallest team with 8% of all WTEs:

---

[19]   The Health Service Executive areas are legally obliged under the *Child Care Act, 1991* to publish an annual report, the function of which is to review the adequacy of child care and family support services in each area. These reports were known as the 'section 8' reports.

[20]   No data provided for administrators and a very small number of other professionals (for example, the public health nurse post in Team 4 was not included in the dataset).

Grade	Team 1 Staff + (WTE)	Team 2 Staff + (WTE)	Team 3 Staff + (WTE)	Team 4 Staff + (WTE)	Team 5 Staff + (WTE)	Total Staff (Persons)	Total WTEs	Grade % by WTE
PSW[22]	2 (1.8)	1 (1)	1 (1)	1 (1)	2 (2)	7	6.8	6%
TL	8 (6.8)	1 (1)	1 (0.8)	3 (3)	3 (3)	16	14.6	12%
SSWP	0 (0)[23]	1 (1)	2 (1.6)	4 (4)	1 (1)	8	7.6	6%
SW	29 (26.65)	7 (5.4)	8 (8)	15 (13.3)	14 (13.5)	73	66.85	55%
CCL	7 (5.72)	2 (1.38)	4 (3.6)	6 (4.46)	3 (2.06)	22	17.22	14%
FS	6 (4.07)	0 (0)	2 (1.38)	0 (0)	6 (3.85)	14	9.3	8%
Totals	52 (45.04)	12 (9.78)	18 (16.38)	29 (25.76)	29 (25.41)	140	122.37	100%*
Team Size by Total WTE	37%	8%	13%	21%	21%	-	-	-

* Does not total 100% exactly due to rounding up/down.

When the child care worker/leader and family support posts are removed from this data (see table 3.2), we see that there are 104 social workers employed in the five teams (95.85 WTEs). The combined social worker

---

21   The data source for tables 3.1 through 3.4 and figures 3.1 and 3.2 is an unpublished 'raw' HSE 'Area A' employee data file (*Microsoft Excel*). The analysis of this data was undertaken by the researcher. The data file contained staff lists for Team 1, Team 3, Team 2, Team 5 and Team 4 child protection and welfare teams for the month of September 2005. The HSE 'Area A' provided updated staff lists in 'raw' format on a quarterly basis which facilitated the researcher to update the sample population dataset and to track employment changes during the fieldwork period.
22   Principal Social Worker (PSW), Team Leader (TL), SSWP (Senior Social Work Practitioner), Social Worker (SW), Child Care Worker/Child Care Leader (CCL) and Family Support Worker/Coordinator (FS).
23   Team 1's senior social work practitioner posts were appointed after September 2005.

and senior social work practitioner grades account for 78% of all social work WTEs:

Table 3.2: HSE 'Area A' child protection and welfare teams by post and WTE (social work posts only)

Grade	Team 1 SW Staff + (WTE)	Team 2 SW Staff + (WTE)	Team 3 SW Staff + (WTE)	Team 4 Staff SW + (WTE)	Team 5 Staff SW + (WTE)	Total SW Staff (Persons)	Total SW WTEs	SW Grade % by WTE
PSW[24]	2 (1.8)	1 (1)	1 (1)	1 (1)	2 (2)	7	6.8	7%
TL	8 (6.8)	1 (1)	1 (0.8)	3 (3)	3 (3)	16	14.6	15%
SSWP	0 (0)[25]	1 (1)	2 (1.6)	4 (4)	1 (1)	8	7.6	8%
SW	29 (26.65)	7 (5.4)	8 (8)	15 (13.3)	14 (13.5)	73	66.85	70%
Totals	**39 (35.25)**	**10 (8.4)**	**12 (11.4)**	**23 (21.3)**	**20 (19.5)**	**104**	**95.85**	*100%*
Team Size by Total SW WTE	*37%*	*9%*	*12%*	*22%*	*20%*	-	-	-

---

[24] Principal Social Worker (PSW), Team Leader (TL), SSWP (Senior Social Work Practitioner), Social Worker (SW), Child Care Worker/Child Care Leader (CCL) and Family Support Worker/Coordinator (FS).

[25] Team 1's senior social work practitioner posts were appointed after September 2005.

Figure 3.1 provides a graphical representation of the relative size of the five teams by the number of social workers and WTEs:

Figure 3.1: Social work posts by child protection and welfare team

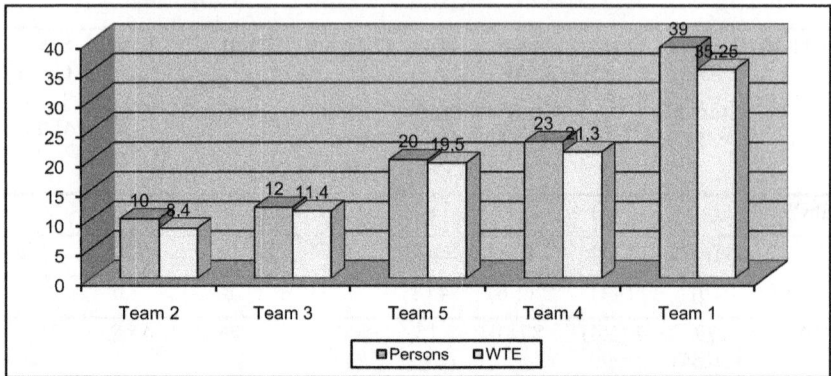

91 of the 104 social workers (87.5%) were women. Men were over-represented in management grades, in particular as principal social workers, relative to the percentage of men social workers in direct service provision:

Table 3.3: HSE 'Area A' child protection and welfare social work posts by grade and sex

Grade	Women	Men	Totals
Principal Social Workers	3 (43%)	4 (57%)	7
Team Leaders	14 (88%)	2 (13%)	16
Senior Social Work Practitioners	6 (75%)	2 (25%)	8
Social Workers	68 (93%)	5 (7%)	73
	91 (87.5%)	**13 (12.5%)**	**104**

Figure 3.2 provides a graphical representation of this data:

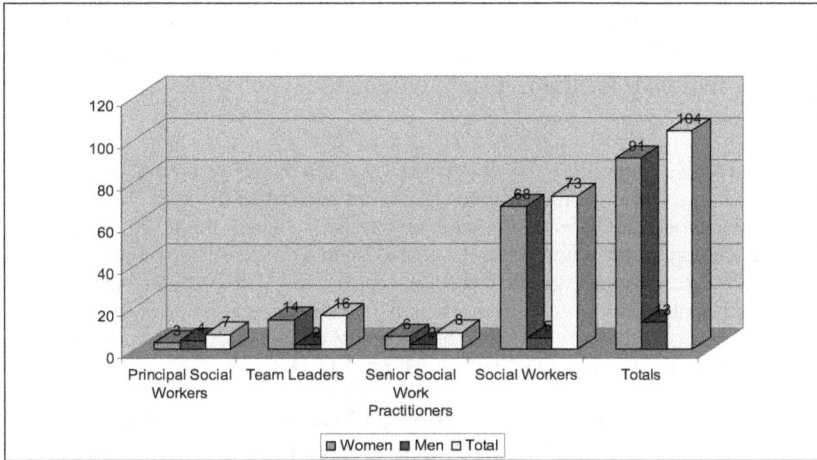

Figure 3.2: HSE 'Area A' child protection and social work posts by grade and sex

From this data, a final sample population was developed, with a total of 81 social workers in direct service provision, the majority of whom were women (74). Table 3.4 provides an overview of the sample population at the beginning of the fieldwork period[26]:

Table 3.4: Sample population by team

	Team 1	Team 2	Team 3	Team 4	Team 5	Totals	Women	Men
SSWP	0[7]	1	2	4	1	**8**	6	2
SW	29	7	8	15	14	**73**	68	5
Totals	**29**	**8**	**10**	**19**	**15**	**81**	74	7
	-	-	-	-	-	-	*91%*	*9%*

---

[26] The sample population changed over the course of the study as the HSE 'Area A' 'raw' employee datasets enabled me to keep updating the sample population. For example, during the fieldwork period, some of the Team 1 social work posts were upgraded to the new senior social work practitioner grade, therefore the number of social workers in the dataset reduced while the number of senior social work practitioners increased.

71

The qualitative research literature highlights the importance of designing samples that take into account participants' 'symbolic representation' and samples should ensure diversity. Purposive and theoretical sampling strategies were employed to select a sample that reflected this sampling population, which included characteristics such as age, experience, gender, regional location, team, nationality and work context (duty, intake, *etc.*):

> Purposive sampling, also known as criterion based sampling, a key feature of which is that sample criteria are prescribed. Sample units are selected on the basis of known characteristics, which might be socio-demographic or might relate to factors such as experience, behaviour, roles etc. relevant to the research topic. Units [*sic.*] are chosen to represent and symbolise prescribed groups or characteristics (symbolic representation) and to reflect the diversity of the study population as fully as possible (Ritchie *et al.*, 2003, pp. 107-108).

Using HSE 'Area A' child protection and welfare social work staff lists (provided on a quarterly basis) which also provided data on gender, number of posts, grades, employment movements and so on; details on the demographic profile of social work in Ireland (age, nationality and experience) (National Social Work Qualifications Board, 2006), and the sampling decisions outlined above, a sample was generated that included:

- At least 30 social workers involved in the direct provision of child protection and welfare services in the HSE 'Area A'.

- At least 5 senior social work practitioners involved in the direct provision of child protection and welfare services in the HSE 'Area A'. Their selection will assist the balance of practice experience in the study.

- Of these 35 social workers, there should be:

  o Approximately 90% women and 10% men to reflect the overall gender profile of these two grades within the HSE 'Area A'.
  o A minimum of 4 social workers from each of the 5 child protection and welfare teams, and after this minimum is reached, participants will be selected based on the relative size of each team.
  o At least 6 social workers who trained outside of Ireland to reflect the national percentage of social workers who were non Irish trained.

- At least 10 social workers/senior social work practitioners with 5+ years' child protection and welfare social work experience.
- Each of the individual teams (duty, intake, long-term) within each child protection and welfare department should be represented on a broadly *pro-rata* basis.

Theoretical sampling within grounded theory supports the expansion of initial sampling strategies and asks '... what data to collect next and where to find them, in order to develop his [*sic.*] theory as it emerges' (Glaser and Strauss, 1967, p. 45). As the research progressed, the data and emerging categories suggested an expansion of these initial sample criteria to include social workers who already resigned their post in child protection and welfare in the HSE 'Area A'. This expansion would help to widen our understanding of how social workers make decisions about leaving. The sample design was refined to add at least 8 social workers/senior social work practitioners who resigned from their post in child protection and welfare in the HSE 'Area A' during the period of the study.

A total of 38 social workers and 6 senior social work practitioners participated in the study (total participants = 44[27]). This total includes the social workers who resigned during the study. The group included 39 women (89%) and 5 men (11%), ranging in age from 26 to 66 (see table 3.5). The average age of participants when they started working in child protection and welfare was 31 years (median = 27). The average age of participants on the day of the interview was 37 (median = 32).

---

[27] In total, 50 invitations of participation were sent. Two social workers declined to be interviewed: no explanation was offered in one case and the other was unavailable as she was about to go on maternity leave. 4 invitations were unanswered - it subsequently transpired that 3 of these letters were never received by the social workers as they had left their child protection and welfare post in the HSE 'Area A', and the fourth invitation is unaccounted for. 44 persons participated in total: 43 were interviewed and 1 email correspondence. 45 interviews were undertaken altogether, where 41 people were interviewed once and 2 were interviewed twice. These two social workers were interviewed firstly as child protection and welfare social workers in the HSE 'Area A' and subsequently as part of the leavers sample.

Table 3.5: Age profile of participants

Age Range	25 and under	26-35	36-45	46-55	56-64	65+	Totals
No.	0	27	6	7	2	2	**44**
%	0%	61%	14%	16%	5%	5%	**100%***

* does not total 100% exactly, due to rounding up

Of those who were asked to participate in the study, one social worker did not want to be interviewed, but entered into an email correspondence with the researcher and gave permission for this data to be included in the study. At the time of interview, 36 of the participants were employed as social workers (30) or senior social work practitioners (6) in child protection and welfare in the HSE 'Area A'. 10 interviews were undertaken with social workers who had left their post as social workers (8) or senior social work practitioners (2) in child protection and welfare in the HSE 'Area A'. Table 3.6 outlines the details of participants' team and department on the day of interview, which is broadly representative of the spread of child protection and welfare posts in this HSE:

Table 3.6: Participants' team and department on day of interview/last post held before leaving

Name of Department	'Generic'	Duty	Intake	Long-Term	'Other'	Totals
Team 1	0	3	3	11	2	**19**
Team 2	0	1	0	4	0	**5**
Team 3	0	1	0	5	0	**6**
Team 4	0	3	3	3	0	**9**
Team 5	5	0	0	0	0	**5**
Totals	**5**	**8**	**6**	**23**	**2**	**44**

34 of the participants were born in Ireland and 10 were born elsewhere. 33 of the participants trained as social workers in Ireland and 11 outside Ireland. 35 (79%) of the participants' first job post-qualification was in child protection and welfare. Of the social workers that trained in Ireland, the first job post-qualification for 91% was in child protection and welfare. All of the participants were professionally qualified and were more experienced in child protection and welfare that social workers/child protection workers in international studies (see, for example, Gibbs and Keating, 1999). Participants in the study had an

average tenure length of 3.5 years in child protection and welfare and two-thirds of the total sample's professional social work careers was in child protection and welfare in the HSE 'Area A'. Table 3.7 summarises the range of participants' child protection and welfare social work experience:

Table 3.7: Range of participants' practice experience in child protection and welfare

Range	No.	%
0 - 2 years	11	25%
3 - 5 years	18	41%
6 - 10 years	10	23%
11 - 15 years	3	7%
16 - 20 years	1	2%
21 - 25 years	1	2%
Total	**44**	**100%**

Data was collected from the study participants through individual semi-structured interviews and a survey form for descriptive demographic and employment data. Data was also collected from the HSE 'Area A' on child protection and welfare social workers' caseloads, turnover and social work employment mobility.

3.4.2 Data collection methods

While reviewing the literature at the early stages of the study, the dominance of quantitative methods suggested that quantitative survey data collection methods would be the best method of data collection using standard questionnaires such as the GHQ-12 or Job Characteristics Survey (JCS) (Bowling, 2005). As the study progressed, I discovered a number of qualitative organisational research studies (see, for example, Ellet *et al.*, 2006) that demonstrated how qualitative methods could be used in organisational research. Reviewing my research questions, I decided that a qualitative research approach was most appropriate. I decided that qualitative research interviews would be the main and most appropriate data collection method in a study where the primary focus is to access the meanings, interpretations and understandings (Kvale, 1996) of child protection and welfare social workers. I also decided to use a short survey form to collect descriptive data from participants and to collect quantitative data to explore one of the research questions which could not be answered by using interviews. The next two sections examine these methods and my data collection decisions in greater detail.

Individual semi-structured interviews

Individual interviews are but one of a number of data collection methods used in qualitative research, including participant observation, focus groups, narratives and the use of visual images and documentary research (Bryman and Burgess, 1999; Silverman, 2004). The use of focus groups and participant observation were examined in the earlier stages of the research design. However, interviews were selected as the main method of data collection and the remainder of this section examines this method and the rationale for choosing semi-structured interviews over the other methods.

45 semi-structured interviews, generally lasting between 1.5–2 hours, were undertaken at a location of the participant's choosing, including the researcher's office, various HSE 'Area A' offices and hotel meeting rooms. All of the interviewees were sent a letter of invitation which included information on the study's purpose, length, a statement of voluntary participation and contact information for the researcher and research supervisor, and a documentation sheet to collect details such as demographic information (e.g. gender, age), employment history details (posts held, length of employment), and educational history (qualifications, year of graduation). All of the interviews were recorded on a mini-disc player and transcribed. A topic [interview] guide was developed from the literature review and adapted during the pilot study phase. The literature associated with work stress and child protection and welfare (Stanley and Goddard, 2002; Ferguson, 2004; European Foundation for the Improvement of Living and Working Conditions, 2005) indicated that there was a moderate to high probability that participants may find some of the material difficult to talk about in front of other participants as part of the data collection process often relates to sensitive topics connected to participants' personal lives.In designing the research, I considered the use of focus groups as a data collection method. I opted not to use this method as it could be embarrassing for social workers to discuss sensitive topics in front of colleagues, to be possibly constructed within groups as someone who cannot 'cope' with the job, and collecting this type of data in focus groups could inhibit participants' willingness to discuss particularly sensitive issues. The pilot study confirmed that individual semi-structured interviews were an effective data collection method, but data collection using this method

only would not allow me to answer all of my research questions. I would also need to employ surveys to collect quantitative data on social workers' workloads, turnover and employment mobility.

In addition to the strength of semi-structured interviews in collecting sensitive personal data, this type of interviewing was chosen as appropriate for the study's chosen methodological approach - providing a way to understand participants' lived world, their behaviour and the meaning of a particular phenomenon or behaviour (Seidman, 1991; Kvale, 1996). Mason (2002a), developing this idea further, argues that qualitative interviews are more than a straightforward information-gathering exercise: the interview is a 'site of knowledge construction' (p. 225). The impact of the researcher on the construction of knowledge, in particular the matching of interviewer and participant characteristics (for example, gender) is identified as significant in the literature (Lewis, 2003). The majority of 'front-line' child protection and welfare social workers in the HSE 'Area A' are women and I was approaching them as a male academic who used to be a male team leader in child protection and welfare in this HSE.

Survey form and HSE 'Area A' caseload/turnover/employee mobility data

To collect data on child protection and welfare social workers' caseloads, their job turnover and employment mobility, I needed to collect data that was not available in the public domain and could not be collected through individual semi-structured interviews. I negotiated with the HSE 'Area A' to provide data on these issues. The data provided was in a 'raw' form and required further detailed analysis. To collect descriptive and demographic data from participants, I designed a survey form for completion prior to the interview. It was not my intention to collect quantitative data by using quantitative surveys as a measure to 'validate' the findings of the qualitative data through 'concurrent/successive paradigm triangulation' or as a means to measure an 'objective' reality and 'improve' the 'validity' and 'reliability' of the study (Sarantakos, 2005; Flick, 2006). However, the quantitative data collected for this study helped me to answer a particular research question that could not be answered using interviews. The quantitative data was also important as in the literature review I had identified gaps in the Irish literature about social workers' turnover and caseloads.

To access basic descriptive data on interviewees which was not included in the employee lists provided by the HSE 'Area A' and to gather initial data on factors which were highlighted as significant in the literature review (sample items: educational history, incidents of violence and threats, and caseload data - see Appendix E), a documentation sheet was sent to all interview participants with their letter of invitation. The documentation sheet was redeveloped after the pilot study to reduce its length, to make it more aesthetically appealing and to remove some minor repetitions.

One of the aims of the study was to explore the level of turnover in child protection and welfare in the HSE 'Area A'. Therefore, the researcher negotiated with the HSE 'Area A' to provide a list of all social work staff in the five child protection and welfare teams in the HSE 'Area A' for the duration of the study (seven lists were provided in total). This provided the opportunity to track staff mobility and turnover over the fieldwork period. This data was analysed using *Microsoft Excel* and illustrative analysis charts were produced using *OmniGraffle* (see Chapter Five). The *Excel* sheets noted when a staff member left and when another social worker was recruited to fill the vacancy. During the fieldwork period, it was necessary to consult with Principal Social Workers, Team Leaders and the HSE 'Area A' Child Care Information Officer to establish the nature of the change for every social work employee movement (retirement, maternity leave, sabbatical, resignation, sick leave) and to establish where the social worker went. This process, while labour-intensive, enabled me to undertake a comprehensive analysis of turnover/employee mobility for five child protection and welfare social work teams, data heretofore unavailable in the Irish literature. The analysis also includes data on the retention of social workers within the HSE, retention within child protection and welfare social work in Ireland and within the social work profession. This process and its findings are described in greater detail in the next chapter, and the data is presented across the four data analysis chapters.

Grounded theory

In his text on qualitative methods in organisational research, Lee (1999) highlights the dominance of grounded theory studies in organisational research. Grounded theory provides specific strategies and approaches for the analysis of large amounts of unstructured qualitative data, and the aim of this method is to develop theory from the data (Punch, 1998; Willot and Griffin, 1999). An overview of the historical development of grounded theory and the 'schism' between the original developers of the method (Glaser and Strauss) is outside the scope of this section (see Charmaz, 2006). Grounded theory has been subject to much criticism over the last 40 years, with critiques focusing on the continual redevelopment of the method, the overemphasis on procedures, eschewing particular ways of making sense of the world while 'elevating' a certain kind of thinking, the fracturing of datasets in the pursuit of order, and the 'dismissal' of people's own accounts of their social world (Thomas and James, 2006). The application of grounded theory in its entirety by researchers in research design and the analysis of qualitative data has been questioned by Bryman and Burgess (1994, p. 220) who suggest that it has '... alerted qualitative researchers to the desirability of extracting concepts and theory out of data. Second, grounded theory has informed, in general terms, aspects of the analysis of qualitative data, including coding, and the use of different types of codes and their role in concept creation'. Taking into account Bryman and Burgess's (1994) observations regarding researchers' selective use of this method and criticisms of the method, the researcher felt there were some merits in using some of the method's procedures and concepts to support the research design and data analysis. The main features of the method used in this study were a focus on memo writing, coding, and the use of theoretical and purposive sampling in the research design.

3.6 Ethical considerations

Research ethics provide a systematic framework to improve the quality of research and as Bryman (2004, p. 506) argues, researchers need to think about how we 'treat the people on whom we conduct research'. This section considers the ethical issues associated with undertaking this study, including informed consent, anonymity and confidentiality, responsibilities towards participants and reciprocity.

3.6.1 Organisational consent and participants' informed consent

A cornerstone of research that involves interviews is the informed consent of interviewees: the process whereby participants are provided with sufficient information to make an informed decision regarding their participation in a research study. Informed consent involves making participants as aware as possible of the nature, purpose and scope of the research, the fact that participation is voluntary, how the data will be used, confidentiality and anonymity arrangements, and that they can withdraw from the research at any point (Punch, 1998; Lewis, 2003; Silverman, 2004). Before the researcher could approach individual social workers to begin an informed consent process, it was necessary to negotiate access from their employer, the HSE 'Area A'.

Consent was first sought from management level in this Health Board (HSE 'Area A') prior to approaching individual teams and social workers. The HSE 'Area A' (Child Care Managers Group/General Manager) was sent a full research proposal indicating the focus, aims, rationale and objectives of the study, research questions, approximate indication of the number of participants and time involved, and a short literature review. Permission to undertake the research was granted and it was agreed that the researcher would have sole control over the selection of participants for interview and that social workers would participate on a voluntary and anonymous basis. Table 3.8 provides a diagrammatical representation of the fieldwork stages, permissions sought and the consent process at each stage:

Table 3.8: Fieldwork timeline, permissions sought and consent processes

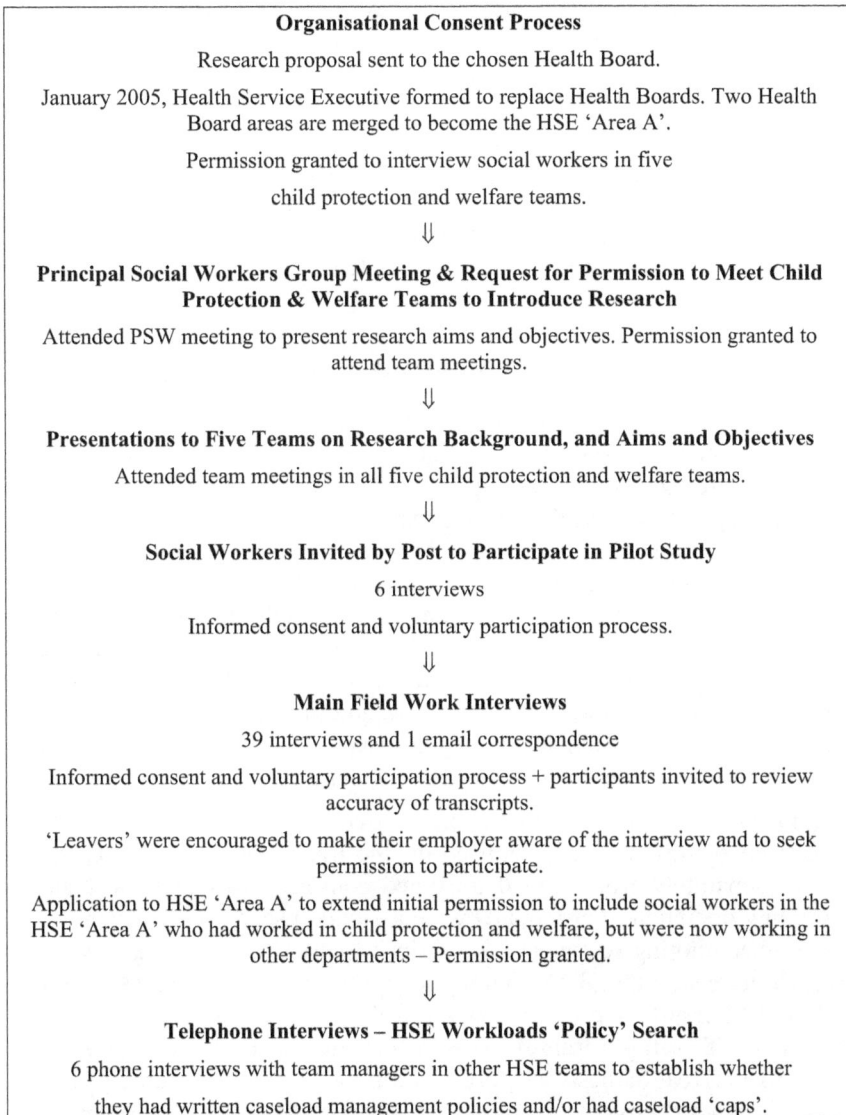

Organisational Consent Process
Research proposal sent to the chosen Health Board.
January 2005, Health Service Executive formed to replace Health Boards. Two Health Board areas are merged to become the HSE 'Area A'.
Permission granted to interview social workers in five child protection and welfare teams.
⇓
Principal Social Workers Group Meeting & Request for Permission to Meet Child Protection & Welfare Teams to Introduce Research
Attended PSW meeting to present research aims and objectives. Permission granted to attend team meetings.
⇓
Presentations to Five Teams on Research Background, and Aims and Objectives
Attended team meetings in all five child protection and welfare teams.
⇓
Social Workers Invited by Post to Participate in Pilot Study
6 interviews
Informed consent and voluntary participation process.
⇓
Main Field Work Interviews
39 interviews and 1 email correspondence
Informed consent and voluntary participation process + participants invited to review accuracy of transcripts.
'Leavers' were encouraged to make their employer aware of the interview and to seek permission to participate.
Application to HSE 'Area A' to extend initial permission to include social workers in the HSE 'Area A' who had worked in child protection and welfare, but were now working in other departments – Permission granted.
⇓
Telephone Interviews – HSE Workloads 'Policy' Search
6 phone interviews with team managers in other HSE teams to establish whether they had written caseload management policies and/or had caseload 'caps'.

After attending the team meetings social workers and senior social work practitioners were invited to take part in the study by letter. This letter included a brief description of the research and information relevant to making an informed decision. The beginning of each interview was dedicated to a process to ensure that participants' questions were answered about the study and that they were provided with enough information so that they could make an informed decision about their participation in the study. The extensive informed consent process undertaken in this research study may account for the very low level of refusals to participate in the study (2 participants). The most significant area of clarification and assurance arising from the informed consent process was participants' concern that the study would use their real name and that the HSE would be advised of their participation. The next section elaborates upon issues associated with confidentiality and anonymity.

3.6.2 Confidentiality, anonymity and data collection

It is not always possible or desirable in a research study to provide cast-iron guarantees of confidentiality and anonymity (Seidman, 1991) and there are often misunderstandings regarding the difference between these two concepts. Lewis (2003, p. 67) explains that 'anonymity means the identity of those taking part not being known outside of the research team ... [and] confidentiality means avoiding the attribution of comments, in reports or presentation, to identified participants'. Due to the small size of the sample frame (81 social workers/senior social work practitioners in total in the HSE 'Area A') and the location of the study in one HSE, the informed consent form and the interview preparation process made it clear that absolute guarantees could not be made, but that every effort would be made to ensure confidentiality.

Tapes and transcripts were labelled with codes and participants' names and team names were anonymised on the transcripts. Transcripts were stored separately from signed informed consent forms and the master sampling document. Participants were assigned pseudonyms which were used when quoting sections of transcripts. Every effort was made, within reason, to ensure that the pseudonyms did not match the names of other social workers in child protection and welfare in the HSE 'Area A' (cross checked with sample frame). A list which linked the pseudonyms with participants' real names was stored within the sampling document which was a password protected *Microsoft Excel* file. As the research data will not be archived, additional measures to further anonymise the transcripts were unnecessary. Efforts were made to avoid direct and indirect attribution in the reporting of the findings by excluding or changing certain biographical characteristics (Lewis, 2003), but the limitations of this process were also discussed with participants.

3.6.3 Responsibilities to research participants

This research project sought to explore the personal/private based knowledges and understandings held by social workers about working in child protection and welfare, and to make these public in an ethical and consensual manner. As outlined above, the informed consent process explored issues of confidentiality and anonymity, and the publication of the research data. It was important to the researcher that the research process and the researcher's behaviour did not distress participants or cause them to experience this research study as disempowering.

Semi-structured interviews in particular require that participants are protected and that interviewers protect themselves from misunderstandings (Seidman, 1991). Seidman argues that because a semi-structured interview encourages participants to share intimate aspects of their lives, this information 'if misused, could leave them [participants] extremely vulnerable' (p. 46). The literature review indicated that studies in this area deal with sensitive themes such as stress, burnout, health, and professional dissatisfaction. Mason (2002b) advises that in order to recognise and confront these issues, researchers should be clear about the purpose of their research, clearly identify who will be affected by the research topic, and what the implications are for participants and other affected parties for constructing the research in a particular way. To address these concerns, the informed consent process covered these areas and participants were advised that they could withdraw from the research at any time, which at the beginning of the interview was clarified to mean any time up until the submission of the dissertation. This potential for distress was revisited before exploring the health and relationships section of the interview and efforts were made to avoid collecting 'prurient or irrelevant detail' (Lewis, 2003, p. 68). Participants were advised that they could take a break or return to a topic during the interview, but at no point in any of the interviews did participants take this option. On occasion, participants were advised of services that may be of assistance (for example, the HSE 'Area A' Employee Assistance Programme), but there was no information arising in interviews which suggested that the participants or others were at risk of immediate harm. However, the researcher was aware that the interview process may open up areas of discussion for social workers on topics which may not have been addressed previously or to which they are guarded about. Also, participation in the study may act as an unintended trigger for social workers to reconsider their position.

3.7 Concluding comments

In this chapter, I have outlined the objectives of the research and detailed the design of the research study. I have argued for the merits of developing and applying a qualitative research design to this piece of organisational research. While I have highlighted the merits of adopting a qualitative approach to examine the research questions, the chapter has also focused on some of the challenges associated with this approach. A rationale for using individual interviews as the main data collection method, supported by the collection of quantitative data, was provided. In addition, I have described the collection of quantitative data from the HSE 'Area A' on caseloads, and staff turnover and mobility.

The methodological approach of this study is interpretivist and seeks to explain how social workers understand, interpret and construct their experience of working in child protection and welfare and how these constructions, and the meanings which they ascribe to these experiences, shape their decisions to stay in or leave their work. To explore these understandings, individual semi-structured interviews were the primary data collection method employed. The sampling strategy, coding, development of concepts, and data analysis, were informed and guided by grounded theory.

It was important to me that the research process and the researcher's behaviour did not cause distress for participants or that they experienced this research study as disempowering. Due to the sensitive nature of some of the topics under consideration in this research, the research design ensured a robust ethical process which highlighted the importance of gaining informed consent, confidentiality/anonymity, and my responsibility towards participants.

In the next chapter, the first of four data analysis chapters, I present and analyse data on statutory child protection and welfare social workers' turnover rates in the HSE 'Area A'. The chapter will help to address a gap in the Irish research on child protection and welfare social workers' turnover. In undertaking this analysis, the chapter will explore a purportedly widely held perception expressed to me by some social workers, and occasionally articulated in the Irish social work literature (see, for example, McGrath, 2001), that the turnover rates for social workers in Ireland are high.

Chapter 4
Turnover and employment mobility patterns of child protection and welfare social workers in the Health Service Executive 'Area A'

4.1 Introduction

In the literature review chapter, I examined the limited available data on the turnover and employment mobility of social workers in Ireland. The only studies that contain such data are the National Social Work Qualifications Board (2000, 2002, 2006) labour force studies. Unfortunately, these reports lack specific data on statutory child protection and welfare social work. To examine the perception held by some social workers that employee turnover in child protection and welfare is high and retention is an issue, a view also expressed by the senior HSE manager and Minister for Children and Youth Affairs (see Chapter One), I analysed the turnover and employment mobility of all child protection and welfare social workers in the HSE 'Area A' during the period of the fieldwork (March 2005 - December 2006). Moreover, I sought evidence of employment growth in child protection and welfare social work in the HSE 'Area A' over the same period. This data was collected at seven time points during the fieldwork.

The definitions of turnover and employment mobility used in this study are presented in the next section. This analysis, for the first time in Ireland, will extend the debate on child protection and welfare social workers' turnover beyond the anecdotal and raise questions about perceptions that turnover is high. What were the turnover and employee mobility rates for child protection and welfare social workers in the HSE 'Area A' between March 2005 and December 2006? During this period, was there any evidence of employment growth in child protection and welfare social work in the HSE 'Area A'?

4.2 Turnover and employment mobility data

The HSE does not systematically collect data on staff turnover and mobility in the child protection and welfare sector, despite being repeatedly identified as a labour force planning issue in the *Dáil* (Houses of the Oireachtas, 1996, 2000, 2003a, b) and despite the fact that the HSE is aware, as evidenced by the former Minister Barry Andrews quote in Chapter One, that it is allegedly a problem. In order to collect data on staff turnover and mobility I negotiated access to HSE 'Area A' raw/uncollated staff compliment data produced on a quarterly basis for each of the five child protection and welfare teams. From this raw data, it was possible to undertake an analysis of the turnover and employment mobility of all social work grades in child protection and welfare over the fieldwork period.

The National Social Work Qualifications Board (NSWQB) surveys (2002, 2006) calculated a turnover rate for all social workers in Ireland of 10.4% in 2005, down from 18.1% in 2001. In these studies, employee turnover was defined as the percentage of permanent social workers who left their post as a percentage of total number of social workers employed in Ireland over a set period of time (usually a 12-month period). Following a request to the NSWQB, they provided me with additional data on turnover in child protection and welfare that was not published in their 2006 report. The NSWQB correspondence indicated that the turnover rate of permanent statutory social workers in child protection and welfare in 2005 was 11.9%. This rate is marginally higher than the overall rate of 10.4% for all permanent social workers in Ireland. A limitation of the NSWQB studies is that their analysis focused on permanent staff only. Using Phillips and O'Connell's (2003) turnover benchmarks as outlined in Chapter Two, a turnover rate of nearly 12% was calculated which suggests a relatively low rate of turnover in child protection and welfare in Ireland in 2005. The report also noted that the 'mobility' of social workers within the profession to take up other social work posts or a secondment was lower than 2001, due possibly to restrictive recruitment practices within the HSE. At this time, the HSE had not publically announced that they had initiated a recruitment embargo/employment ceiling policy. However, HSE staff were aware that if they left their post that it was unlikely they would be able to return as a result of these policies. This may have contributed to a lowering of turnover rates and employment mobility within the profession during the period that the NSWQB data was collected.

Between March 2005 and December 2006, data was collected on the total social work staff compliment in the identified five child protection and welfare teams in the HSE 'Area A'. By comparing each dataset, it was possible to establish how many staff resigned from their post, went on secondment, took a career break, retired, went on maternity leave or long-term sick leave. This data also allowed me to analyse whether the HSE 'Area A' were filling vacancies. The datasets also allowed for an analysis of Whole Time Equivalent (WTE) posts across this time period to see if there were any fluctuations. The diagram in figure 4.1 presents the study's findings on the turnover and employment mobility of child protection and welfare social workers in the HSE 'Area A' (a detailed diagram for each individual child protection and welfare team is presented in Appendix A). It also describes the total number of child protection and welfare social workers and WTEs at the end of March 2005 and December 2006. In between these two dates, the model illustrates social workers' movements in and out of the teams, and as resignations are not the only reasons for personnel changes, the analysis also includes data on secondments, career breaks, retirements, long-term sick leave and maternity leave. In designing this model, a decision was made to track the movements of all social work grades in child protection and welfare in the HSE 'Area A' (locum and permanent staff). This decision was taken in order to provide a more detailed picture of turnover and employment mobility than was presented in the NSWQB (2006) study; locum social workers, who are most likely to change employment due to a lower level of employment security, and who were not included in the NSWQB analysis, are accounted for in the analysis below.

Before presenting the data analysis, it may be useful to restate the definition of turnover from the literature review chapter that is used in this research. Turnover refers to the voluntary cessation of membership of an organisation by paid employees, with an emphasis on the separation of employees from an organisation rather than on promotion, transfers and internal mobility within the organisation (Mobley, 1982; Hom and Griffeth, 1995). There are different interpretations in the literature as to what constitutes voluntary turnover; some consider pregnancy and moving job because of a spouse as voluntary turnover, whereas others define such moves as involuntary. Moreover, it is difficult to establish the exact reasons for moves as researchers are not always able to access personnel files, and these files may be incomplete to protect an employee's privacy, and/or to guard against legal action. Similarly, exit interviews with employees may not always be complete as employees may censor themselves so as not to damage their chance of getting a good reference (Hom and Griffeth, 1995).

In this study, *turnover* means social workers employed in child protection and welfare in the HSE 'Area A' on either a permanent or locum contract who voluntarily ceased their employment. Maternity leave, secondments and career breaks are also not included in the turnover calculation as their separation from the organisation is temporary: many of these social workers returned to their posts in child protection and welfare in the HSE 'Area A', and the others may yet return. Employment *mobility* on the other hand, refers to all other changes in employment status, where the social worker is temporarily not occupying their post in child protection and welfare. The model developed from this data is presented in figure 4.1:

Figure 4.1: Employment mobility and turnover of child protection and welfare social work staff in the HSE 'Area A', March 2005 – December 2006

COMBINED TEAMS [5]

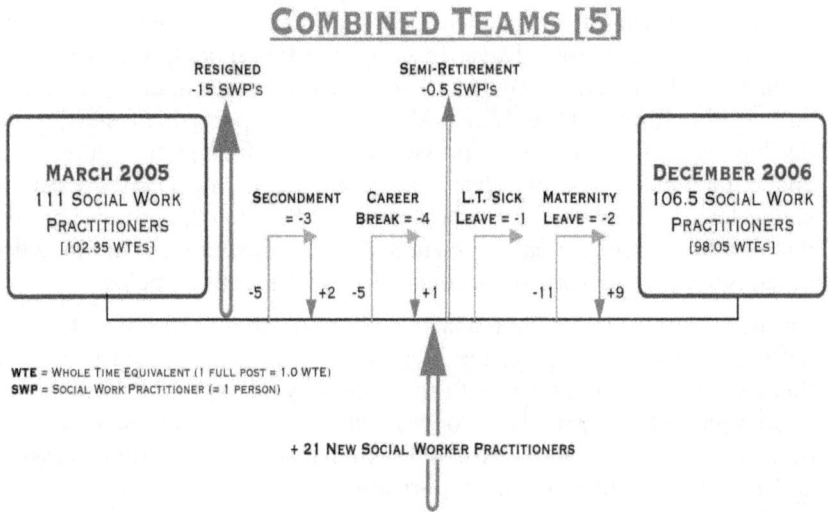

The above diagram shows that 15 child protection and welfare social workers resigned their post in the HSE 'Area A' during the 22-month[28] research period. Employee mobility for reasons of secondment, retirement, career breaks and maternity leave accounted for the other employment mobility seen by social workers. Many of these social workers returned to their post once their special leave period came to an end. For example, 11 female social workers had gone on maternity leave and 9 had returned to their posts. Taking into account the age and gender profile of social workers in child protection and welfare, it is not surprising there are so many maternity leaves[29]. 8 of the 11 maternity

---

[28] The HSE 'Area A' stopped collecting this data in month 22, so it was not possible to complete a full two-year cycle.

[29] The average age at which women in Ireland currently have their first child is 28.7 years. In 1977, this figure was 24.0 years (Central Statistics Office, 2008). Nearly 60% of social workers in child protection and welfare in Ireland are under the age of 35 and over 90% are female (National Social Work

leaves were based in Team 1, which is disproportionate to its size relative to the other four teams[30], but this is possibly explained by the relatively older age profile of female social workers on the more 'rural' teams. 12% of the total population of female social workers in child protection and welfare in the HSE 'Area A' were on maternity leave at some point during the fieldwork period. While this may not be surprising due to stated demographic factors, the over-representation of young and female workers in this practice setting, and consequently the high number of maternity leaves, may affect the continuity of service delivery due to a change in HSE policy in covering maternity leaves. The current HSE policy of not covering all maternity leaves and the specific demographic factors outlined above will particularly impact on child protection and welfare social work compared to other social work sectors. Maternity leaves which are not covered place an increased caseload burden on other staff and potentially impact on the quality of service to children and families.

Secondments were all internal to the HSE 'Area A', whereas career breaks were used to move outside of the HSE for international travel, work in other countries or caring responsibilities at home. A number of social workers interviewed said that there had been a reduction in social workers taking breaks because the HSE human resource policies at the time made it hard for teams to fill vacancies, which meant that social workers were concerned they would be unable to return. Furthermore, managers were less likely to approve a break unless they were assured they could fill the newly vacant post. The figure for career breaks may have been higher, except that the employment climate within the HSE restricted some social workers from taking this option. The very small number of retirements is also unsurprising, given the primarily young age profile of staff in this sector as described in the methodology and literature review chapters.

It is perhaps surprising that the number of resignations (15) is quite low and contrary to the opinions of some social workers in the interviews who believed that there was a significant turnover of staff in their office (additional data presented in Chapters Five and Seven to support this point). Social workers often had contradictory views of the turnover rate in their own office. For example, three social workers in the same team

---

Qualifications Board, 2006). See also data on the demographic profile of child protection and welfare social workers presented in Chapter Three.

[30] Team 1 employed 45 of the 111 (41%) child protection and welfare social workers in the five HSE 'Area A' teams that participated in the research study.

who were interviewed within two months of each other, indicate the variety of views amongst social workers regarding turnover:

> With our own team at the moment there seems to be a very high turnover (Ryan).

> I think it's very stable [referring to turnover] (Evan).

> I don't think the team has been as stable for so long. By that I mean that the same people are here. Like the changeover, people aren't changing as fast. There is...the same staff have been here (Denise).

What were the turnover rates of child protection and welfare social workers, specifically in the Health Service Executive 'Area A', between March 2005 and December 2006? The following turnover calculation uses the definition of turnover outlined earlier in this section:

Calculation:

Average numbers of total social work staff at start (March 2005) and end date (December 2006): (111 + 106.5)/2 = 109. 15 social workers left child protection and welfare in the HSE 'Area A' divided by 109 = 14% over a 22-month period. Adjusted for 12 months = approximately 8%[31].

Thus, we get an approximately 8% turnover rate for the five child protection and welfare social work teams. This figure represents both permanent and locum social workers and is even lower than the NSWQB (2007) rate of 11.9% for the year 2005. Using Mobley's (1982) definition of turnover as being only those who separate from the organisation, then only 9 of the social workers who resigned from the HSE should be counted in the calculation, as the other 6 were still working for the Health Service Executive outside of child protection and welfare in the HSE 'Area A'. Using this approach results in an even lower turnover rate again (4.5%). As discussed in Chapter Two, the turnover literature further stratifies turnover into 'avoidable' or 'unavoidable' turnover[32](Hom and Griffeth, 1995; Phillips and O'Connell, 2003). In Chapter Seven, I present data from interviews with 10 of the 15 social workers who resigned from child protection and welfare, and this analysis will

---

[31] % figures are rounded up/down.

[32] 'Avoidable' turnover (employees leaving for better pay, better working conditions, problems with managers) and 'unavoidable' turnover (death, retirement, geographical move, not coming back to work after birth of child).

examine the reasons for their resignations and whether their resignations could have been avoided.

There were differences between teams on the rate of turnover and the analysis of resignation by team and turnover percentage is presented in table 4.1:

Table 4.1: Resignations and turnover by team

Team	No.	Turnover % (12 month period)*
Team 1	*9*	*11%*
Team 2	*1*	*5%*
Team 3	*2*	*8%*
Team 4	*2*	*5%*
Team 5	*1*	*3%*
Total	*15*	

* Rounded up/down

Team 1, the largest team, had the highest rate of turnover (9 of 15 resignations, 11% turnover rate). The lowest turnover rates were on the smaller and more rural teams. However, due to the relatively small number of social workers in these teams (see table 3.1 and Appendix A), it is hard to make hard and fast conclusions. Of note in the analysis of turnover in Team 4 is that despite there being collective action amongst social workers concerning their working conditions during the period of data collection which led to conflict with management and the instigation of industrial relations mechanisms, the turnover rate of social workers was surprisingly small.

Does a low turnover rate and low rate of employment mobility indicate that social workers are satisfied in their work, feel valued and supported by the HSE and want to stay? Isabelle, a social worker with nine years' experience in child protection and welfare, and therefore well placed to note changes over this period, explains:

In previous years they could leave. The situation at the moment with no jobs going and if you look in the papers for the last three years or whatever it is, there is no jobs going. So what's happened here on the team is that a lot of the same people are here and haven't moved for a long time because they can't move, which in itself causes a lot of ... a lot of problems ...They are not moving on to another team like...like we would have done before in fostering or adoption. And there is just no posts coming up at all. My feeling is that the whole thing is stagnated, and the people that are in child protection at the moment have no way out of that (Isabelle).

Thus, the high turnover rates in child protection and welfare identified in the 1990s (McGrath, 2001; National Social Work Qualifications Board, 2002; Burns and Murray, 2003), appear, at least in the HSE 'Area A', to have reduced significantly during the period of data collection (March 2005-December 2006). This reduction may be explained by (these explanations are examined in subsequent analysis chapters):

a) social workers who want to leave their job in child protection and welfare find that the decision to leave becomes harder as there are fewer alternative employment opportunities due to a tighter labour market.

b) the HSE recruitment embargo/'pause' applied to the whole HSE and as the HSE is the largest employer of social workers in the State[33], these policies restricted internal transfers to other areas such as fostering, adoption and medical social work;

c) the supply of social work graduates from the universities has increased steadily since 2001 (National Social Work Qualifications Board, 2002, 2006), which reduced opportunities to move internally within the HSE or externally, due to increased competition for posts;

d) social workers who resigned their post in the HSE may not be able to return (career breaks, or if a job outside the HSE was inappropriate) as the HSE were recruiting fewer social workers than in previous years;

---

[33] The Health Service Executive employs 59% of all social workers in Ireland. The second and third largest sectors are 'Voluntary/Community/Private' at 14% and Probation Service at 13% (National Social Work Qualifications Board, 2006). These three sectors account for 86% of all social workers employed in Ireland.

e) managers are less likely to approve leave as the new HSE labour policies do not guarantee that the departing employee's post will be covered; and

f) the HSE employment contract is considered by social workers to be more secure and 'better' than other available jobs (supporting data presented in Chapter Five).

It might also be possible that more social workers like their jobs and want to stay in child protection and welfare. All of these possible explanations were explored in the interviews with social workers and these findings will be presented in Chapters Five, Six and Seven.

As regards the 15 social workers who resigned from child protection and welfare in the HSE 'Area A', 14 went on to work in other social work positions, indicating a very low attrition rate for the profession; however, 3 of these social workers were working in social work outside of Ireland. 6 continued to work with children and families in child protection and welfare or fostering as indicated in Table 4.2:

Table 4.2: Subsequent occupations following resignation from child protection and welfare post in the HSE 'Area A'

New Post	No.
Child Protection and Welfare (Ireland 2 & International 1)	*3*
Fostering (Ireland 2 & International 1)	*3*
Disability – Social Work Post	*3*
Mental Health – Social Work Post	*1*
Older Adults-Social Work Post (Ireland 1 & International 1)	*2*
Hospital-Social Work Post	*1*
Social Work Education	*1*
Not working in social work	*1*
Sub Total: Social Work Posts (Republic of Ireland)	11
Sub Total: Social Work Posts (International)	3
Sub Total: Not Working in Social Work	1
Total Resigned	**15**

The number of social work posts, however, seems to have remained stable as indicated in the next section.

4.3 Social work labour force 'strength'

The data presented earlier in figure 4.1 clearly shows that the number of social work posts in the sector remained stable during the period of data collection. A closer analysis of the staff turnover and mobility dataset showed that the HSE tended to quickly fill vacant WTEs, which suggested that the supply and recruitment of new social workers was not an issue during this period, and there was no evidence of the HSE leaving vacant posts unfilled. The fieldwork for this study took place before the introduction of the 'official' recruitment embargo and employment ceiling. Anecdotal reports from within the HSE 'Area A' since the fieldwork was completed indicate that managers are finding it increasingly difficult to get permission to fill vacancies.

The number of WTEs was virtually identical 22 months after the beginning of the study (-4.3 WTEs, but this can be accounted for in the usual time-lag in replacing staff). The lack of growth in WTEs is explained by the 'official' and 'unofficial' HSE employment ceilings in place since 2003, and in fact the total compliment of social WTEs in child protection and welfare in the HSE 'Area A' has not changed since 2003. This HSE labour force policy sought to curb the expansion of new posts as part of a fiscal tightening programme. However, this situation changed in 2009 following the publication of the Government's action plan (Office of the Minister for Children and Youth Affairs, 2009) to respond to the recommendations contained in the *Commission to Inquire into Child Abuse Report*(Ryan, 2009) to strengthen the protection of children in Ireland. Despite a very tough economic environment, 270 additional posts were created in child protection and welfare and vacant child protection social work posts were filled.

The factors outlined in this section so far are important to place this chapter's findings in context. A further important limitation of the data presented in this chapter was that it was collected during a particular set of political and economic conditions which are likely to have influenced the turnover rate. Furthermore, the dataset is small: it is for five child protection and welfare teams in the HSE 'Area A' over a 22 month period. Due to the exploratory nature of this small study and the lack of availability of datasets for other years, it would not have been feasible to have done anything else. The HSE and former Health Board HR systems have lead the HSE to remark in 2012 that it is unable to determine exactly how many social workers it employs in child protection and welfare(Health Service Executive, 2012, p. 12). The proposed establishment of a new Child and Families Support Services Agency in 2013 may create a "clean" and up-to-date staff database which could be used to track all staff changes. Such a thorough analysis of turnover would generate a larger dataset of teams and over time, may assist with an analysis over a wider span of years. Therefore, it is important not to generalise too much from this data, nor use it to make predictions or infer statistical probabilities.

4.4 Concluding comments

In this chapter, I presented data which showed that the turnover of social workers in the five child protection and welfare teams in the HSE 'Area A' is relatively low and I explored some of the possible reasons for this situation. At the time of the study, there was still some mobility within the profession with social workers moving to other posts, career breaks and secondments, and the HSE 'Area A' were filling vacancies as they arose. The data does not support reports of high turnover and low retention levels in child protection and welfare social work. If reports earlier in the 1990s and earlier in this decade of high turnover in child protection and welfare are accurate, the findings in the HSE 'Area A' at least, suggest that a number of factors have changed that may have influenced social workers' decisions to resign or stay in their posts. Firstly, social workers perceive that the labour market for social workers has tightened, resulting in less employment opportunities (internal or external) – perceptions which are supported by a significant reduction in the number of social work posts advertised in the job vacancies pages of the main newspapers. Secondly, the HSE labour force recruitment embargo and employment ceiling policies have impacted on the demand for social workers, who may therefore be less likely to leave a 'secure' job in an uncertain labour market climate. Thirdly, the supply of social work graduates from the universities has increased to fill an ever decreasing number of vacancies as fewer social workers are moving within the profession; the total number of posts in the sector had at the time of the fieldwork declined slightly since 2001.

The literature review chapter and interview data to be presented in the next chapters indicated that the HSE has never specifically implemented a labour policy to address the turnover of social workers. The reduction of turnover can be largely explained by demand and supply considerations, rather than as a result of a specific HSE policy initiative. An implication of this finding for the HSE's labour force planning is that there may be a cohort of social workers in child protection and welfare who want to leave, but are 'stuck' – a theme which is explored in subsequent data analysis chapters. Taking into account reports of higher turnover earlier in the decade and the now relatively low level of turnover, the question arises as to whether there are particular groups of social workers in child protection and welfare social work in the HSE 'Area A' who are dissatisfied in their post and want to leave, but are unable to do so due to certain factors, for example, the current public sector employment embargo and funding cutbacks to government services and civil society organisations. This question will be examined as part of the qualitative data analysis in Chapters Five and Six.

The findings in this chapter help to set the context of employment changes within child protection and welfare teams within the HSE 'Area A'. In Chapter Seven, I will return to present data from qualitative interviews with ten of the social workers in this chapter who left their job in child protection and welfare in the Health Service Executive 'Area A'. This analysis will explore their professional experiences in this sector and identify the particular factors which they described as influencing their decisions to leave.

The next chapter explores in greater detail the turnover and retention of social workers by analysing qualitative data collected from 35 social workers who are presently employed in the HSE 'Area A'. The chapter describes social workers' professional experiences in child protection and welfare in the HSE 'Area A' and examines whether these social workers want to stay or leave. It also identifies and examines the individual, supervisory, social support and organisational factors which influence child protection and welfare social workers' decisions to want to stay or leave.

Chapter 5
Analysis of individual, supervisory, social support and organisational factors that influence social workers' retention

5.1 Introduction

In earlier chapters, I argued that there has been little research in Ireland examining the factors that influence child protection and welfare social workers' decisions to stay or leave their jobs. I also argued that child protection and welfare work is particularly challenging and demanding as workload demands are high and it is a job that places considerable responsibility on individual workers to ensure that children's welfare is safeguarded and promoted (Ferguson, 2004; RTÉ, 2008c). Therefore, this work can place social workers under considerable risk of stress. Furthermore, international studies and Irish commentaries have indicated that the working conditions, organisational factors and statutory responsibilities associated with child protection and welfare contribute to high employee turnover rates(Anderson, 2000; McGrath, 2001; Stanley and Goddard, 2002; Mor Barak *et al.*, 2006). However, in the preceding chapter, I examined data on turnover rates and employment mobility of social workers in the HSE 'Area A' and described how the turnover rate was relatively low. Contrary to my expectations, which were shaped by my experience of working in the sector and from a review of the literature many child protection and welfare social workers were being retained. This raises the question of why social workers were staying in child protection and welfare in the HSE 'Area A'.

Within the sample of social workers interviewed, there were diverse opinions regarding the issue of social workers' retention in child protection and welfare in the Health Service Executive 'Area A'. The following illustrative quotations taken from the interviews highlight these views. Mya and Sophia question the commonly-held perception that there is a high turnover of social workers in child protection and welfare:

> … maybe I came at a good time but I'm not quite sure where that idea of such a high turnover, 'oh my God' you know, you think people are leaving after six months (Mya).

> No, I don't think people are dropping like flies in the agency ... There is great craic in the office. There is great camaraderie ... A lot of that is just baloney, it's trumped up. Do you know ... the stereotyping that bears little relation to reality, you know (Sophia).

However, Anna explains that while turnover rates on the child protection and welfare team on which she works are relatively 'stable', she believes that all of her team colleagues are talking about leaving. Also, Hannah, a social worker on a different team appears to confirm this view while also suggesting that a theme from the last chapter – that of a tight labour market – limits social workers' options to leave:

> The team is stable but I don't think there's one person that I have heard saying that they want to stay there forever ... everybody I know there talks about leaving (Anna).

> ... everyone wants out [of child protection and welfare social work] if there's another job out there (Hannah).

This chapter presents the findings from qualitative data collected during interviews with 35 social workers in direct service provision in child protection and welfare in the HSE 'Area A'. These interviews explored social workers' and senior social work practitioners' experiences of 'doing' child protection and welfare work, and the factors that they identified as important in shaping their decisions to stay or leave. This chapter discusses the key findings under three main headings: individual factors, supervisory and social supports, and organisational factors. These factors are not always discrete, therefore data relating to some factors is presented in more than one section.

5.2 Individual factors

In this, the first of three main sections, I examine the personal/individual factors that influence social workers' decisions to stay or leave child protection and welfare in the HSE 'Area A': making a difference with children and families; professional commitment to child protection and welfare work; age and educational background, and social workers' health.

5.2.1 Making a difference with children and families

The ability of a job to 'engage, enable and support staff to make a positive difference to service users and communities' (Audit Commission, 2002, p. 59) was found in research studies to be an important factor in the turnover and intentions to leave of workers(Reagh, 1994; Rycraft, 1994; Mor Barak *et al.*, 2006; Ellet, 2007). 'Making a difference' has acquired the status of a *cliché* within social work. In my experience, it is often the main reason social work students give for wanting to become a social worker. However, the term encapsulates a very broad and ambiguous commitment to safeguarding and promoting the welfare of children and families. Rycraft (2000) describes it as the 'mission' associated with the work and as a central factor in the job retention of staff. In the job characteristics theory, making a difference, or 'task significance', is a crucial component of designing a positive job (Morgeson and Campion, 2003) – your job makes you feel like you are making a 'substantial impact on the lives of others' (Hackman and Oldham, 1980, p. 79). In this study, social workers defined making a difference as occasions when they made some positive contribution towards safeguarding and promoting the welfare of children and families. For example, Grace, Jessica and Ava, who want to stay in child protection and welfare, said:

> I do make a difference in a family and I do get on their wavelength and you mightn't be able to cure everything, but you certainly make a better difference - they are usually better when you come out/leave, when you close the case (Grace).

> I like it in there and I suppose about, to me, it's about meeting with families and seeing what's going on and seeing what level of risk there is for the child and just about making a safe and secure environment for the child, whether that's at home or somewhere else (Jessica).

> What we do it's very important stuff for people, you know … a parent having a problem with a child, a child having difficulties, a child experiencing abuse, sort of behaving… kind of acting out, a child rejected, grieving. I mean it really is very meaningful stuff - hugely meaningful stuff. It's very basic. It's very powerful stuff (Ava).

Within the sample of social workers interviewed, social workers who wanted to stay generally thought they could make a difference. However, a number of factors impacted upon social workers' assessments of their ability to make a difference with children and families: the crisis orientation and long-term nature of the work; definitions of success and accomplishment; difficulties in accessing essential but finite resources for children; high caseload/workload demands, and the 'stress of conscience' (Glasberg *et al.*, 2007) associated with not having enough time to do the work. Lucy and Hannah, two social workers who wanted to stay, remarked about their decision to stay and making a difference:

Yeah, definitely. I think I wouldn't do it if I didn't. No I do, definitely think you see, especially when you are with children who have had positive experiences. You really do see the meaning then (Lucy).

Well there are lots of good things it's the little things that happen on the cases that are the good things it's watching those children in care you know coming to eighteen and actually going off to university or it's watching you know returning say a child where the parents have really done the work and seeing it working out (Hannah).

Social workers who felt they did not make a difference highlighted the long-term nature of the work and the lack of immediate feedback from their input. Caoimhe explains:

When you don't see any change and for me I think, I'm an instant gratification woman, I like to see change happen fast and when it doesn't happen, it frustrates me. But I do know that then what work you put in now might, in ten years time, reap the benefits of it. But, it frustrates me, and I know that's my issue, because I am about instant gratification but I know that when I don't see change occurring in a shorter time frame, then I get frustrated (Caoimhe).

Aoife, a newly-qualified social worker with less than one year's experience who has decided she wants to leave her job, identified the crisis nature of the work and the lack of hands-on work as factors that inhibited her ability to make a difference in the lives of others:

I'm kind of a bit disillusioned with it. I went in to it thinking, I was going to make a difference in people's lives, but I don't think I do and I think it's more the job is very much crisis driven so you don't get to do the things that you want to do ... obviously I expected the families to have problems right, because they wouldn't be coming to the attention of the Social Services otherwise, that's fine, but I thought that I would be doing hands-on work with the family and that I would be able to see a difference in the family over time (Aoife).

Aoife explains that the lack of face-to-face work with clients, and the actual crisis nature of the work, inhibits her ability to make a difference. Later in her interview she goes on to describe how the large volume of the work, not having time to do the work, and subsequent worry about all the work that she cannot get done, contributes to her frustration. Caitlin, a social worker with over 4 years' experience who wants to leave, said she felt 'useless' when she described her inability to access an essential resource for a child at risk. She described how as a representative of the HSE she received negative feedback from a parent about the lack of child psychiatric services. Although the provision of this service was outside of the control of the social worker, her inability to provide the service was experienced as her own 'failure':

> Caitlin: Like even recently now I called to a woman who has a little boy who is seven and he has been on a waiting list for a psychiatrist since he was three, do you know? Yes. And he is out of control. And like there is nothing to offer her ... your hands are tied then really in what you can do for people. And like there is nothing to offer her ...

> *KB: And how does that make you feel?*

> Caitlin: It just makes me feel kind of useless really. Because obviously I mean it's just human nature. These people are going to direct that at you...their frustration at you. You know a case of, oh you are doing nothing for me and I have come to you looking for help and you are not doing anything.

Such difficulties with accessing finite resources for children were identified as a particularly frustrating issue which prevented both these social workers ability to make a difference. The following quotations are taken from interviews both with social workers who wanted to stay and those who wanted to leave. Social workers highlighted critical problems in the availability of alternative care placements, mental health/therapeutic services, and an apparent lack of recognition and support from senior management in the HSE 'Area A' in acknowledging and addressing these issues (for greater detail on resource deficits, see section 5.4.3). There was also some evidence in the interviews to support the general view that the policy of spending reductions in health and personal social services is significantly affecting the health and welfare of children:

> I suppose one of the stresses that we would have in child welfare and child protection, especially in relation to children coming into care, is finding placements for them (Clodagh).

> At this stage I have worked within child protection for [greater than 5 years]. I am fatigued by the work, and I feel I need a change of scenery. At the moment it feels like a new case with the same old story. In addition to this, it is so difficult to keep up energy and motivation for clients as what I can offer clients is so limited. Support services are close to non-existent and so all I can offer is regular visits to clients. This can only bring about limited change, and is frustrating for both the client and I ... repairing the same old worn out tyre repeatedly. Major investment is needed, but this is not a priority for Senior Health Board Management (Majella).

Burnout theory (Maslach *et al.*, 2001) and research on self-efficacy (Ellet, 2007), as noted in Chapter Two, suggest that when workers have a sense of inefficacy (low feelings of personal accomplishment), they are at increased risk of burnout. This in turn increases the likelihood of workers starting to think about leaving. These social workers are critical of a system that was unable to provide them with some of the essential resources for promoting the welfare of children, such as alternative care placements and counselling. Of particular concern is the difficulty for some workers of finding care placements for children who are left at home in 'unsafe' home conditions. Furthermore, Majella's quote represents a broader view expressed by social workers in the interviews that 'Senior Health Board Management' were well aware of these resources issues.

Tara and Ciara, two social workers who want to stay, stressed the often-contradictory nature of defining 'making a difference' in child protection and welfare. Making a difference to a child, for example by removing them to a place of safety, may not be understood in the same way by the child, their family or the wider community. On the contrary, the fact that a child is taken into care can be perceived as a failure of the State to provide services under the Child Care Act 1991 to ensure that children remain within their family:

> Even taking children into care and going into court, there are no winners in that situation. You might get your care order, but it is like - there are no winners really (Ciara).

> You make the decision in the best interest of the child but that doesn't necessarily mean that they are going to appreciate that or they are going to cope with that or it's not going to do substantial damage to them. So, I think the impact of our work is huge ... Well, I would have to say more positive. I wouldn't do it if I thought it was more negative (Tara).

Taking a child into care can also be defined as a positive difference, as the child is safer. However, Tara noted how a social work intervention also has the potential to do 'harm', as an admission to care may not be synonymous with achieving good outcomes in an under-resourced care system. Such dilemmas regarding the meaning of 'the best interests of the child', competing opinions on what this means in each case, and an awareness of the limitations of the system to provide adequate resources to promote and safeguard the welfare of children, can lead to social workers feeling an enormous sense of individual responsibility and an uncertainty that their work will make a difference. It may mark a change in the child's welfare, but it is not always possible to assess immediately what that change is or whether it is 'positive' or 'negative'. Nevertheless, Tara clarified that overall, she feels that she makes more of a positive difference and this perception helps her to stay in the job.

Social workers who had made a decision to leave highlighted how their ability to make a difference was influenced by the availability of resources. Additionally, they also identified how working with 'involuntary'clients impacted on their ability to make a difference. The experience of working with involuntary clients was noted as a factor in social workers leaving child protection and welfare work in Australia (Barber, 1991), and social work education has been criticised for not equipping social workers with adequate skills and theoretical frameworks to work with involuntary clients (Ferguson, 2005). Anna, a social worker who wanted to leave and who during her interview described feelings of accomplishment in her work as 'rare', links working with involuntary clients and her feelings towards the job:

> Sometimes you do feel like you make a difference but sometimes if you have a resistant client ... It feels crap sometimes ... it's difficult knowing that you're going to somebody's house and they don't, they're, they really hate that the fact that you're coming to see them. It's difficult to face that all the time. I think just knowing that you are not welcome or you know, people hate to see you coming (Anna).

Caitlin and Aoife associated working with involuntary clients with their decisions to leave child protection and welfare work. They emphasised the stress associated with working with resistance and the difficulties associated with improving the welfare of children when families do not engage:

> I suppose when people are very resistant to any kind of change or any kind of intervention, and very hostile towards the service. And.............I think sometimes with cases where....where people will tell you what you want to hear but you know they are not following through on it, and the children continue to be put in situations where they are at risk (Caitlin).

> I have an awful lot of clients who won't engage with me and that's very stressful. That's really really stressful for me and won't take phone calls from me and won't have me in the house (Aoife).

Thomas, a social worker who said he had a long-term commitment to working in child protection and welfare social work, described how he felt he had the skills to develop relationships with 'involuntary clients':

> ... if you look at involuntary clients, obviously we have loads of them, but I so far - knock on wood, I always found a way to actually work with people, to build a working relationship even if they are very reluctant in the beginning and sort of slam the door in my face and shouted at me and then threatened with solicitors, but, eventually I always found a way to actually sit down with them and work on the problems (Thomas).

Social workers in the study who constructed small and achievable definitions of success and accomplishment or making a difference, were more likely to describe themselves as wanting to stay in child protection and welfare. Social workers acknowledged that their definitions of making a difference may not be shared by, or visible, to the community, or even meet the standards of agency performance indicators, but are significant for them in achieving job satisfaction. Thomas suggested that it is important to moderate one's expectations of success and that meanings of success and making a difference could be relative. His advice was to have low expectations for change to reduce the potential for frustration:

> If I can be sort of a catalyst to get things a little bit going, then that's the best you can [do]. You know people are always asking you as a social worker, how much success do you actually have and of course success is very relative. If you think success is sort of solving ten cases and everything is hunky dory afterwards, you'd be disappointed and frustrated. So success is something different, you have to define it for yourself. Success can even be to, whatever, establish a relationship and make them, maybe get their agreement to look at a parenting programme, even that's a success. If you can improve their relationship between the kid and the parent in the slightest bit, that's a success. So, don't set the bar too high, I think that's very important for me because otherwise there will be frustration (Thomas).

This quotation from Thomas can be interpreted in at least two ways. Firstly, that it is reasonable and practical to moderate your expectation of change, particularly when working with what Ferguson and O'Reilly (2001) describe as 'extremely complex, often intractable problems for children and families', while trying to manage large caseloads under less than optimal working conditions. Secondly, it can be interpreted as the social worker reducing his expectations to such a level that he is uncritical of the child protection and welfare system and being pessimistic regarding families' potential for change.

In summary, social workers who experienced their work as satisfying and chose to stay nearly always felt that they were making a difference, or enough of a difference, in the lives of children and families. These social workers were able to feel that they were making positive changes with children and families, however small, and this perception sustained them in the work. Using job characteristics theory, these social workers' perception of task significance (Hackman and Oldham, 1980) meant that they were more likely to come to terms with working in an imperfect system, even though they had inadequate resources which limited their ability to make a difference. They were also less frustrated by working with involuntary clients than those who wanted to leave. Being able to see positive differences in the lives of children, and believing that the social worker had made a contribution was also significant:

> Yeah, definitely ... especially when you are with children who have had positive experiences. You really do see the meaning then (Lucy).

On the other hand, nearly all of the social workers who wanted to leave felt that they made little or no difference in the lives of children and families (low task significance). Erin, a social worker who had decided to leave, explained:

> *KB: Do you think you make a difference ...?*

> Erin: No. ... No. No. I would like to think I do ... go back a little bit and say that there is little differences that maybe I am making, but not the amount of differences that I wanted to make when I set out. And that for me is very disappointing. But I don't know is there a certain level of hopelessness in that. In that am I thinking to myself, this is the way it is? (Erin).

These social workers found working with involuntary clients particularly difficult, and were extremely frustrated at the lack of services and resources to safeguard and protect children. Even if they sometimes felt that they made a difference, it was not enough to sustain them in the work.

5.2.2 Professional commitment to child protection and welfare work

While professional commitment to child protection and welfare work is presented as a discrete theme in the literature review, when compiling this findings chapter it became clear that social workers' commitment to the work spanned across quite a number of the themes. So as not to fragment this data from related factors or unnecessarily repeat data, I have decided to present the data related to social workers' professional commitment to child protection and welfare across the chapter. Thus, data relating to social workers' commitment to children protection and welfare work is addressed in the following sections: making a difference with children and families; organisational climate and culture; 'farming' out the work; accessing finite resources, and caseload size/workloads. Professional commitment to child protection and welfare work will also be examined in Chapter Six.

5.2.3 Educational background and age of social workers

Studies in the United States of America (U.S.A.) found differences between child protection and welfare workers' educational background and their retention and turnover (Jones, 2002; Robin and Hollister, 2002). Workers in these studies with a social work qualification, particularly an MSW, were more likely to be retained that workers who did not have a social work qualification. However, unlike the U.S.A. and some other countries, in order to be employed as a statutory child protection and welfare worker in Ireland you must have successfully completed a minimum of four years' social work education at university. All of the social workers in this study had a professional social work qualification; therefore it was not possible to undertake an analysis of differences between different professions undertaking this work. While there are other professions working in child protection in the HSE 'Area A', their role and tasks are different to social work staff and they were not interviewed as part of the study.

Regarding social workers' age as a retention factor, a U.S.A. study noted that older workers have lower intentions to leave as they may see advantages in staying in their post and value their employment benefits (Mor Barak et al., 2006). Overall, age is rarely noted in turnover and retention studies. An analysis of the ages and experience level of the 35 social workers in this study indicated that the median age of social workers who wanted to leave was 30, while the median age of social workers wanting to stay was 35. There was also a difference in level of experience, where those who had more experience in child protection and welfare were more likely to want to stay[34]. This suggests that there may be some correlation between being older and having more experience

---

[34] Those who wanted to stay had a median of 4 years' experience in child protection and welfare, whereas those who wanted to leave had a median figure of 3 years' experience. The sample size is too small for such an analysis to have any statistical significance, and is included for illustrative purposes only.

and wanting to continue their employment as social workers in child protection and welfare.

While age did not appear significant in an overall way, it may have some relevance for certain social workers. Social workers in the study who were of a particular age and were applying for a mortgage saw the advantage of the security of tenure which the job offered, as the following quotes explain:

> When I was looking for a mortgage, the bank were saying, oh sure you have a very safe job, this kind of thing (Ciara).

> ... they are having to start making decisions. Right after I am there three years then I can make other choices again in relation to...say do you know do I go a sabbatical or do ....now that I am permanent can I apply for the mortgage or can I get the car or....those sort of things (Ryan).

Grace and Robyn, two social workers who were coming up to retirement age, did not see their age as a factor in relation to their retention and they wanted to stay working in child protection and welfare beyond the statutory retirement age[35]. In the literature review chapter, job embeddedness theory suggests that the greater an employee's links with the community and the organisation, the less likely they are to leave. Older workers may have had more time to establish such links in the local communities in which they work (for example, through their children attending local schools, involvement in local organisations and clubs), and the longer one works in an organisation the greater the likelihood of more established social networks in and through work (the implications of having children and running a household are addressed later in the chapter). The non-city-based (Team 5, Team 3, and Team 2) teams have 'older' workers than the two city-based teams (Team 1 and Team 4), which in conjunction with fewer employment opportunities in rural areas, may contribute to higher retention on these 'rural' teams. Anna explains:

> There's a good few people [social workers] who are actually living in the area and who would be older and for that reason like, there's isn't as much work opportunities I suppose, in the [name of social work department] area itself (Anna).

Anna, in her interview, explained how older workers are less likely to move as they have more connections in local areas than younger

---

[35] Social workers are public servants and are legally obliged to retire at age 65.

workers. They usually have chosen to live in the particular town/area, and these factors, in conjunction with the limited availability of alternative employment opportunities, increase the likelihood that they will stay in child protection and welfare. In retrospect, the interview guide should have included more specific questions to examine the issue of age and experience with participants.

5.2.4 Social workers' health

The impact of child protection and welfare work on the welfare of those who undertake this work has been a consistent feature in the literature, most specifically connected with the impact of burnout (emotional exhaustion) on turnover (Dickinson and Perry, 2002; Strolin *et al.*, 2007). In this section, I consider the data connected with social workers' health in a broader sense and whether it impacts on their decisions to stay or leave. Social workers in the study described how the work impacted on their physical health, sleep, feelings of stress, and emotional exhaustion, and how taking sick leave could sometimes be 'problematic'. Both Thomas and Jenna described some of the health implications of working in this area:

> ... a lot of viral things....chest infections, throat infections, just things that won't go...like kidney infections. I mean half the staff are prone to bladder and kidney infections.... [and other health – identifying information removed] problems. You know, I suppose those viral things that just linger and not....like colds and....just don't go away (Jenna).

> ... there are loads of experienced colleagues here and people I know who had mental health problems, who had tumours, who had heart attacks who had all kind of things and I think a lot of it is certainly, I'm not sure if it's primarily the work, but as I said, if there are problems outside the work, it can be the last bit, the last straw that breaks your back (Thomas).

In his description, Thomas questioned whether it is work or other factors that affect social workers' health. However, he suggested that physical illness could be a factor in social workers' decisions to leave the profession.

On the other hand, Ava, a social worker who wanted to stay, clearly linked her ill-health with her work:

I found by the end of the week I was actually physically sick, like I would have some sort of an infection or a cold or something. I wasn't going into the weekend able to enjoy the weekend. I was going into the weekend needing to recover … I went full time when I applied for the permanent post. I was full time for a year. And I came out of that year convinced that I had cancer, which I didn't have, fortunately … my neurosis was telling me, this is too much. So there was something telling me, my body wasn't going to survive this … And so it was like I feel it was my way of telling me something has got to change here … I would be getting worried that I was going to get cancer, do you know. No, I mean, there is absolutely no way on this earth I would have done it full time … (Ava).

This quotation starkly highlights how work can influence the perception of social workers' health and home life. Ava wanted to stay in this work so she reduced her hours to part-time as she felt that working full-time took too much of a toll on her health and gave her insufficient time to recover from the impact of the work. A further example of the physical and emotional affects of the work can be found in Caitlin's transcript. Caitlin is a social worker who wanted to leave and she describes how the stress of the work impacted on her:

I had a constant feeling of stress. Well I suppose my experience of stress would be, I would get …like an almost…a physical feeling of not being able to breathe, do you know. And I would have that regularly. Again if I am stressed I would lose weight. I was losing a lot of weight. I suppose it got particularly bad maybe in the last six months before I took the career break. Just that general feeling of panic, of not being able to sleep, of waking up in the middle of the night, just kind of going, how am I going to get all this done. I suppose it got to the worst point where, shortly before I took my career break, I woke up one morning and I actually physically was unable to move. I couldn't get out of bed. And I ended up…I ended up being off for two weeks. And I was at the point where I actually couldn't stay awake for more than a couple of hours. There was actually nothing really physically wrong with me. It wasn't like a bug or a virus or anything like that even. I was just purely burnt out from being stressed for so long. And yes, it took two weeks to actually be any way right, you know, to be able to even go into work. It was actually quite frightening because you don't…you know you….I wouldn't have expected …it to affect you in that much of a physical way you know (Caitlin).

In this lengthy quotation, Caitlin describes how persistent levels of stress from the work contributed to her reduced mobility, energy, physical and mental health. Caitlin refers to a career break which she took to 'recover' from the impact of the work on her, and to evaluate whether to come back to child protection and welfare work or to seek a job in another social work practice setting. Taking a career break from this work as a result of burnout, ill-health or disillusionment with the work was also a feature for some other social workers in the study. For example, Isabelle a social worker who wanted to stay, said:

> The career break was taking time out … coming towards the start of the career break, I definitely would have been burnt out … I would have had a lot of physical symptoms, like back problems on a very regular basis, waking at night worried about cases, feeling very unsupported, and what else… just… just the stresses and strains of that … I couldn't deal with the amount of work that was there anymore. And I would literally come in and feel, oh, I can't even look at this, which is a sign literally of not being able to deal with it at all (Isabelle).

All of these social workers returned to the work, but with a revised orientation to the work. They felt they were better able to accept its limitations (i.e. too much work, too little time and resources), they reduced their expectations regarding the contribution they could make, even it was at odds with their commitment to the work, and they placed stricter boundaries around home/work life. Nicole, a social worker who wanted to stay, pointed out that a strong commitment to the work when connected to the unsupportive culture in the HSE can contribute to burnout for social workers:

> I can see how people would get burnt out very easily here…..very easily. You know, you are always going to be expected to do more. You are never going to be told …or rarely are you going to be told, you know, pull back there and take it easy, you know, you are affecting your own health or whatever. We do look out for each other alright like…but I suppose it's your own sense of….I don't know, it's not pride, but you want to do what is best and you want to do the best for people you know. So that keeps pushing you and pushing you [until] breakdown, yes (Nicole).

Close to two thirds of the social workers reported how the work intruded on and disturbed their sleep:

> When I am getting really stressed - I dream about my clients (which) is a clear indication to me that I need to switch off a bit (Grace).

> … something that happens and then it sticks to you then and your mind starts to race and ultimately, you know, and then when you start dreaming about your clients, that's just the worst yet 'cause they are in your dreams as well as in your daily life (Caoimhe).

110

> I'd find I'm lying in bed at night and I can't get off to sleep cause I'm thinking about work and that really annoys me ... (Hannah).

> ... almost a physical sense of just being so stressed and so wound up. And like going home at night and waking up in the middle of the night going, oh my God, I didn't do this, I didn't do that, do you know (Caitlin)?

The impact on sleep and intrusive thinking was also reported by Ferguson (2004) in his study of child protection and welfare social workers in the Mid-Western Health Board. Having reduced energy for life and family as a result of the work was also an issue for social workers. Denise, Anna and Abbey, three social workers that wanted to leave, said:

> ... there are times when I find it very very emotionally draining and exhausting. But that's the nature of ...of the work, you know (Abbey).

> I just find that I'm exhausted after the day (Anna).

> I would have seen the quality of my own personal life change very significantly, and not necessarily for the better in the last number of years. I don't have the same energy when I go home in the evening. I found the last year there was a considerable amount of illness for no particular...you know, nothing...nothing else I can attribute it (Denise).

For these social workers, the job led to being physically tired and exhausted. This is increasingly a feature of work for many Irish workers. As described in Chapter One, 44% of workers in Ireland who participated in a study on attitudes towards work said that they came home from work exhausted and 36% were too tired to enjoy home life after work (O'Connell et al., 2004). Some social workers in my research said that the pace, stress and nature of the work contributed to them reaching a point where they felt they were no longer able to function in the job. The next three sample quotations are from social workers who described taking sick leave because of the impact of the work on their health:

... in the last year I suppose I would have found times where I had to take time out for myself to survive. And I hated doing it. And it seemed like ....how will I put it....it seemed nearly dishonest to take it. But I actually felt if I didn't I would end up ill, or you know in the sense of being physically ill. And there was also ...I suppose I have come to terms with the fact that there are times on those particular occasions where I actually felt I couldn't function (Clodagh).

I just, I burst into tears. I, I couldn't believe it. She [GP] did put it down as stomach problems which she felt wasn't a real lie so but I the thought that I was off for two weeks made me feel that I couldn't do my job. That I wasn't strong enough. That I was weak. That I was letting people down. What was I going to do for two weeks? It felt like I was knocking off school you know. That, that I wasn't ill (Claire).

Lucinda: I definitely think stress is...is a major factor, you know.

KB: And what does stress mean for you in this job?

Lucinda: When I go through...through periods where I feel stressed to such a level that...that it is affecting me....the sleepless nights, it is worrying ...it is...and I have...I mean I have been on sick leave because of stress on ....one occasion....two occasions. So yes it actually means that I...you know, that there are times where you feel .....you would obviously do yourself a disservice if you continued working, but you certainly would do your clients a disservice. And that is a major issue ... When I came to that stage where I went on sick leave? That I got up in the morning and just dreaded going in and couldn't stop crying.

When social workers did take time out as the result of stress at work, they often felt, such as Claire and Clodagh suggest above, that in some way that they were not worthy of the time off; it was a sign of their 'inability' to cope and they would be letting clients down. A strong commitment to co-workers and client care underpinned these social workers' decisions. Despite data which repeatedly recounted signs of stress, emotional exhaustion and physical ill-health, there appeared to be a surprisingly low sick leave rate for social workers in the study. When this trend became obvious in early interviews, the researcher made a request to the HSE 'Area A' for access to composite data on sick leave levels for child protection and welfare social workers. Unfortunately, the HSE 'Area A' was unable to provide this data. However, social workers in the study self-reported an average of 5 sick days in the 12 months leading up to their interview, which is less than the national average of 6 sick days per year[36]. In 2004, workers in Ireland had the second lowest sick leave rate in the European Union after Greece, the highest being Sweden with 25 days per year (Organisation for Economic Co-operation and Development, 2005).

As noted above, there was evidence of a strong ethic of care amongst the social workers who continued to work even when it affected their health. For example, in Chapter Two (see Dressel, 1984; Morris, 2005), I highlighted how the gendered nature of social work and the socialization of women as carers may contribute to this mainly female social workers making decisions to stay in this work because of this strong ethic of care, particularly when they feel that they are making a difference, and despite the negatives affects on their health and welfare.

It is unsurprising that social workers reported high levels of stress, as the profession is nearly always towards the top of lists of stressful occupations (see, for example, Millet *et al.*, 2005). For those that wanted to leave, feeling exhausted and 'drained' from the work was a consistent theme in their interviews. However, it was also often raised in the interviews with social workers that wanted to stay. The impact of the work on their health, as described by social workers in these quotations, suggests a need for the HSE 'Area A' to examine this issue and to introduce a strategy to lessen the impact of the work on social workers. In the interviews, there appeared to be little evidence of the HSE 'Area A' taking pro-active steps to reduce the stressful working conditions for social workers. Such a strategy could include: ensuring that social workers had quality and frequent professional supervision; ensuring that they felt valued and support by the organisation, and that their workloads were fair and manageable. Perceived organisational support theory suggests that workers who feel that the organisation cares for their well-being, are more likely to be retained (Eisenberger *et al.*, 2004). The data in this section suggests that for these social workers at least, that they do not perceive the HSE 'Area A' as supportive or caring in this way. The data here suggests the need for further research on the impact of occupational stresses on social workers' health. The role of supervision and social supports to lessen the impact of some of the negative effects of the work is addressed in the next section (5.3), and the role of workloads is examined in a subsequent section (5.4.1).

---

[36] As this figure is based on a self-reported study, it can only be considered as an estimate of the actual number of sick days taken by child protection and welfare social workers in the HSE 'Area A'. OECD figure based on full-time equivalent employees.

5.3 Supervision and social supports

Studies have consistently shown that quality professional supervision and social supports can reduce the occupational stress experienced by social workers (Rushton and Nathan, 1996; Gibbs, 2001; Jacquet et al., 2007). In Chapter Two, the importance of social exchange relationships between workers and supervisors, and its importance in employee retention, was emphasised in the discussion of social exchange theory and perceived organisational support theory. In perceived organisational support theory and research, employees' perceptions of supervisor support contributes to perceptions that the organisation is supportive, and ultimately, their retention (Eisenberger et al., 2002). Supervisors provide social workers with professional supervision as well as other types of supports and guidance. Due to their daily contact with social workers, supervisors are best positioned to convey through their actions whether the organisation is supportive, values their contribution and cares about their welfare. This section explores social workers views about the HSE's ability to meet its part of the exchange relationship in terms of the provision of social exchange resources (support, supervision, praise, information). Social workers' views on the HSE's ability to meet its part of the exchange relationship in terms of economic exchange resources such as salary and employment benefits are discussed in section 5.4.5.

There is evidence to suggest that supervision is not always available or of a sufficient standard in child protection and welfare social work in Ireland (McGuinness, 1993; Buckley, 2002). Irish government policy governing the assessment and management of child abuse stipulates that those who undertake this work should receive adequate and regular supervision, although what exactly this means is undefined (Department of Health and Children, 1999; Department of Children and Youth Affairs, 2011). The HSE 'Area A's' own supervision policy states that experienced workers should receive supervision of an hour and a half in length at least monthly and every three weeks for new workers during the first year. The supervision policy outlined in the national guidelines emphasises the important role managers/supervisors play in acknowledging the actual and potential strains on staff in child protection and welfare. The policy also affirms the importance of regular and adequate supervision of staff, a regular review of caseloads and the acknowledgement of positive achievements, where the acknowledgement of positive achievements is one example of a social exchange resource.

Social exchanges between worker and supervisor, as described in Chapter Two, can also be an important source of social support, as can social work colleagues. The quality of social supports provided by both supervisors and co-workers play an important role in retaining child protection workers (Gibbs, 2001; Weaver and Chang, 2004; Nissly et al., 2005). In her study of social workers' decisions to leave their work in Sweden, Tham (2007) concluded that inter-personal relationships with managers and co-workers were of greater importance than workloads or job demands in the retention of social workers.

Normally, professional supervision and social supports would be placed under organisational factors, but given their central position and importance in the literature, they are presented in this chapter under their own heading. The section begins with an analysis of the data concerning social workers' experiences of supervision, the quality of social supports provided by managers, and the impact of both of these factors on social workers' retention. The second part of the section examines inter-personal relationships between co-workers, the quality of social supports provided by work colleagues, and the impact of both of these factors on social workers' retention.

5.3.1 Supervision and social supports from managers

In this section, I present data from interviews with social workers examining their experiences of supervision, their inter-personal relationships with managers and the quality of social supports provided by social work supervisors. This data is analysed to examine the impact of these factors on social workers' decisions to stay or leave. The literature on supervision highlights the influential role that social work supervisors play in containing social workers' anxieties, affirming workers, providing feedback, facilitating skills development and contributing to workers' feelings that they are 'looked after' and protected by the employing agency (Morrison, 1993, 1996; Ruch, 2007). Separately, perceived organisational support theory also links employees' perceptions of being 'looked after', or the extent to 'which the organisation values their contributions and cares about their well-being' (Eisenberger et al., 2004, p. 204), with retention.

The frequency and length of supervision arose as a significant issue for social workers in the study. Despite evidence from research studies and government policy emphasising the importance of regular and adequate professional supervision for child protection and welfare workers (Rushton and Nathan, 1996; Department of Health and Children, 1999; Jacquet et al., 2007), and also despite the HSE 'Area A's' own supervision policy, participants described long periods where they had no structured supervision or had very short supervision sessions. Jenna, a social worker who wants to stay, described the frequency of supervision sessions:

> Jenna: ... and supervision happened very rarely.
>
> *KB: Can you define rarely for me?*
>
> Jenna: Twice in seven months ... I had it more than the rest of the team ... They only had it once. ... I think it's important to have it on a regular basis. I think monthly to every six weeks, uninterrupted as much as possible, phone off the hook, note on the door, [for an] hour.

Jenna's experience of infrequent supervision was a consistent feature on all of the child protection and welfare teams. The following sample quotations are taken from interviews with social workers from the other four teams:

> My supervision at the moment is irregular. It wouldn't be what I would like. I would like it at least on a monthly basis. But I mean there is several months have passed now since I had my last supervision. That is compensated by the fact that in theory there is an open door policy that you can go in and address your supervisor (Jessica).
>
> The last time I had supervision ... [was] a few months ago maybe for half an hour (Holly).
>
> We can come in and out at any point. If she is here, we...you know, we would bat things back and forward. So we kind of have informal supervision in a way. So there is no....you are not left on your own with it. But formal supervision would be maybe once every two to three months (Nicole).
>
> I hadn't had supervision for about six months, partially because it hadn't happened between us, partially because I consciously decided to avoid it [identifying reason removed] (Deborah).

Within teams, there were some exceptions where social workers did receive what they described as regular and adequate 'formal' supervision. Both Evan and Holly, two social workers who wanted to stay, had positive experiences of supervision. Evan defined regular supervision as occurring once a month. Holly also had a positive experience of supervision, which she found to be supportive and significant in her willingness to stay:

116

You have the formal supervision sessions every month or whatever they would be. But then you have that constant kind of resource that you can check in. You know, that it is informal and it can be over a coffee, it can be passing in the corridor, it can be...whatever, you know. You run by....things, you know, that's the way I work anyway. And that....I find that excellent (Evan).

KB: Does professional supervision influence the way you think about your job?

Oh. Definitely. Definitely yeah. Yeah. Because I am actually changing team leaders now soon and I think it's the continuity for me as well. I've actually had the same team leader since I started which would be pretty unusual (Holly).

The quotations from Jessica and Holly indicate that some supervisors make themselves available through an open door consultation policy and that some social workers find such 'informal' supervision supportive. Holly explained that part of her positive experience of supervision was the consistency that came from having the same supervisor, which allowed time to build a relationship. Quality and regular supervision is important for social workers that are new to this work, particularly newly-qualified social workers. As outlined in Chapter Two, supervision, according to Hawkins and Shohet (1989), must attend to the educational and supportive, as well as the administrative functions. Caoimhe, a newly qualified graduate in her 20s who wants to stay, described how during her 'crucial' first six months in the job she was rarely supervised, which is contrary to the advice provided by the National Social Work Qualification Board (2004a) on the induction of newly qualified social workers. Her supervision focused primarily on the administrative function, with little attention paid to the educational and supportive functions:

In my first week when I eventually had to get some guidance [from her team leader], I got 'short thrift', and I was to get on with it, that's what a social worker does. So, I thought to myself right, obviously I'm not going to get any support from you so I went elsewhere and I got it from my co-workers and more senior members of the team. Only for them, I probably would have walked out after the first week ... So, that was for a period of about 6 months, basically there was no support, there was no supervision, when I did have supervision it was more often than not cancelled, it was never rescheduled, six months of this. This is the most crucial phase of becoming a child protection social worker and I had nothing. When I did have it, the supervisor talked about themselves and twiddled with my cases on the computer (Caoimhe).

This first experience of supervision did not meet Caoimhe's expectations of what supervision should be, but in another part of the interview she was able to contrast this first experience of supervision with a later experience with a different supervisor where her expectations of supervision were met. This later good experience of supervision, and the support of co-workers in her early months, helped Caoimhe to stay. The response from her supervisor gives some indication of the organisational culture of support and induction for new staff in child protection and welfare in the HSE 'Area A'. Caoimhe described the first six months as her 'baptism of fire'. Mya, a colleague of Caoimhe who now wants to stay, but for the first six-nine months regularly thought about leaving, described her 'induction' to child protection and welfare:

There was virtually no induction. The induction, induction quote unquote that was there was just a joke ... off you go. It really was that. No exaggeration! And it's, it's extremely daunting ... I was crying going in to work. I was crying going home. I was having nightmares. I was, it was one of the worst times I think I've, I've experienced in my life in terms of stress levels ... When your starting out in [name of social work department] is, is done on an *ad hoc* basis you know. There's no kind of consistency you know and it's almost a culture thing. I don't know if it's, it's, you know, sink or swim and if you're able to swim, then you're great and you can stay (Mya).

When social workers did receive 'formal' supervision, it was invariably described as 'case-management' supervision. Social workers defined case-management supervision as supervision that focuses on the administrative function to the exclusion of the educational and supportive functions. Grace explained that though her supervision was case-management in orientation there was still not enough time for this type of supervision:

... supervision for that sort of workload and the complexity of the problems it is not there. There is case management, but even case management is impossible. You don't even get enough of case management, there is absolutely no emotional, what I call emotional supervision available. There is no time. It is not even the managers or supervisors fault because they [are] managing seven to eight different, you know, different people at a time. You just can't do it (Grace).

These criticisms of narrow supervision practices limited to an administrative or 'case-management' format were echoed by social workers on all of the teams. These quotations are from social workers on other teams that want to stay:

I think the supervision we get is just about case direction, what will I do here? Nobody asks you how you're feeling (Ciara).

I think the supervision that we get within the child protection area anyway is there's too much emphasis on, just on looking at cases and case management, that kind of thing (Thomas).

... with social workers and the risk for burnout and just maybe lacking energy that you also need to be minded a little bit. I feel that they are treating us like, more or less a number and that number should have 20.5 you know families in a case load, it's very much, there's nothing kind of, oh how are you and or how are you managing at the moment? (Laura)

The following quotations are from social workers on other teams who want to leave:

I would say my view of the supervision that is available is very negative. First of all, it's not supervision, it's case management ... because of the....the demands I suppose that are put upon people because they are not here as much as they could be or should be, the...the chances of interruption during your supervision have increased greatly. So your case management isn't even managed well (Denise).

Supervision is seen as what are you doing on your cases and here is new cases (Simon).

Both those who wanted to stay and those who wanted to leave mostly experienced supervision as case-management, thereby mainly addressing the administrative aspect of supervision in Hawkins and Shohet's (1989) model. In this type of supervision the anxieties, feelings and emotions of social workers arising from this emotional labour and their need for 'containment' (Ruch, 2007), are not addressed. Social workers described how there was little acknowledgement of actual or potential strains from the work, as recommended in the national child abuse guidelines. Social work supervisors themselves were not interviewed in this study, and data on their experience of supervising social workers would provide important additional insight into their needs as supervisors and the challenges of providing regular supervision that attends to all aspects of supervision. Further research on supervision in child protection and welfare would be welcome and would contribute to addressing a significant gap in this research in Ireland. When social workers experienced the quality of support as not being what they expected, some were able to identify the factors inhibiting social work managers from being resourced to provide the quality of support social workers felt they required. When discussing supervision in her interview, Ava said:

> And that's not to say that… if I were to go and you know seek out that support, in an immediate sense, that it wouldn't be there. Well what I would ideally want I suppose wouldn't be there, but that there would be some support there. But…you know, and often it's sort of…..I mean I suppose I recognise the limits of that. But….but also you know that people are quite stretched in terms of …the line managers are quite stretched in terms of time and commitment (Ava).

In the interviews, most social workers said that social work managers were generally available for 'immediate' support, which in this sense means a consultation, but this form of support has its limits. Some social workers questioned social worker managers' awareness of the need to provide quality supports to staff, which in turn affected the quality of inter-personal relationships with social work managers and also social workers' perceived levels of support from managers. Deborah said:

> They just don't have the relationship, don't have the trust. And the managers concerned I don't think have an awareness of the need for it. Unless somebody is sitting there crying in front of them, I don't think they really see that, you know, somebody who never sheds a tear is feeling it as much as somebody who is…you know…that it's always there, it's a constant. It impacts all of us all of the time. I don't think they …they are aware of that, and wouldn't have the same skills as other managers may have had in managing the emotional welfare of the team … they wouldn't have the skills, but they would certainly have the intention and the….you know, the willingness, and that's why we have co-worker support, which I know every social work team doesn't have… (Deborah).

In Deborah's team, a co-worker support/supervision group was established to acknowledge and address these needs. She suggested that supervisors were not even aware of the need to provide emotional support and a recognition of the strain of the work on workers, even though these roles are clearly ascribed to supervisors/managers in the national child abuse guidelines (Department of Health and Children, 1999; Department of Children and Youth Affairs, 2011) and the HSE 'Area A' supervision policy. When managers do not provide these supports, it affects social workers' perceived levels of support and feelings of being valued by the organisation. Tara spoke about the role of supervision as a mechanism to protect the organisation, rather than a mechanism of addressing the administrative, support and educational needs of workers:

> ... it's all geared around keeping a corporation ticking over, it's not geared towards actually supporting the people who are there, or acknowledging any of the fears or the anxiety or the stress or the absolute depression some people actually go through. I think that it looks good on paper that they care for their staff, but I don't think they do (Tara).

An organisational culture that fails to validate the feelings and experiences of the workers, even if they are negative, does not contribute to workers' feelings of being valued and supported by the organisation, and may suggest low levels of organisational support (Eisenberger *et al.*, 2004). In the earlier quote from Deborah, she questions social work managers' skills and other social workers in the study also questioned the level of training for social work managers. Both Grace and Isabelle were critical of the way they were managed:

> ... the supervisors mightn't have done any particular training in how to supervise, which is something I have a big problem with myself, because I think it is vital that managers get trained to be managers. Trained to be managers, both case management and emotional ... supervision. But you have to be able to go to somebody after a bad case and say 'I am wrecked'. 'I don't know how I am going to cope with that'. 'I didn't sleep last night'. You have got to be able to go to someone, if you are going to maintain your, I won't say sanity - it is not as bad as that, but I mean your stress levels are going to shoot sky high if you don't have an opportunity to get to debrief to get yourself out, of you know, what you go through ... My job satisfaction with clients has not diminished over the years. My dissatisfaction with the admin' side and with management - I would give it 0 (Grace).

Very poor management would be another aspect of that. But having said that, I would also identify that say team leaders or principal social workers are asked to do a managerial job that they are not qualified to do. They are...they are social workers, they are not managers. They haven't been trained or don't have expertise in what a team is, how a team works, what team dynamics are, how to deal with conflict on a team, how to deal with low morale, how to do any of that. So in fairness to them as well, they don't have that expertise ... there would be absolutely no confidence in some of the management (Isabelle).

Both Grace and Deborah identified a role for managers in providing emotional support to social workers, but question whether social work managers in the HSE 'Area A' are being trained and supported to develop their knowledge and skills in these areas. If what these two social workers suggests is representative of the wider experience of social workers, then investment by the HSE 'Area A' in regular and quality training for social work managers and resourcing them to have time to undertake the complete supervisory range of functions could pay dividends in terms of team development, strengthening support networks, improving inter-personal relationships between supervisors and co-workers and social workers' perceptions of organisational support.

The negative impact on retention of inadequate supervision and poor quality inter-personal relationships between a worker and supervisor is again illustrated by the following quote. Robyn is a mature-age social worker with a longer than average experience of child protection and welfare social work who wants to continue to work in this practice setting[37]:

I felt every day was like a dread coming in here do you know. My only thing about that is the wider team at the time ... that this lady [social work supervisor] supervised me so at least it was the support within the team that, that mitigated it and, and I, I said well, I'll just bear with her ... I stayed (Robyn).

Robyn described how a poor experience with one supervisor led to job dissatisfaction, but the role of social supports from co-workers helped to mitigate this negative experience. In another part of the interview, she explained that once she changed supervisors, the 'dread' of coming to work diminished. This experience underlines the critical impact of supervisors on social workers' experiences of the job, and in Robyn's

---

[37] In this study, the median length of social workers' practice experience in child protection and welfare was 4 years (see Chapter Four). The actual length of Robyn's service was removed to protect her anonymity.

case, if she had not had the support of co-workers, she would have left because of her supervisor.

Feedback from social work managers as an social exchange resource was identified by social workers as a factor which affects their feelings of being supported and valued by the organisation. The acknowledgment of workers' positive achievements during supervision is identified in the national child abuse guidelines as something which helps to 'acknowledge the levels of actual or potential stress that may affect their staff'(Department of Children and Youth Affairs, 2011, p. 43). Social workers perceived that their dedication and hard work was not valued by the organisation as supervisors and managers provided insufficient verbal affirmation, in supervision or otherwise, for good work undertaken:

> I think every day, we do unbelievable work and I think we go beyond sometimes what our job description is and I think it's never, ever, ever acknowledged ... I think that even the most contentious clients, if you work a case in a professional manner, and if you are continuously respectful towards them, I think that you will develop a certain kind of rapport. So I would definitely say the clients value you. Do management? No (Tara).

> I mean you might say, well Jesus I did a good job there you know. But it certainly wouldn't be coming from management or that like you know (Simon).

> Pats on the back are absolutely non-existent. Nobody will ever say you did that job well, I think I had one supervisor in the whole of my [5+] years who would be saying - well you did a good job there. How do you feel about that now - you had a fierce problem there with that case. How do you feel after it? That was about five years ago, I think. Nobody has ever said that was a job well done - and I know there have been loads of them. There were jobs well done (Grace).

Social workers expect praise, affirmation and constructive feedback as social exchange resources from their supervisors. Social workers in the same child protection and welfare team can have very different experiences of being affirmed, depending on who is supervising them. Holly and Mya are social workers on the same team:

> She's brilliant [team leader]. Yeah. Really good. Always praises me and just do you know, commends me you know, for work done good or reports or a good decision or do you know ... She's no problem at all in you know, telling you if you have a job well done. Then she has no problem telling you know, if you messed up there (Holly).

The social exchange between the supervisor and social worker is experienced as positive; in this case the exchange resource is praise. However, the following quote from Mya reinforces how some can experience the organisational culture as less than affirming, and she hypothesises why this may be:

> It's almost like, oh you can't you know, if we give them too many strokes they'll just get lazy [social worker laughs] kind of, kind of attitude! You know, kind of mentality of you know, we'll only speak up when things aren't being done the way they should be done. There's no point saying things when things are going grand (Mya).

Again, the lack of positive feedback led Hannah to question whether she was 'good enough' to do this work, but co-workers played an important role in affirming that she was:

> … a lot later when I'd be saying God I feel that I'm just not up to it when I look at so and so and everyone [co-workers] will go, my God everyone thinks you are really good at this or really good at that. You don't get that feedback. Your team leader would never say to you, you have done an excellent job (Hannah).

In nearly all the research on retention in child protection and welfare, one significant constant is the social support role played by supervisors and the quality of professional supervision (Rycraft, 1994; Mor Barak *et al.*, 2001; Smith, 2005). Research shows that when employees perceive their supervisors to be supportive, their commitment to the supervisor and the organisation increases, leading to job retention. Conversely, when supervisor support is perceived to be low, this leads to turnover (Smith, 2005). Thus, the quality of the relationship with one's supervisor can be the difference between a social worker leaving and staying (Samantrai, 1992).

In summary, social workers expect high quality and frequency of supervision, and it has been shown to be significant in job satisfaction levels, burnout and retention (Warman and Jackson, 2007). Social workers in this study described what they consider supervision should be: it should attend to professional development issues; consider workers' feelings about the work and impact of this emotional labour; be frequent; be greater than an hour in length; be provided by skilled social work managers, and all of the supervisory functions of education, support and administration, should be attended to. Social workers in this study were critical that too little time was given to supervision, and when it did happen it was 'imbalanced' towards dealing primarily with the administrative function. Furthermore, quite a number of social workers questioned whether their managers had the skills and training to provide quality supervision. There were incidences of social workers describing their supervision as good or excellent, but these were in the minority.

Social workers differentiated between social supports provided by co-workers and support from social work managers. Social work supervisors were nearly always available for consultation, which social workers defined as supportive, but were less available for structured professional supervision, which social workers found unsupportive. These affected social workers' perceptions of the quality of supports from, and inter-personal relationships with, their managers. The social workers who wanted to leave identified the poor quality and infrequency of their professional supervision as one of the core factors that contributed to their decision to leave. These social workers did not feel supported by their employer and were not 'contained' (Ruch, 2007) to hold and process the anxieties and pressures of undertaking this work. While supervision and the social supports from managers were not the only factors which contributed to these social workers' decisions to leave, it was amongst the most consistent factor that mediated their experience of doing the work.

Most of the social workers who wanted to stay had more positive experiences of supervision and support from managers, but not all described having good or excellent supervision. Overall, both social workers who wanted to stay and those that wanted to leave were critical of the quality and availability of supervision. However, social workers that wanted to stay expressed that they had other support networks that lessened the impact of the deficiencies of their supervision. They could also see other positive aspects and had positive experiences of the job. In the next part of this section, I examine support networks and social exchanges between workers and co-workers, which were one factor which social workers repeatedly spoke of and which they felt influenced their experience of the work and their retention.

5.3.2 Social supports from work colleagues and being part of a social work team

In this section, I present data from interviews with social workers examining the importance of the atmosphere in, and friendships gained from, working on child protection and welfare social work teams; social supports from and social exchanges with their co-workers; the experience of being part of a social work team; and how these impacted on their experience of 'doing the work' and their retention. Both Lucy and Shauna, social workers who wanted to stay, explained:

> ... a lot of it is made a lot easier by the fact that I have good friends there. They would have been people who have come from college with me and people who didn't. In terms of even if something has happened, that you're upset about, they are there to talk to but, there's also good fun (Lucy).

> I really like my team mates. I find them supportive, great company; I look forward to seeing them in the morning or the afternoon whenever I get here. I think that's a big part of it (Shauna).

Ava explained how working in a team of social workers and the co-worker support are contributory factors in her decision to want to stay, particularly when contrasted with her experience of 'single-handed' social work posts:

> I suppose the thing that comes to mind first would be team and sharing with colleagues really and supporting each other, and sort of being in it together you know. I think that's hugely helpful ... I have done single-handed posts and I have not stayed in them a really long time and I think it's just the difference between having that support from colleagues and not. And that's not to say that you are going to get on with everyone or that you know it's always going to work out perfectly. But, it's a huge plus [being] on a team (Ava).

Being supported by co-workers, which contributes to a supportive climate within child protection and welfare teams, can ameliorate other demanding aspects of the jobs. Nearly all of the social workers interviewed identified co-worker support and team atmosphere as being significant in their decision to stay working in child protection and welfare. Robyn and Ciara, two social workers who want to stay, described how co-workers helped with the processing of the emotional strains of the job, provided social outlets, and contributed to a shared experience of dealing with the struggles of the work, which helped to reduce the isolation felt by workers:

Robyn: I think a lot of people in social work have such a good insight into people and everything that social workers in general you know, even though we all make our jokes and oh my God listen to social workers and all of that. I think they, they really are kind of generally insightful bunch and humorous and I think it's, I've really enjoyed a lot of the time do you know. Ok, it was all in little spells but overall if I look back, I think of all the do you know, the kind of good, good times and good laughs and good sharing of being in the same boat together do you know, that whole sense.

KB; If you didn't have that would you still be here after [number

removed] years?

Robyn: No, definitely not. If I was with the same kind of pressures - very isolated - I would not.

I think only that, it's a nice team and I would be long gone only that I feel it's a nice place to work and that the team are very nice. That keeps me there (Ciara).

Social workers that had decided to leave also found the support of co-workers crucial in terms of dealing with the work and being retained longer. Clodagh and Aoife, two social workers that wanted to leave, explained that they would have left the work much earlier had it not been for the support of their co-workers. In Clodagh's case, 'team' means co-workers, as in another part of the interview she is highly critical of the lack of support from social worker managers. Even though she wants to leave, Aoife explained that such decisions were rarely clear-cut and the supports from colleagues helped to sustain her longer in the work:

The team is probably the reason why I have stayed so long, because there is good co-worker support in the team. And there has been....I suppose really that has been the attraction for me and for my colleagues. We would say that the team makes it worthwhile to come in (Clodagh).

I think that is the thing that keeps you in the job is the support you get from the people around you and I have got a very supportive team that I really like and if I didn't have that I wouldn't be in the job still (Aoife).

A positive aspect of the increased stability on child protection and welfare teams as a result of decreased employee turnover is the potential for inter-personal relationships to develop, as staff are together longer. Denise described how support networks on teams were improving due to the increased retention of social workers:

I think it has definitely improved in the time that I have been here ... I don't think the team has been as stable for so long. By that I mean that the same people are here. Like the changeover, people aren't changing as fast. There is...the same staff have been here. The relationships between people as opposed to between social workers have evolved (Denise).

Throughout the study, most social workers described very poor or non-existent induction for new staff when they first enter child protection and welfare in the HSE 'Area A'. The data suggests that the NSWQB (2004a) induction framework, which was produced to guide employers in the induction of newly-qualified and 'non-national' staff, has limited currency in this HSE. Despite the absence of a formal induction system, social work colleagues appear to play a key role in inducting new colleagues. Claire, an experienced social worker, found that in the absence of a formal induction it was the support of her colleagues that helped her to stay:

I wouldn't have survived if it wasn't for them [co-workers] as much as I've said I feel I'm a competent social worker. In, in that environment the, the newness of it and the difficulties that are involved, difficulties that are involved with the high numbers, with a different legislation, with different services that are not available in Cork, I don't think I would have lasted at all (Claire).

In summary, while there were many factors that influenced social workers' decisions to stay or leave child protection and welfare, one particular factor stands out from the others for its frequent occurrence and importance in the data. Social workers in this study repeatedly and consistently identified the quality of inter-personal relationships with, and social supports from, work colleagues as *the* factor which had the strongest influence on their willingness to continue working in child protection and welfare. Social exchange theory contends that social relationships formed between two partners, in this case a worker and their co-workers, can influence workplace behaviour such as turnover (Cropanzano and Mitchell, 2005). Nearly all social workers on the five social work teams highlighted the high quality of social supports and inter-personal relationships with their co-workers, which influenced their commitment to colleagues and team, and which social workers' explicitly linked with their retention. In the absence of regular and adequate supervision from supervisors, co-workers were addressing some of the unmet functions of supervision. For example in one team, they had developed a co-worker support group for social workers, and another team had developed a 'buddy' system between co-workers for new staff. Most teams arranged team days where staff had a day out, part training and part team-building, to help develop the cohesiveness of their team. It would appear that these initiatives are important and play an essential role in developing inter-personal relationships between co-workers. In an unintended way, the HSE recruitment embargo may have contributed to the capacity of teams to develop social support networks, as social workers are staying longer, which increases opportunities for the development of friendships and support networks. An analysis of the data also suggests that there is a camaraderie which can develop when working under duress as a result of criticism, lack of resources and a perceived lack of support from management and the organisation.

Given their seminal role in the literature, professional supervision and social supports/exchanges as organisational factors influencing job retention and turnover were presented in their own section. The next section examines the other organisational factors implicated in the turnover and retention of child protection and welfare workers.

5.4 Organisational factors

In this section I examine organisational factors identified in the literature review as being important in influencing child protection workers' decisions to stay and leave. The organisational factors examined in the following sections include caseload size and meeting the needs of children; 'farming' out the work and the perceived deskilling of social workers; accessing finite resources; organisational climate and culture; salary and promotional opportunities; variety in the work; alternative employment options, and other factors including violence, social work education, and 'the buzz' associated with the work and court work.

5.4.1 Caseload size and its impact on meeting the needs of children

The size of social workers' caseloads and the resultant workload is a constant theme within the literature, but its influence on retention and turnover is much disputed (see, for example, Smith, 2005; Tham, 2007). In the research interviews, social workers were most animated when talking about two factors in particular: supervision and the size of their caseloads. Social workers complained of high caseloads which they felt impacted on the quality of service given to children and families due to time pressures, the 'stress of conscience' associated with reconciling the quality of service they would like to provide with what is actually possible due to caseload size and time constraints, the impact of these factors on their sleep, and how such high caseloads negatively impact upon the reputation of the sector. This section examines these issues, but to set this theme in context, it was important to first establish the exact caseload numbers and children that social workers were responsible for.

As outlined in the literature review chapter, the quality of data on the number of children for which the HSE is responsible is either incomplete or out-of-date. The Minister for Children and Youth Affairs is on record acknowledging the poor quality of statistical data in this area (Fitzgerald, 2011)and there is an on-going project (Health Service Executive, 2009) to address this issue, which should be completed in 2013/14 .

Initially, I asked social workers to provide data on their caseloads when completing their documentation sheet (Appendix E), but the quality of the data collected in this way was unreliable as many social workers admitted that the figures provided were estimates. To collect more accurate data on caseloads, an exercise was undertaken in the HSE 'Area A' in November 2006 to gather data on the number of children each social worker was assigned at the end of the month[38]. The HSE 'Area A' Child Care Information Unit supported the collection of this data and table 5.1 presents the findings on the number of children assigned to each social work Whole Time Equivalent (SW WTE) in each of the five child protection and welfare social work teams. The table also shows how many children each internal department were responsible for:

---

[38] From a statistical perspective, relying on caseload figures from one month is far from ideal. Due to the absence of other datasets for comparison, it is difficult to say whether November 2006 was a representative month. Nonetheless, given the persistently high number of reports received by this HSE and little change in the compliment of staff, it is likely to be an adequate representation. In 2012, I spoke with a Principal Social Worker on one of the teams who ran a report on this system to compare this table with social workers' present caseload levels. The number of children each social worker is responsible for at the end of 2012 has remained more or less the same as the end of 2006, despite the increase in staffing due to an expanding rate of referrals.

Table 5.1: Caseload analysis, November 2006, HSE 'Area A'

Team	Department	SW WTE	No. of children	No. of children per SW WTE
Team 1	Duty	4	304	76
	Intake	4.8	231	48
	Long-Term	20	670	34
	Subtotal		*1,205*	
Team 2	Intake	1.6	62	39
	'Generic'/Long-Term	4.9	195	40
	Subtotal		*257*	
Team 3	Duty	1.8	140	78
	Intake	0.6	25	42
	Long-Term	5.7	277	49
	Managers[39]	2.8	23	8
	Subtotal		*465*	
Team 4	Duty	4	168	42
	Intake	4	182	46
	Long-Term	8.6	340	43
	Aftercare	0.5	14	28
	Subtotal		*704*	
Team 5	Duty	1	30	30
	'Generic'/Long-Term	12	508	42
	Managers	3	48	16
	Subtotal		*586*	
Total			**3,217**	**Average = 41.3**

The findings presented in this table confirm social workers' perceptions that they had high caseloads and were responsible for very large numbers of children. Most of the social workers in the HSE 'Area A' were responsible for 40+ children (average = 41.3 children), with duty team

---

[39] Social work managers in Team 3 and Team 2 'carry' caseloads, whereas social work managers in the other teams do not have children 'assigned' to them.

social workers in Team 1 and Team 3 having more than that 70 children assigned to each SW WTE. At the end of November 2006, child protection and welfare social workers in the HSE 'Area A' were assigned a total of 3,217 children. At the end of 2006, the HSE had 781 children in care, received 411 children into care during the year and dealt with 2,388 new reports of suspected child abuse and requests for support (Child Care Information Unit, 2007). This is demanding and important work with vulnerable children and families, and the work can often be slow and labour-intensive, with supportive and preventative work being particularly so. How long would it have taken for a social worker to see each child on their caseload once?

If one were to set an unrealistic scenario (no sick leave, planned work only, no emergencies, no court work, and so on) for a generic/long-term worker in Team 5 who was responsible for 42 children, it would have take them from 1st November to the end of December to see each child once[40]. In the reality of everyday practice, the social worker would have at least 4-5 high-profile and intensive cases requiring daily contact, would spend days in court and other meetings, and would be constantly negotiating funding for, and access to, finite support resources for these children. Under these conditions, it could be six months before a social worker got time to visit some children and families on their caseload. How realistic is it then for these social workers, with such high caseloads, to provide a quality service to these children and families?

In the literature review chapter, I presented Irish research which indicated that the 'saturation' of social workers' caseloads is as important as the number of cases. Saturation refers to the small number of intensive and time-consuming 'crisis' cases which take up a disproportionate amount of social workers' time (Social Information Systems, 2005). Caoimhe and Jessica explain:

---

[40] There were 40 working days in November and December 2005. The calculation takes into account travel time, time for recording, duty days, report writing, telephone calls with other professionals, form filling and other tasks which social workers normally undertake in their daily work.

We all experience where there is one family for a particular time frame that will take up your entire week, your entire month, an entire 6 months and then the rest of your cases then just get abandoned, they shouldn't but they do, because, whoever shouts loudest gets the attention, then all of a sudden the cases you have neglected for 3 months, 4 months, 5 months, 6 months they start to jump and things start to happen in those case loads because you've neglected them (Caoimhe).

... they don't see us for months, then we often get that - Who are you? I thought that case was closed? You know, 'cos you haven't been able to get back to them (Jessica).

The consequences of the saturation effect of these cases is that the other children on the caseload become 'neglected'; not only are they not receiving a service, but only when they reach a certain threshold of 'crisis' do they receive attention, by which time it is often too late to engage in preventative and supportive work. This practice reality is far from the 'milk van' approach ('low key, discreet, inobtrusive [*sic*.], nurturing, regular, reliable, long term') to building a therapeutic alliance and relationship building and more in common with a 'fire brigade' type response ('sudden, one off, invasive, crisis driven, hyped') (Harris, 1993 cited in Gilligan, 2004, p. 97). Jessica's account highlights the difficulties of establishing and maintaining relationships with services users when there are such lengthy breaks between visits. Caoimhe's use of the word 'neglect' is interesting in that a system that is supposed to identify and address issues such as neglect in families is itself 'neglecting' these children due to high workload demands and time pressures as a result of high caseloads. The metaphor of 'skimming' was used by Nicole, a social worker who wants to stay, to emphasise succinctly the challenge of finding time to do in-depth quality social work with large caseloads. This point was also raised by Erin, a social worker who wants to leave:

Nicole: ... I suppose extra staff really ... yes, case loads.

KB: And what way would extra staff help you?

Nicole: I suppose just like cases, you know, that we wouldn't have so many cases that other people could take...divide them out equally you know. So that we could spend more time actually on the work itself ... Yes, I feel a lot of the time I am skimming and I hate that. Like I would love to just get into it and do it properly. But you are under such time constraints with everything and everybody wants something yesterday ... a lot of it is just crisis driven.

> I just feel that I am kind of barely touching everything instead of doing something in-depth (Erin).

These social workers suggest directly and indirectly that child protection and welfare teams in the HSE 'Area A' are understaffed and that there are unrealistic expectations regarding social workers' caseloads. The Child Care Manager's office responsible for Team 1 in personal correspondence indicated that they have not received development funding for their social work departments since 2003 (Health Service Executive South, 2007). The lack of growth in WTEs in the sector since 2003, together with the increasing number of children and families coming to the attention of these services (see figure 1.4 in Chapter One), results in social workers being responsible for greater numbers of children (waiting lists were not operated in this HSE at the time of the fieldwork and there were some reports that some of the teams are experimenting with waiting lists, although caseload numbers remain high). Social workers can get spread too thinly, 'skimming' over the caseload which Jane, a social worker who wants to stay, connects with the quality of her practice:

> At times the size of the caseload, trying to meet all of your client's needs as I might perceive them. That can be quite frustrating that I feel that I'm not maybe maintaining a level of practice for each of those individual cases that I might wish to … (Jane).

The link between high caseloads and feelings of not being able to 'do a good job' as highlighted in Jane's quote has also been associated with a loss of job satisfaction and as a factor in retaining social workers (The Scottish Parliament Information Centre, 2002). Making a difference with children and families becomes harder as cases that were 'neglected' may become worse due to a lack of attention. This may lead to emotional stress for social workers, who experience a 'stress of conscience', which is having insufficient time to provide quality care, being unable to live up to others' expectations, deadening one's conscience and lowering expectations regarding quality of service provision (Glasberg *et al.*, 2007). The following quotations from social workers that want to stay (Ava, Caoimhe and Abigail) and Aoife, who wants to leave, illustrate this issue:

Because things have fallen apart for … for want of being taken care of, or being addressed. And you know, or you end up having to deal with something on duty…or one of your own cases that has sort of just got further and further down to the bottom of the heap, even though you are kind of aware of it. But it's…it's just, you know, been left there. And you see things go badly wrong, and you think, well, I could probably have prevented that, or gone some way towards preventing that. So you actually feel….you can feel almost destructive. You can take on too much responsibility (Ava).

… the guilt around not having enough time in the day and then when you don't have enough time in the day the guilt around not being able to see the children that you need to see. I think the guilt, the guilt is huge about to what you're not getting done as opposed to what you are actually doing (Caoimhe).

… it's stressful. It's stress inducing, you know, when you have cases that you don't get to (Abigail)

I just focus on the things that I haven't done and there is an awful lot that I haven't done that I should have done and it's families that are entitled to services and they are not getting it because they are on my caseload and I can't get around to them and that is frustrating (Aoife).

These social workers, who were all highly critical of the organisational conditions in child protection and welfare, highlight the stress for them of having insufficient time to provide a quality of care and having to lower expectations regarding this care. This must be a particular stress for social workers, as the children who are not in receipt of a service, or an inadequate quality of service, are children living in families where they may be at risk of abuse or their needs are not being met. Why, then, do social workers not seek to change these conditions? Nicole spoke about negative experiences of trying to make small changes on their team and feeling disempowered:

… you have been knocked down so many times or whatever that people just feel like….what is the point in making any complaints that we don't have this, this and this, because nothing changes. We would often have this at team meetings, that you know we don't have, you know, x amount of foster placements for …we don't have emergency placements. And we have often, you know, written a letter or whatever. And nothing comes out of it. So you just feel like, what's the point? (Nicole)

Nicole's team's experience of not being listened to or having their views acknowledged or validated contributes to workers not feeling valued by the HSE 'Area A'. Further evidence of the HSE's approach to criticism from within could be seen in their response to the *Prime Time Investigates* (RTÉ, 2008c)programme on child protection and welfare. In the face of evidence presented by RTÉ,which mirrored the concerns of social workers in this chapter about the chronic under-resourcing and numbers of children at risk who were not receiving a service[41], the first response of the HSE and the Minister of State for Children and Youth Affairs was to seek to undermine the veracity of data provided by social workers, to deny that the system was under strain or that there were children at risk in the community who were not in receipt of a service (RTÉ, 2008a, c).

Furthermore, being seen to be critical of the HSE may result in negative consequences for social workers (social workers who participated in the *Prime Time Investigates* documentary were silhouetted and were not identified by name or team). For example, Tara suggests that there can be consequences in promotional terms:

> I know there would be a kind of an ethic, I think in general among social workers that you keep your head below the parapet and by nature all of us go in wanting to put our heads above it and wanting to actually take on the system or fight a little bit and that kind of sense of justice and injustice. I think there is a huge ethic of how you do your job, you keep your head, if you in any way go against the grain well then you are going to meet that person across the desk at an interview. You may have forgotten, but they will remember (Tara).

In this instance it is unsafe to 'go against the grain' and social workers are socialised by the organisation not to be critical. On the other hand, there were social workers that were less critical of the system and more 'accepting' of the conditions. For example, Jessica is less questioning and we can interpret her quote in two ways: either this is a coping strategy to survive the workplace or evidence of the social worker's socialisation by the organisation:

> At the same time I'm quite happy with the way things are working, I suppose, you just get used to the system that's in place and you have to work with it, I think like, I wouldn't be challenging it all the time. It's just I suppose like the reality of it is, is this is how it is now (Jessica).

---

[41] The HSE (Health Board) have a statutory responsibility under section 3 the Child Care Act, 1991 to identify and protect all children in its area who are not receiving adequate care and protection.

The impact of large caseloads on social workers' health was also evident in the data. Clodagh highlighted how doing the work and large caseloads impacted on her sleep and resulted in unmet expectations of her social work practice:

> And you wake up in the middle of the night thinking, what is happening with that family, you know. I mean when I signed up, I signed up for working with people and giving them…maybe it's an idealistic viewpoint of social work, but I definitely did think I would be going to their home on a regular basis, I would be seeing them, you know, I would be working as part of a multi-disciplinary team. There are cases now where childcare leaders work, I don't work with the children, because I simply don't have the time (Clodagh).

Social workers in child protection and welfare, as illustrated here by Clodagh, are not always seeing children or doing direct work with children. A more in-depth analysis of social workers' reduced involvement in 'direct work' with children and families is undertaken in the next section (5.4.2). The concerning aspect of this quote is the reduction in social workers' frequency of visits to family homes. In a child abuse inquiry in the UK (Lord Laming, 2003), a key recommendation was that social work home visits were crucial in the assessment of children's circumstances and were directly related to the capacity of the system to protect children. Any reduction or cessation of social work home visits is highly questionable, irrespective of the reasons.

To return to the theme of workloads and social workers' health, a clash between excessive caseloads and social workers' own professional expectations can lead some to attempt to keep up with these demanding work conditions 'at the expense of their own emotional health, with high levels of burnout as a result' (Mor Barak *et al.*, 2001, p. 653). Shauna, a social worker that wants to stay, points to the implications of high caseloads on her work-life balance:

> Shauna: Of course that creates stress which I'm trying to find ways of managing. Because one of the ways that I manage it is to work after hours or to take things home with me and I've pretty much put a stop to that. But as the role is right now, it's not realistic.
>
> *KB: And do you want to say a bit more about why you think it's not realistic?*

Shauna: The amount of meetings, the expectations and desire to work with clients in a professional manner in a way they deserve you know, their integrity and the demands that are put on the social workers. It's not logical for our caseloads.

Shauna's coping strategy was to take work home in an attempt to try and keep up standards and cope with volume. She explains that expectations of social workers in child protection and welfare are unrealistic, with the effect that they are stressed about their integrity and their ability to provide a service and make a difference to clients who deserve a quality service.

In this section, I have presented data on the high number of children that child protection and welfare social workers are responsible for in the HSE 'Area A'. Both social workers that wanted to stay and those that wanted to leave were highly critical of the HSE 'Area A's' expectation that they 'carry' and work with such high caseload numbers, which contributed to social workers' perceptions that the HSE 'Area A' was not a supportive organisation which valued their contribution or cared for their well-being. Social workers outlined the negative consequences of this policy for both clients and themselves: social workers were under increased strain and clients were in receipt of a reduced-quality service. Social workers were particularly vexed at the HSE's lack of investment in staffing and support services (for example, alternative care placements) to cope with the increased volume of work. For social workers that wanted to leave, the impact of high caseloads was significant in their decisions. What is clear from the data is that caseloads, but more specifically the impact of high caseloads on service users and social workers, is a key mediating factor in social workers' experiences of child protection and welfare in the HSE 'Area A'. Social workers that want to stay are also unhappy about high caseloads, but other factors such as their commitment to the work, supervision, and social supports from peers helped them to stay. There may be a point reached where the stress and risk associated with carrying the responsibility for this volume of children may lead social workers that want to stay to change their decision, leading to avoidable turnover. Another consequence of high caseloads highlighted by social workers in the study was their increased distance from direct service provision, a theme which will be examined in the next section.

5.4.2 'Farming out' the work and the perceived deskilling of social workers

A recurring theme in the interviews was that of social workers becoming increasingly removed from direct service provision with children and families. Family support and prevention, while given credence in government policies and organisational practice guidelines (Department of Health and Children, 1999; Government of Ireland, 2000) had little resonance for many social workers in the study, who routinely called themselves - in a derogatory sense - 'case-managers'. Social workers repeatedly described professional identity conflicts resulting from a variance between their expectations of professional practice, their training and the reality of the work. Research with social workers in UK mental health services found that social workers value face-to-face direct contact with clients above all (Carpenter *et al.*, 2003). Social workers professional identity conflict had its genesis in a perceived shift towards their work being defined in managerial terms (case-manager), rather than working with people. Anna, a social worker who wanted to leave, explained how the quantity of work led to the 'farming out' of work to others and Aoife, who had also decided to leave, described herself as being a delegator of work (a managerial function):

> As opposed to farming it out to other people because I hate just the idea of just ok you do this, you do that and you know referring to every, all these different agencies and, actually not doing the work yourself and then you are getting so many people involved in people's lives as well (Anna).

> What I am doing is getting other people to do all the work. I didn't see it like that before I went in to it. I didn't see it that I was basically just a case manager who delegates work to other people. That's the way I essentially see it now is that I just get some family that have a problem and I get on to other people to sort it out (Aoife).

This 'farming out' of tasks results in social workers being increasingly removed from providing face-to-face interventions with clients and concern associated with the impact on service users of having multiple professionals involved in their lives. As entry thresholds to the system rise in response to rising workloads (Buckley, 2008), social workers increasingly work with the most serious cases, leaving them with a caseload of the most difficult and challenging ones. Using concepts from job characteristics theory (Oldham, 1996), this affects social workers' capacity to experience contributing to change in the lives of children and families (task significance) and the variety of their skills used in the work (skill variety). Also, social workers feel deskilled as they are using less of their inter-personal and direct work skills:

> It is only the ones who are almost impossible to get an outcome that we are left with. Yeah, this is where burnout is going to come in … because if you don't have a few good cases - preventative work you are not going to have any feel-good factor … if you don't have the few nice cases, what we would call the feel-good cases, it is doing more harm than good, because even though they might take up time, they sort of give you the spark to keep you going (Grace).

> So having that balance of the caseload so that there is nice stuff in there that you are occasionally visiting foster carers who are smiling giving you a cup of coffee coming in after your five visits to people that are literally you know flicking cigarettes at you as you go out the door. The balance is important (Hannah).

Hannah and Grace both use the word 'nice' to describe the need to have 'balanced' caseloads where there are some cases with lower levels of risk and conflict, with a possibility of undertaking some supportive and preventative work. In other parts of their interviews, these social workers described how with increasing caseloads, many social workers are 'left' with the highest-risk and complex cases which are harder to work on. Abbey described the lack of emphasis on social work *practice* development and her role in 'processing' cases: closing them as fast as possible by being a case-manager:

> Abbey: I don't necessarily feel that there is a motivation always to develop a team in a practice sense, that we essentially become case managers and our role is to keep taking on the cases, do the work, close them off, here is your next pile to…..

> KB: OK. Where do you think that message comes from?

> Abbey: I think….I suppose some of it is naturally driven by the work load that we have. A service has to be delivered.

Social workers in the 'rural' teams were most likely to say that their teams still facilitated them to do more supportive and preventative work. Being on a 'rural' team allowed social workers to use a greater variety of their skills and talents, and to have more direct face-to-face contact with clients, which resulted in less 'farming out' of work to others. In the next quotation Jenna, a social worker in one of the 'rural' teams who wants to stay, compared what she believed happens in the city teams in the first part of the quote with her experience where she gets to do preventive work. This experience is shared by Shannon, a social worker in one of the other 'rural' teams:

> [Referring to one of the primarily city based child protection and welfare teams in the HSE 'Area A'] It's very much case management, very crisis driven, a lot of paperwork, a lot of referring the families out. If you are not bad enough, you know, we don't even open the case. You know, there is not a lot of preventative work being done, which I like here. You know, we are opening cases that may not have been necessarily opened in other places, trying to do some prevention…trying to keep families together, and not just work with families who are in constant crisis. Do you know…trying to get to families in an earlier stage (Jenna).

> I think so. I do…yes. But then you have to take the time to do it. And I suppose if I didn't do it, so I am responsible in a way. Because I do plan my diary. I have to put scheduled appointments in….over say three months I will have…and that has saved my sanity as well. Because if you plan your diary and you do a bit of direct work each day or something nice each day (Shannon).

Anna, a social worker in a 'rural' team who managed to run a supportive parenting group, identified her positive move away from the dominant practice orientation towards a different method of intervention which improved her relationship with clients:

> And like it was really positive to actually to have my clients there and do that work with them and for them to see me in a different light I think and I actually built a very good relationship with a couple of my clients (Anna).

Relationship-building is also illustrated by Mya who believed that the bureaucratisation of social work (Howe, 1992) affected the reputation of the sector and social workers. Social workers who had decided that they wanted to leave were most likely to perceive that they had less opportunity to engage in preventative-type work than they expected, felt de-skilled by becoming more of a bureaucrat than a social work practitioner and highlighted the negative impact on service users:

> Frustrated. I think the children get a bit of a raw deal in that respect. I think that's also part of what plays in to social workers having a bad rep you know and getting, you know, social workers maybe don't care or aren't as concerned about the child's welfare. That we're kind of aloof and busy doing our paperwork as opposed to you know, being hands on with the child (Mya).

Aoife, a social worker who had decided to leave the work, described the value she placed on direct practice with children. She got most satisfaction from the work when she able to use her skills:

> … you could have a great day where you'd do a good piece of work with a child and that's very satisfying as well (Aoife).

However, Aoife, in other parts of the interview, described how this experience was infrequent, and in her next quotation she alluded to a growing 'jealousy' within child protection teams at the division of labour between social workers and community child care leaders, whom social workers saw as doing the 'nicer' pieces of work. Aoife's decision to want to leave was directly related to her not being able to do enough direct practice with children and families, and she should be seen as an 'avoidable' leaver:

> I did honestly think I would stay because I love working with children, I love working with families. Do you know, I do generally love the work but just see I see childcare leaders going off and I go, I'd love to be doing that now. Taking kids places, doing things I'd like to do like (Aoife).

In her interview, Ciara extends the analysis of social workers feeling deskilled by implicating social work managers in the process. She explained her work was largely bureaucratic and social work managers allocated the direct work to others as they believed she does not have the skills for this type of work - work which traditionally would have been seen as a core social work task:

> I suppose you lose the skills, but a lot of the work I feel we do, we are writing court reports and writing reports for case conferences and all this and trying to get children into residential units and then any sort of direct work with children say if children need work managing their anger, that is done by a child care worker and it's like, the child care workers are held in very high esteem. I'm sure I could do that work but it's like - No a childcare worker would have to do that work because it is so specialised. What more qualifications do they have than I have? And I think a lot of those kind of skills they learned on the job through experience and by reading up on stuff. It's not like they are counsellors either (Ciara).

The impractical nature of social workers taking on too much planned work with children is underscored by Claire, who identified the need to respond to crises. Her reluctant response to these pressures was to 'farm out' this work out to 'therapeutic' social workers on her team:

142

We didn't seem to have the time to do that and that would, that would need to be referred to others and that was frustrating that we were sort of clock-watching quite a lot. Well, if we did try to take something on then a crisis would come up and we wouldn't be able to commit to say six sessions every Thursday at three o'clock you know. So I did find, I did find that hard. I just find it hard that any activity such as life story work was passed on to do by the other team within [Name of Social Work Department] (Claire).

Clodagh and Mya perceived that the HSE valued social workers fulfilling their managerial functions first and were less concerned about social workers actually meeting clients:

> ... the mandate, have the paperwork done irrespective of how long it takes and how cumbersome it is ... I would say 60% of my time is in the office doing paperwork. I signed up for working with people and giving them...maybe it's an idealistic viewpoint of social work, but I definitely did think I would be going to their home on a regular basis ... I don't work with the children, because I simply don't have the time. So I may meet them, but the work is done by childcare leaders ... (Clodagh).

> ... if we were pulled up on our managing of the case, it would not be about, how much time have you spent with the child, what kind of quality time do you spend with the child as opposed to, are your case notes up to date and have you done such and such a form? I mean, I have nightmares at night sometimes that I haven't filled in some kind of form. Whatever, it never makes any sense but, yeah and I think unfortunately day to day [that's] what it's, what it's more about sometimes (Mya).

A BBC *Panorama* documentary which examined the death of 17-month-old 'Baby P' in the United Kingdom, also made the point that child protection and welfare social workers spend too much time on administration and computer work, which limits their contact time with service users (BBC, 2008).

In summary, social workers expressed disappointment and a sense of disillusionment at the limited amount of time they spent with children and families compared to the demands of their administrative tasks. However, social workers on the 'rural' teams were more likely to feel that they could structure their workload to engage in planned direct work with children and families and preventative work. It is difficult to see how social workers with large caseloads, with even fewer opportunities for 'nicer' pieces of work, can sustain themselves in the work. They are left mainly with the most complex, conflict-laden and high-risk cases, where opportunities for changes are fewer. It is important for social workers to feel like they can grow and develop, and to have a variety of work that utilised their skills and talents. Unfortunately, some social workers in the study felt that the opposite was the case; they were becoming more deskilled practitioners and more able bureaucrats. For the social workers that had decided to leave, another job that would provide them with more time for face-to-face work with clients and more opportunities to use their skills was significant in making their decision.

Another organisational theme which arose in the data was the challenge associated with accessing resources to support these clients, and this issue will be examined in the next section.

5.4.3 Accessing essential resources

Social workers consistently identified what they considered to be the poor resourcing of services for children as being a significant factor in measuring feelings of accomplishment and success in their work, as was the perceived value of their work by the organisation and by society. To extend the analysis of this theme, which was briefly examined in the personal factors section (making a difference), social workers explained that their ability to meet the needs of children and families was reduced due to difficulties in accessing finite resources within the HSE for children and families. Social workers repeatedly described the lack of resources to implement care/protection plans as being significant in their ability to meet the needs of children, which, in turn, affected their job satisfaction and increased job stress. Social workers placed particular emphasis on difficulties associated with accessing two particular resources: alternative care placements for children who could no longer live at home, and mental health/therapeutic resources. Clodagh and Nicole described their feelings of 'impotence' and 'inadequacy' as a result of not being able to access such resources, which contributed to a sense of powerlessness:

> ... a sense of impotence as well as a professional. And you had of course the...the real sense that this person's needs were not being met by the then SHB and that you were colluding at some level with depriving this young person of what they needed (Clodagh).

> ... you just feel inadequate in many ways because you don't have the resources to fulfil the needs that are there (Nicole).

Social workers recognised that they were only one part of a larger system for children and families: without the support of other community services (for example, mental health services, school placements, alternative care placements, psychology, and so on) social workers can only make a limited difference with their clients. Social workers compete within the organisation to secure finite resources on behalf of their clients, and their reconciliation with these conditions can be significant in their feelings of job satisfaction and stress. In the following quotes from two social workers who want to stay, we can see the frustration connected with not being able to access an essential resource such as alternative care placement:

> ... a lot of it is resources. You feel sometimes like you are banging your head off the wall. We don't have any teenage fostering placements. We have...only a select few have supported accommodation, you know, fostering placements are just impossible to find. And we have a lot of the teenage kids now out of home. And you feel like putting them into a hostel or whatever, it's just not good enough. And you...you feel then that you are failing the teenager (Nicole).

> I mean it's.....it's utterly abusive. It's ridiculous what is happening, you know. I mean someone who was at the admissions panel for the applications to residential care the other day was saying that there were 16 applications in for that month, and one residential placement available (Ava).

Caoimhe points out the consequences of this lack of resources, namely, that unsafe practice decisions were being made based on service availability rather than on need:

> Caoimhe: Foster placements, and I'm not talking about for troubled teens, I'm talking about babies, there are no foster placements. Full stop.

> *KB: How does that affect your job?*

> Caoimhe: It means that we are working in a situation where we are basing our decision on whether or not to take a care order on a child and whether or not we will get a placement for them. There are children on my caseload that we probably should have in care, but we cannot go into a courtroom and ask them to admit these children to care without a placement.

> *KB: How does that make you feel?*

> Caoimhe: Horrible, because they are living in conditions that they shouldn't be living in. It has far-reaching consequences.

Workers' feelings of stress are compounded by the responsibility of keeping children at home in potentially unsafe conditions and the possible consequences for these children. Overly bureaucratic processes can act as a disincentive to apply to admission panels for residential care, which leads to further stress for social workers. Social workers described their engagement with extensive and lengthy bureaucratic admission application processes, not because there were placements available to protect children, but as a means for the organisation to protect itself by being seen to do something. Both Evan and Simon explain:

> Evan: ... referral doesn't stand a chance you know.
>
> *KB: And why don't they stand a chance?*
>
> Evan: I suppose the pressure....the pressure on resources, you know, the....the....it arises particularly now with the special care units and that type of thing ... I notice increasingly is that it's serving a kind of a gate keeping role....you know, having multiple copies of applications, do you know. And there is one unit now ...it's gone from eight copies of everything to eleven copies of everything you know. And it's...it's a couple of day's effort...work tracking reports and then just...you know, photocopying them. You know that tedium of ...of just photocopying. And then of sending off a box that high...a foot high of stuff you know...for the third or fourth time. And then the refusal coming back.
>
> I would have a number of cases at the moment, one in particular, and you know the child that is clearly in need of....of protection for himself and for society and there are no places there for him. That's...that's the bottom line here you know. And I suppose there is a huge ....I wouldn't say a huge...but there is a large emphasis on the process involved in trying to get this child a place, even though there may not be a place there for him. But you have to be seen....I suppose, there is sort of a liable issue at play here. Like that you have to fill out you know these huge documents you know and....and fair enough they have to be filled out. But when you know that you are not going to get a place, what's the purpose of all this, you know, when you could be out in the field I suppose and still trying to be there for him (Simon).

There are at least two issues with the situation as described by Evan and Simon. Firstly, they are participating in lengthy and time consuming administrative processes to apply for placements which do not exist or which their clients are unlikely to secure, which takes time away from their direct work with children and families. Secondly, it appears that children are being left in unsafe environments as the HSE 'Area A' is unable to provide a safe alternative placement. This is in direct contradiction to the HSEs statutory responsibilities as outlined in the Child Care Act 1991 and the *Report of the Working Group on Foster Care* which highlighted that 'health boards have a corporate responsibility towards those in their care ... [and that] there is a need to ensure that adequate attention and resources are allocated to the alternative care services' (Department of Health and Children, 2001, p. 22). Given the pervasive nature of this issue in the data, there appears to be an avenue for further research to examine the extent of children being left in unsafe environments and being 'supervised' by social workers at home due to an inadequate supply of alternative care placements. I will address some of these research opportunities in the conclusion at the end of this chapter.

The second set of resources which social workers described as problematic were the poor provision of therapeutic and mental health services for children. The need to develop counselling care and mental health services for children have been well documented (see, for example, Mental Health Commission, 2004; Houston, 2007). The social workers interviewed found that they were unable to access therapeutic services for their clients - children who had lived with adverse home conditions or who had been subject to severely abusive behaviours:

> [I] expected I would be able to have these resources, I would be able to refer people on say for counselling. Say child abuse or children in care for instance, children in care don't have any counselling unless they are presenting with extreme difficulties ...there is no budget in child protection for anything, no budget for counselling, it is only very extreme cases that you would apply for counselling. You have to apply to the child care manager and put it out there that this person needs extra, whereas it should be an everyday event, it should be available as part and parcel of the service (Grace).

Social workers' descriptions of little money for counselling supports reemphasises critiques of the child protection discourse which focuses on the identification and assessment of children and families in need, with less weight on the provision of therapeutic resources post-assessment (Ferguson, 2001). Aoife's experience highlights the changing fiscal climate within the HSE in recent years and its impact on support services for children:

> ... there is a waiting list so if somebody drastically needs counselling then tough, they can't get it ... They can't get it because there is no money there and then you hear stories like oh if that was five years ago now there was loads of money ... (Aoife).

The responsibility and commitment that social workers feel towards children on their caseloads, particularly when the child's home situation is affecting their welfare, leads to frustration when they are not able to access essential and indispensable resources. Social workers in the study appear to be questioning the HSE 'Area A's' support for child protection and welfare work. Children that come into the contact with the system requiring family support, counselling or alternative care should be provided with these services as a right. However, social workers' time is increasingly invested in bureaucratic processes and competing with each other for access to what appears to be a limited supply of these resources:

> ... it generates an expectation ... having a social worker etc. And it generates an expectation that we will find the resources or that we will be able to do x, y and z and we can't....particularly, you know, making your decision to receive a child into care, saying that their situation at home isn't adequate for them to be cared for by parents. And then we don't even have a psychologist available to meet that child's needs. Do you know...that is....not OK (Deborah).

> I think the consequences of it is very often that we have children who have been in very you know traumatic abusive situations and those children I suppose have got a message that, I have made a disclosure about something, I may have come into care because of it, why isn't somebody helping me now? Why ....why can't I ...you know, go and talk to somebody? I think it...it's a very ...it gives them a very poor message in terms of what we now think about them. Do you know....that we....we can't you know provide a service to them. And I suppose you know there are kids that become a bit more messed up because of it (Abbey).

These quotations from Deborah and Abbey, two social workers who had decided they wanted to leave, illustrate the potential consequences of the limited supply of these services for children. This theme played a role in social workers' decisions to stay or leave, but it was not a key factor on its own for social workers' decisions to want to leave. It appears to be a mediating factor which can compound other factors. Social workers did not expect that there would be a bounty of resources, but neither did they expect it to be quite so bad. Social workers' abilities to reconcile themselves with the reality of this situation appear significant. The deteriorating level of resources as a result of a fiscal tightening policy under way in health and social services, may suggest that services for children and families could be even more stretched, and there is a need for social work as a profession to collectively engage with the HSE and government to advocate on behalf of these children and families. Furthermore, the challenge of accessing resources contributed to social workers' perceptions of the climate and culture of the organisation and this theme is examined in greater depth in the next section.

5.4.4 Organisational climate and culture

Other sections in this chapter also address themes which contribute to social workers' experience of the organisational climate and culture within child protection and welfare social work in the HSE 'Area A'. These themes included: perceived organisational support from the HSE; administrative burdens; quality of supervision; relationships with and social supports from managers; job induction for newly-qualified graduates; salary; working conditions, and being listened to by the organisation. This section presents additional data on the culture and climate in child protection and welfare in the HSE 'Area A'. This data examines: the organisation's response to the impact of the work on workers' health; 'proving' that you can do this work; what it means to be constructed as a 'good' or 'reliable' worker; not being able to control your workload; an ethic of care and commitment to clients, and the degree of autonomy experienced by social workers.

Ava, a social worker who wanted to stay, described the organisational culture in child protection and welfare as an unsafe environment where you could not be seen to be affected by the work:

> … it just isn't acceptable, it's not safe to say that you are stressed by the job, and that it's affecting you in the sense that you need time off, or that you….or that it's affected your physical health. It's not safe to put out …that out there clearly to your line manager … It's not safe in terms of your employment. And people wouldn't consider that it was safe to….you know, if you reached a point where, for instance, you were being asked to attend the occupational physician. But that could affect…that can affect your employment, your contract and your employment, you know, the viability of that with the HSE. Or how you will be viewed maybe in terms of being a whole or reliable sort of person, yes (Ava).

This very experienced social worker who in another part of the interview described how she had stretched herself to respond to children and families in need despite the serious personal affects on her health, felt that it was important to be seen to be a 'reliable' worker in spite of the consequences. Ava's description suggests an unsympathetic organisational culture and climate towards social workers who feel stressed or whose health is affected. In conjunction with the findings presented in the supervision section, it is concerning that social workers perceive their managers and the organisation in such a manner, and in Ava's case, to feel unsafe to articulate feelings for fear that it could affect her employment and/or reputation.

To build on Ava's description of the organisational culture and climate social workers explained that they must be able to cope with the high demands of the work and wanted to prove that they could do it. Robyn, Mya and Sophia, three social workers that wanted to stay, used interesting language to describe their efforts to stay in this work: 'failure', 'beaten' and 'not wanting to throw in the towel':

> ... not being this big failure who was beaten by the system do you know (Robyn).

> ... it's a bit of a, a, a pride thing and kind of, you know, not wanting to throw in the towel (Mya).

> ... when I am having bad days, and I am saying, well feck this I am out of here you know. And then when I have calmer days where I would sit and think, I say I am not going to be beaten by this. There is work to be done here. I think I can do it. I want to see what I am like (Sophia).

In their interviews, these social workers all described their working conditions as challenging, but are actively working at trying to stay, despite these conditions. This type of strategy may be a defensive strategy to counter ambivalence and conflicted feelings, by fighting rather than flight. These social workers were in a 'battle' not to allow the system to beat them, suggesting a less than supportive organisational culture and also a desire to prove themselves in these conditions. I will return to this theme of 'proving' oneself in child protection and welfare in significant depth in Chapter Six.

Erin, a social worker who wants to stay but has decided to leave because of a lack of organisational support, expressed a view that setting limits and saying no to more work may be interpreted negatively within the organisational culture. Like Ava above, who described what she understood to be a 'reliable' worker, Erin questioned what it meant for her to be a 'good social worker':

I was given a new case five weeks ago that I knew ....like you know I was told to hold it. But you know there is no holding in long-term. And I already felt...I mean I was doing on average maybe you know five hours TOIL [time off in lieu] you know a week and I was being told not to be doing that. So it certainly wasn't by choice that ....that I was doing it. And being given a new case then on top of that. So that's ...you just wonder then how am I meant to do this, you know? And then you wonder should you make noise? And then you are wondering, if you make noise, does that mean you are not a good social worker? You don't know how far you can push that. You don't know who you can...I suppose I mean human nature being human nature you don't know who you can....you could trust with that you know (Erin).

Erin's description of the HSE not protecting her caseload by setting limits on its size has been a common theme in the study. During the period of the research, the HSE 'Area A' did not operate waiting lists, therefore the responsibility and anxiety for pending new cases was felt at the 'front-line' practice level rather than being contained by higher management. This led to social workers feeling unprotected by the HSE 'Area A' as they were unable to 'control' the size of their workload and the volume of the work. As part of the study, I spoke with principal social workers on child protection and welfare teams in other parts of the country that operated waiting lists. It is not possible to discuss the merits and demerits of waiting lists in child protection and welfare departments here. It is my intention only to note that there are child protection and welfare teams in other parts of the country that acknowledge that there is a limit to the amount of work a social worker can do and that it is the responsibility of the agency to manage and hold extra work beyond a certain threshold.

Even though some social workers did not feel valued by the organisation, they were prepared to work exceptionally hard to ensure their clients got a good service and to protect their reputation, suggesting a strong ethic of care and a commitment to clients, rather than a commitment to the HSE 'Area A':

I think because of the, I think because of the clients. I felt bad because the caseload that I got had had a high turnover before me. Some of the clients on my caseload had had five social workers in four years and I just felt, I can't walk out on them now you know. I was just getting to know them and if I walked out, you know, I just would have felt very guilty. And also it's a bit of a, a, a pride thing and kind of, you know, not wanting to throw in the towel ... Seriously though, the working with, with clients definitely makes me want to stay (Mya).

Thus, Mya's commitment to her clients contributed to her decision to stay, despite a low level of commitment to the organisation. Similar to the finding of the Mor Barak *et al.* (2006) study, nearly all of the social workers expressed low levels of commitment to the organisation, but high levels of commitment to the work and service users. However, despite some social workers' commitment to the work and clients, their use of language suggested that the organisational culture and climate gave the message that they were 'expendable':

> I don't particularly feel valued by management. I think, in some ways I think we're looked at as quite expendable (Mya).

> They got a lot of fresh meat for the fodder, you know. There is a lot of new.....newly-qualified social workers started working there, who were all incredibly enthusiastic, who are all now thinking of leaving (Kelly).

> I could never get my head around it. I said, but like why…why would we not ….why would we not be supported in…in as much as we possibly could be to do the job, rather than going the opposite, completely the opposite direction in no support and everything else, and working conditions and all that. Why would that be? Like and why wouldn't…why wouldn't the Health Service [Executive] want to have people that are there on a regular basis on a permanent basis and that sort of thing? And then my thinking around it at that stage was, sure you just get people coming in and out and it churns around and churns. So there is no change to it (Isabelle).

Words such as 'expendable', 'churn' and 'fodder' suggest an organisational culture with a low incentive to address retention: there will always be a new supply of graduates willing to take your place if you are troublesome or cannot cope with the work. Isabelle pointed out that the HSE 'Area A' is fully aware of the issues, but is puzzled by its apparent lack of interest in making changes. She argued in another part of the interview, that a good supply of new graduates at the time reduced the need for the organisation to make changes.

In addition to the support of colleagues, which contributed positively to the climate on teams, the data analysis identified one other specific positive factor which contributed to the organisational culture and climate. This positive related to the degree to which social workers felt that they had autonomy in undertaking their work. Autonomy and control over decisions is identified in job characteristics theory and the literature as an important factor that influences a worker's experience of the work and attitudes towards the organisational culture and climate(Audit Commission, 2002; Stalker *et al.*, 2007a). Sophia and Lucy, two social workers who wanted to stay, compared their current high level of autonomy in child protection and welfare with previously held non-social work jobs:

> In comparison to my old job where I used to work in the [business sector]....one other positive thing is, and this is hugely important...that you have a degree of autonomy (Sophia).

> Coming from where I came from, where you would have to check everything, it's very business environment, I think [in child protection and welfare] you have an awful lot of freedom in terms of when you meet people or putting in appointments or, except for huge decisions, you obviously have to talk to a line manager about it (Lucy).

Social workers in the study defined autonomy in terms of their ability to schedule their work, and freedom and independence in undertaking and choosing how to approach the work. Job characteristics theory examined in Chapter Two, argues that workers are more satisfied in their work when their job facilitates a good degree of autonomy (Hackman *et al.*, 2000). The following quotations, taken from a large file of quotations on this topic, illustrate this theme:

> I really love what I am doing and I really appreciate that I feel that within the work I still have, sort of, a little bit of leeway of where I want to put my emphasis and what I want to do ... Like for example, working with the students, there was no problem doing the course the 10 months post-graduate degree, I ran parenting courses, for a couple of years I was very interested in asylum seekers, that kind of work ...I would hate a job where I would know exactly whatever from 9-5 and from Monday to Friday that's what you do and there is no leeway whatsoever (Thomas).

> I haven't been told yet that's something you can't do (Jessica).

> The discretion is huge (Aoife).

> ... that was always my experience (high autonomy). Yes. And that was, that was one of the positives that kept me here ... I think people respond to being given I, I, generally I think. You get the odd few but in general I think people respond to being given the, that kind of control over their own (Robyn).

> in just practically like from scheduling you know your work load, yes I think...yes, I would say that there is quite a fair bit of autonomy (Lucinda).

the managers have never…they have allowed you to develop practices as opposed to bringing down too much on all the red tape and the….although the forms and all that has come in and keeps coming in. There was….somehow there was always a balance I think (Shannon).

Yet a deeper analysis of the data showed some limitations regarding some social workers' sense of autonomy. They were autonomous in scheduling their diary and choosing intervention methods, but high caseloads and policy and legislative imperatives limited their autonomy when it came to their desire to undertake more preventative work. Both Jessica and Lucinda, two social workers who want to stay, explain:

Not always because, I find you're so, you know, because you're so tied to high case loads and tied by laws and guidelines, that you don't get to focus on prevention all the time, which probably is very frustrating, because there are sometimes you could probably, if you had the time and the resources you could do fabulous pieces of work with families but you just can't … can't because you have fifty something other families that need you … (Jessica).

I think they think we are robots and just should do it … Just do our jobs according to you know the nice ethos and the standards and the procedures. … I do, I think we do get freedom, I mean I would practise maybe different from a colleague, but I mean, obviously within reason (Lucinda).

Overall, the level of autonomy, freedom and independence to manage their own diary and work without close supervision was highly valued by social workers. Having high levels of autonomy and flexibility was consistently identified by social workers as an aspect of the organisational culture that they rated highly. Most of the social workers, both wanting to stay and leave, felt that they had high levels of autonomy and flexibility, which they defined as a positive in the work. Despite the increasing amount of bureaucracy as a result of legislation and practice procedures, social workers still felt that it was not pervasive enough to stifle their autonomy, but limitations on their autonomy to chose an intensive preventative practice approach with a family was imposed by caseload size.

5.4.5 Salary and promotional opportunities

Economic theories of turnover consider the role of labour markets in explaining turnover and focus on factors such as the availability of job alternatives or perceived job alternatives, reward and investments or 'sunk' costs' (Morrel et al., 2001, p. 227). Also, in social exchange

154

theory, employees have expectations that their efforts are reciprocated by employing organisation through the exchange of economic resources such as salary and promotional opportunities (Cropanzano and Mitchell, 2005). Social workers in this study were asked whether they felt they were adequately rewarded for the job that they undertook, which included views on their salary. Table 5.2 provides a comparison of salary scales for social workers in Ireland, the United Kingdom, and the United States of America:[42]Table

5.2 Social work salary scale comparisons (Ireland, UK and USA)

Country	Grade	Entry salary and date	Maximum salary and number of points on scale
Ireland	Senior Social Work Practitioner	€50,001 (Mar. '08)	€64,925 (8 points)
	Professionally Qualified Social Worker	€44,701 (Mar. '08)	€59,211 (10 points)
United Kingdom	Hackney (Central London)	€36,937 (Jun. '08)	€46,074
	Social Worker (general scale)	€24,963 (Oct. '07)	€36,935
United States	Social Caseworker I (Rhode Island)	€25,708 (Jun. '07)	€29,640 (5 points)
	Social Caseworker II (Rhode Island)	€27,532 (Jun. '07)	€32,032 (5 points)
	Chief Casework Supervisor[43] (R. Isl.)	€41,667 (Jun. '07)	€47,219 (5 points)

Sources: (Andalo, 2006; Swift, 2007; Department of Health and Children, 2008; Prospects, 2008).

---

[42] Salary scales for the UK and the USA are not intended to be indicative of their respective country but a general guide. Unlike Ireland, each county/state/borough has a different salary scale for child protection and welfare staff. Currency conversion rates used were August 2008.

[43] Equivalent to the Principal Social Worker grade in the Republic of Ireland.

Social workers working in child protection and welfare in the Health Service Executive are well paid compared to child protection workers in other countries. Social workers in Ireland also have better salaries than many other professions in Ireland, and compared to Gardaí and teachers, have a significantly shorter time before they reach the top of their salary scale. A comparison between these Irish professions and grades is presented in table 5.3:

Table 5.3 Salary scale comparisons between HSE social work and other professions/ grades in Ireland

Grade	Entry Salary	Maximum Salary
Senior Social Work Practitioner (HSE)	€50,001 (Mar. '08)	€64,925 (8 points)
Professionally Qualified Social Worker (HSE)	€44,701 (Mar. '08)	€59,211 (10 points)
Social Care Leader	€45,683 (Mar. '08)	€53,685 (7 points)
Speech and Language Therapist	€39,017 (Mar. '08)	€51,979 (12 points)
Social Care Worker	€34,357 (Mar. '08)	€45,939 (10 points)
Staff Nurse	€31,098 (Mar. '08)	€45,406 (11 points)
Teacher (Primary, Secondary & VEC)	€31,028 (Mar. '08)	€61,816 (25 points)
Probation and Welfare Officer[44]	€31,628 (Mar '08)	€62,074 (15 points)
Community Welfare Officer	€30,026 (Mar. '08)	€59,587 (16 points)
Garda Síochaná	€26,439 (Mar. '08)	€47,507 (19 points)

Sources: (Department of Education and Science, 2008; Department of Finance, 2008; Department of Health and Children, 2008; Department of Justice Equality and Law Reform, 2008).

---

[44] Probation and welfare officers are paid under the 'Engineer Grade III and Professional Accountant Grade III' civil service salary scale. Probation officers with a professional social work qualification would be offered a salary commensurate with their training and practice experience and would therefore be unlikely to begin at the entry point of this scale.

156

There were mixed views amongst social workers in the study as to whether they felt that the level of remuneration was adequate for the work undertaken. Social workers that wanted to stay said:

It is a well-paid job (Jessica).

I'm not a martyr. We get well paid (Holly).

I think it's a good [salary]. You know, the increment system, the way it works ... the overall package I think is pretty good, yes (Evan).

I wouldn't consider the salary good. It's only OK, for the job we do, it's an OK salary (Isabelle).

... what people actually work hours wise. You know, and I they think they should be paid more. Because there is more responsibility involved (Kelly).

... we are actually on the same salary as Community Welfare Workers, who do a six weeks training course[45] ... Irish Social Workers are well paid in comparison to [name of home European country removed] ones[46] (Laura).

I feel we're paid quite well. Shortly after I arrived I found out that the childcare leaders and workers on a very similar scale and the work is vastly different or the demands of the job are vastly different so I have dissatisfaction with that (Shauna).

Social workers that wanted to leave said:

No. I don't think it is good at all ... I feel that the job is very much mentally draining and I know people who do work that's just far easier who are on more money and again they say, there like two of my brothers they are on away more than me and it's for like and electrician and plumber and I'd be thinking oh my God and they don't talk back to you you know they just work with wires and you just work with pipes and they're on more money and they but then it's all relative isn't it? Like as far as, but no to answer that question, I don't think I am on enough money at all (Aoife).

---

[45] See table 5.3 above for exact comparison between HSE social work and community welfare officers.

[46] Name of home country removed as it would lead to the identification of this social worker.

> ... if you want to attract, not so much attract the best, but keep the best, because there are some fantastic social workers that I work with at the moment. They are brilliant like. And they need to be commensurate you know in a similar fashion like, whether it's the...on the probation officer scale or stuff like that like you know (Simon).

In short, social workers that wanted to stay were more likely to define their pay as good or sufficient, whereas those who wanted to leave were more likely to define their pay as inadequate. Dissatisfaction with salary was often linked with a comparison with salaries in other professions/disciplines, tasks and responsibilities *vis-à-vis* the salary, and tasks and responsibilities of a child protection and welfare social worker. Simon argued that if the salary was improved in line with the grade of probation officer then there may be an increased likelihood that social workers would be retained[47]. The Irish government since the late 1990s have specifically increased the pay of social workers to reflect more accurately their responsibilities and to aid retention. In addition to pay, other general employment conditions were perceived by social workers to be valuable, such as: time off in lieu (TOIL), security of tenure through permanency, state pension scheme, career break scheme, flexibility in taking time off, length of holiday leave, and so on. Isabelle, a social worker who will stay, but would probably leave were it not for her mortgage and bills, explains:

> Why I stay? I stay because I have a mortgage and I have bills and it's a permanent position. I have...the Health Service have been excellent around taking time off, taking the career break. That's a very nice perk to have. It ties you into pensions and stuff like that (Isabelle).

Denise, another social worker who wants to leave, described how the salary and employment conditions contribute to her staying:

> *KB: And why didn't you leave ...?*

> Denise: Mortgage and three children. They are an expensive commodity ... if I am being very very honest with you I would say I am still in this job because I have a mortgage, right, that's the primary reason. Very closely in behind that is I...I am still deriving great satisfaction from what I do (Denise).

---

[47] See table 5.3 for a salary comparison. A pay 'relativity' between HSE social work and the 'general service grade' of probation officers (civil service) is unlikely, as previous benchmarking processes have not established such a link. Nonetheless, table 5.3 clearly shows that any historical gap in pay between these two posts is no longer the case.

Other social workers in the study also noted how a permanent job with a good salary and some 'perks' (see sample employment conditions above) are helpful in meeting the financial needs of having a family and children. Social workers' job searches led them to conclude that other social work jobs in the community were unable to match these employment conditions, a factor which helped to keep them in the job.

A welcome and progressive policy initiative in the HSE has been the introduction of a new senior social work practitioner grade[48] designed to value and retain experienced social work staff at direct service provision level who were looking for a non-managerial progression option. Such a grade was proposed in an article in the *British Journal of Social Work* (Healy *et al.*, 2009), with the authors arguing that it could assist with the retention of experienced workers in child protection. The link between this grade and the retention of social workers was also noted in an IMPACT (2006) trade union discussion paper on social work structures. Social workers in the study had noted that opportunities for promotion to managerial grades were more limited as fewer managers were leaving their posts in child protection and welfare. However, this new grade was still being implemented in Ireland during the fieldwork period of this study, therefore there was insufficient time and data to analyse its affect upon retention. This might be an interesting focus for future research.

5.4.6 Variety in the work

The broad scope of the work in child protection and welfare was seen by these social workers as being another important factor which contributed to their job satisfaction and experience of the work. The following sample quotations, selected from a voluminous file of quotations on variety, illustrate this. All of the quotations are from social workers who had decided to stay, except for Caitlin who wanted to leave:

> I think it's so diverse really. Child protection is never, there's never a dull moment ... I think every day is kind of different (Lucy).

> You would never be bored, plenty of variety (Ciara).

---

[48] The responsibilities of the new senior social work practitioner grade include: the induction of new staff, training of social work students, development of training plans for social work staff, and 'holding' a practice caseload (Health Service Executive South, 2005).

I like meeting the variety of families we meet, I suppose the different categories, like you know even looking at child welfare and all the different parts that come with Child Welfare, it's so broad. I mean I like the variety in the job (Jessica).

I like the variety of it. I...I wouldn't be a type that I would....you know, I like being out of the office. I like, you know, that there is some...a new challenge really...most days in a way, even though it is repetitive as well. It's kind of a funny mix. It can be very repetitive. And yet it's ...it's new all the time. So it doesn't get boring in that sense (Lucinda).

There is plenty of variety, yes. Yes, yes, definitely. I mean you have links....I mean even linking in with other professionals, you know, there is so much variety there....GPs....the mental health, anything, you know. You....in families you have all different sorts of issues you know. And no two families are the same, or no two people are the same. It's... there is constantly variety. You could never say this job was boring (Nicole).

It is hugely varied, you know. Like no two days are the same. You are not sitting behind a desk all day. I mean you are out and about, you are meeting different people. You are going to meetings. You are going to court. You are meeting families. You are meeting children. I mean there is...I think there is huge variation in it (Caitlin).

Social workers described the variety of the work, in terms of where the work was undertaken, the diversity and volume of people and services with which they interacted, and the wide scope of practice issues which they had to deal with. As a result, social workers were unlikely to feel 'bored' with the job. However, despite the general view that this variety was a positive, there were some exceptions to this view. Lucinda, a social worker who wants to stay, said:

The variedness can have its disadvantages as well, because I mean the way we work....I mean we are not specialised in any one area. I mean we are not specialised on you know families with alcohol problems. You are not specialised on sexual abuse or whatever. So you are kind of.....you are a jack of all trades which can be a bit dodgy at times too you know (Lucinda).

Lucinda questioned whether having such a wide variety of work, which contributes to social workers having a more generalist knowledge and skills base rather than one or two specific areas of expertise, was the best approach to practice. Aoife, a social worker who wanted to leave, also raised questions about the variety of the work:

The variety of work. It's basically the same. I think there's not much of a variety really. It's the time I'd say because you would have to get the time off work but no the variety of work it is like there's a lot of variety but it's the same then like as in the work varies a lot but you do it all the time if you know what I mean. It's, there's a lot of variety but it is repetitive like. I do it every day (Aoife).

On the one hand she was saying it has some variety, but on the other hand it could still become repetitive.

In summary, social workers in the interviews described how even though there was huge variety in the work, over time the tasks and roles could become familiar, leading to fatigue. They also talked about the desire to develop specialist knowledge in a particular area (child sexual abuse, domestic violence, children seeking asylum, and so on) as a way to keep the job interesting, and others describe the merits of rotating jobs within their team. Team 1 operates a rotation system where staff can apply to move every two years, which social workers described as a positive factor. These social workers clearly enjoyed the variety of the work, which included the diversity of the locations in which it was undertaken, the variety of practice issues, and the diversity of families, professionals and services with whom they came into contact. Social workers who enjoyed the variety of the work invariably highlighted a link between the variety and the opportunities that this offered for professional growth. A recurring theme in the data was social workers highlighting the fact that the work was at least 'not boring', particularly when making comparisons with previous jobs. While social workers in the study did not explicitly say that they had decided to leave because the job was not varied enough for them, some social workers did feel that after a number of years in a post they felt the need for a new challenge. Furthermore, internal rotation policies and opportunities promotions contributed to social workers' feeling that they could continue to learn and grow and this helped them to stay in the work. Social workers who perceived that they were stuck in their caseload with no opportunity for change were more likely to express dissatisfaction. When social workers feel the need to grow and develop and the organisation does not offer this opportunity either through promotion or job rotation, they may decide to leave for alternative employment outside the team or outside of the organisation altogether. In the next section, I examine the role of the availability of job alternatives in retaining social workers in child protection and welfare.

5.4.7 Alternative employment options

Economic theories seek to explain turnover by emphasising the role of the labour market. Such an analysis places a focus on the supply and demand of labour, job search behaviours, the availability of job alternatives or perceived alternatives, and rewards such as salary and employment conditions. In this section, I examine data that relates to social workers' perceptions of job alternatives and their analyses of the relative merits of child protection and welfare as a job when compared to job alternatives. A dominant theme in the study, both in data from those who wanted to stay and those who wanted to leave, was the perception that the labour market for social work was presently tight, with few job alternatives:

> In previous years they could leave. The situation at the moment with no jobs going and if you look in the papers for the last three years or whatever it is, there is no jobs going. So what's happened here on the team is that a lot of the same people are here and haven't moved for a long time because they can't move, which in itself causes a lot of …a lot of problems …They are not moving on to another team like…like we would have done before in fostering or adoption. And there is just no posts coming up at all. My feeling is that the whole thing is stagnated, and the people that are in child protection at the moment have no way out of that (Isabelle).

Isabelle describes how traditional exit pathways from child protection and welfare internally within the HSE to adoption or fostering were perceived to be restricted and also that external jobs were now in limited supply. Some social workers felt this limited availability of job alternatives, or the perception of this limited availability, was a factor which contributed to their retention:

> I see, well I hear everyone desperately looking for any other job that's out there and there's just nothing at the moment (Hannah).

> No jobs to go to … in fact more people would be gone if there were jobs to go to (Kelly).

On one of the teams where there has been considerable unrest amongst social workers concerning their working conditions, leading to conflict with management and the instigation of industrial relations mechanisms, there was a 5% turnover rate. When this very low rate was queried with one of the social workers, she commented that the lack of available employment resulted in stability and lower turnover:

KB: I did understand from the 'grapevine' that the atmosphere on the team was.....

Kelly: Sucks.

KB: Why was nobody leaving? ...

Kelly: No jobs to go to.... and in fact more people would be gone if there were jobs to go to.

The limited availability of job alternatives was a particular issue for the more 'rural' teams (Team 2, Team 5 and Team 3) due to the small size of the towns and potential long commutes to access alternative employment. Nicole, a social worker who wanted to stay, said:

Nicole: I suppose convenience is one thing. OK, I am not going to travel out of the county or whatever. So...and the options here are limited. You do get a sense of satisfaction from the job, despite all the negative things that I have said....through all of this, but you do get a sense of satisfaction from it. And it's a good feeling.

KB: It's a good feeling?

Nicole: You know, it's a good feeling to get that, you know. And when you do see changes it's good. Every job has its stresses...everything...you know, there is problems in every job. So why not be in this one?

Nicole describes her job satisfaction from the work, but also the stress and the negative aspects of the job. The convenience of staying in child protection and welfare was also part of her decision to stay as she would have to relocate or commute out of the county to take up an alternative job. Nicole is also balanced in her decision-making as she is realistic when identifying that all jobs have their challenges. Lucinda, a social worker in a different rural team to Nicole, who wanted to stay, identified the upheaval of moving if she left her job in child protection and welfare:

I do like the team. I do like the people I work with. I do like some aspects of the work. And for me to make a different choice, which I have considered at times, but so far hasn't...would have meant huge upheaval for me...for my personal life in a sense. So you have to balance these I suppose you know ... it's where we are ...that people choose to be in [Name of Rural Area]. And I mean that...that obviously influences whether...whether you...you decide, OK, I actively look for somewhere else to work, and I have to travel to Cork or move altogether or whatever. And it's I suppose ...it's the age as well. We are all geriatrics (Lucinda).

Job embeddedness theory, as outlined in Chapter Two, helps to explain Lucinda's decision to stay. In conjunction with the positives of the job described (fit), the myriad strands of her and her family's social connections with the local community (links) means that costs of leaving would be high for Lucinda (sacrifice). This experience was similar for other more mature-age social workers in the rural teams who had families, and by extension greater commitments and social connections with the community, all of which contributed to their decisions to stay. Holly, a social worker under 30 who had decided to leave, explained that following through on this decision would involve an assessment of rewards of the alternative compared with her job in child protection and welfare:

> I probably would. I probably would even though I'd probably struggle with it. I'd probably be thinking but then it would depend if it was a permanent job. Because you have to think of that as well at the end of the day. It is a job and you have to think about which you know, which perks are better? (Holly)

Aoife, another social worker under 30 who had decided to leave, was unable to follow through on her decision to leave as she was waiting for a job alternative that would 'fit' with her career goals. Even though she wanted to leave, she would not leave for any job, while in another part of the interview she acknowledged that there were few job alternatives at that time:

> I won't leave unless I get something that I really want because I do like the work so I have a couple of things in my head that if I got, I'd leave tomorrow but it depends on the availability of those because I won't leave the job for something that I don't want (Aoife).

For social workers who wanted to stay, the availability of job alternatives was of lesser importance to them, and even when they were aware of alternatives, it was still their preference to stay:

> There's just not that many opportunities out there but the reality is I really do, I'm very happy with what I'm doing (Shauna)

> I used to always think that. That if another job came that I really wanted I would leave. But actually, probably thinking about it, I don't ….I don't actually know if I would….at this stage….until I became so frustrated that it was time to go (Jenna).

In the next and final part of this section, I address some other factors identified in the literature review and data analysis as influencing social workers' experience of the job.

5.4.8 Other factors

In this final section, I present data relating to 'peripheral' themes identified in the literature review and the data analysis. These themes include violence, social work education, 'the buzz' associated with doing this work, and court work.

Violence and threats

In Chapters One and Two, I highlighted violence as a theme within the literature which appeared to influence social workers' experience of child protection and welfare social work. In my study, social workers were asked about their experiences of violence and aggression in the last 6-12 months. In the main, there were very low levels of actual physical violence towards social workers. Of those social workers asked about violence and threats[49], only two reported that they had been physically assaulted on one occasion in the identified period, and one other social worker was 'nearly' assaulted. Social workers in general were surprised at the low levels of assault as they were familiar with a literature which suggested that it might be higher:

> God, it surprises me alright, yeah. It surprises me that I haven't ever been as well, because you're getting yourself into really tight knit situations in some cases where you're calling to a house and you go in and there could be a mother and father there who would have drink on them. It does arise, it's very risky (Lucy).

At least three quarters of social workers in the study, had at some point in the 12 months before the interview, experienced behaviour or threats from clients which they found upsetting. Both Ciara and Jessica explain:

---

[49] The five social workers in the pilot study were not asked about violence and threats.

Yes, one man was desperately aggressive towards me, he didn't strike me now, but I thought he was going to. I filled up an incident report because [name of secretary] told me to fill it up but there was nothing about it. I think it was only filed away, I gave it to [name of team leader] and he said grand. To be honest with you now, it frightened me and do you know something, when he left it was like I had flashbacks or something (Ciara).

I suppose I've only been in a situation where I was genuinely afraid of my life once and I did come back and say it to my team leader at the time, I'm never ever again going out there unless, there was another social worker with me actually which didn't make any difference. I mean it was this particular person anyway that was very physically threatening and the guards did say to me - yeah he would carry out his threats of burying me in a bog - he has been known to actually do things like that (Jessica).

Social workers found these experiences upsetting, but they were usually short-term in nature and occurred infrequently. The impact of these events should not be minimised, but a perception that social workers in child protection and welfare are subject to regular assault, at least for this sample of social workers, is not borne out. The study collected a significant amount data on this topic, but as no social worker in the study said that they were leaving the job as a result of violence, aggression or intimidating behaviour towards them by service users or other persons, this data is not presented here. This finding supports Tham's (2006) conclusion that social workers' intention to leave was weakly related to violence and threats.

Social work education

Social workers' preparedness for the realities of social work practice in child protection and welfare arose in interviews with a small number of social workers. This theme was addressed more comprehensively in the earlier section which addressed the induction of, and supports for, newly qualified social workers. Social workers offered specific advice for colleges regarding certain modules and course changes which may have been helpful, but no social worker linked this theme with their retention, despite this theme being flagged as one of possible interest in the recent literature (Healy and Meagher, 2007; Healy et al., 2009). Social workers' experiences in the colleges in a wider sense did appear to play a role in their motivations for entry and their career pathways in the profession and played a significant role in their retention. More than half the social workers in this study said that, during college training, a view was

166

formed that all social workers should work in child protection and welfare. These views developed primarily from their practice placements and from class peers, rather than lecturers. This theme is a core focus of Chapter Six, therefore this data is not presented here.

The 'buzz'

Another peripheral theme was the 'buzz' and excitement which the work can offer. The crisis orientation and the unpredictable nature of the work, as well as feelings arising from making a positive difference, can contribute to social workers experiencing a physical/adrenaline 'high'. Both Grace and Robyn, social workers who wanted to stay, explain:

> I need the buzz of the everyday work and I think to keep me occupied (Grace).

> There's kind of a strange mixture of being fascinated by interest in people's lives which we are all very interested in and the desire to do good and then the desire to have that bit of power to change things and I think all of those things are the very, are positive ones at the beginning. And I think they, it's, it's a really, it's probably, I, I think it's the most interesting job in the world because your, these, these children that are at risk in the society. If, if there's any opportunity that anything the state does can improve their lot, it's, it's a great buzz (Robyn).

From these two quotes we can see that social workers are getting a positive dividend from the job, which meets some need in them for excitement. Even social workers that wanted to leave described similar attitudes towards the excitement:

> It's great actually to see children who may have been physically neglected as well. I think that's a real buzz to see them actually you know, grow and develop and get tall and fat and it's great ... sometimes it's such a buzz and it's just great and you go, wow I love this job and you could be after applying for something else and you go, I don't even think I'm going to take that now if I get it and next week then you could be having an absolutely terrible week (Holly).

> And sometimes I like the adrenalin buzz as well, do you know, I have responded to an emergency situation and you know going in, doing what you have got to do, and knowing that you have made the right decision ... there is this mania sometimes that surrounds the place and you know...which I quite enjoy (Abbey).

For both Holly and Abbey this excitement was insufficient to keep them there, although it is an aspect of the job that contributed to their job satisfaction, but other issues are more critical for their decisions to want to leave. There were also some critical voices of this need for excitement. For example, Evan, a social worker who wanted to stay, was critical of some of his peers who were more orientated towards the aspects of child protection and welfare work with the most excitement:

> ... it is being driven in some respects then by the social workers themselves. That some social workers ... not say realistically why they are in the job, but what needs are they actually meeting? Because they....it's the aspects of say do you know the crisis or the drama that is attracting them more ... I have seen that some people then do kind of say come alive when there is a crisis or that they work better in a crisis (Evan).

Gilligan (2004, p. 98) commenting on social workers' apparent preference for 'fire brigade' responses with the associated excitement and interventions, suggests that there is a need to temper social workers' notions of 'rescue and omnipotence [as] people may become very attached to the excitement and action of intervention'. In this regard, Evan described in the preceding part of the transcript how some of his colleagues placed a reduced value on cases that were going well and may be more interested in meeting their own needs by being attracted to, and deriving satisfaction from, the 'drama' of emergency/crisis work. For a small number of social workers, the 'buzz' associated with the work contributed to their sense of job satisfaction and influenced their decision to stay in the work.

Court work

Finally, social workers had much to say about their experience of bringing cases to the family law courts, but there was no clear evidence to suggest that these experiences resulted in social workers leaving. Social workers presented equally mixed views on their many positive as well negative experiences in the family law courts, but as the data was not significant in social workers' decisions to stay or leave, the data on this theme is not presented here. Therefore, there was no evidence in data to support the link between court work and the legal ethic on turnover in child welfare as suggested by Vandervort and colleagues (2007).

5.5 Discussion and analysis

In the chapter so far, I have examined the individual, supervisory and social supports and organisational factors that impact on social workers' experience of the job and influence their decisions to stay or leave. In this section, I draw together the key themes for these two groups of social workers and develop the analysis of the factors implicated in social workers' decisions to stay or leave child protection and welfare in the HSE 'Area A'.

5.5.1 Factors that influence social workers' decisions to stay

Of the 35 social workers/senior social work practitioners in direct service provision in child protection and welfare in the HSE 'Area A', two thirds indicated that they wanted to stay in their job and were not making plans to leave. There were eight main factors contributing to their decision. Firstly, they perceived that the social supports provided by co-workers were crucial in terms of providing friendships, helping with the work, compensating for some of the supervision functions not addressed by their supervisors, and contributing to a positive work environment. Secondly, these social workers perceived that they were making a difference, or enough of a difference, in the lives of children and families. Thirdly, high levels of autonomy and freedom in undertaking their work was important. Fourthly, a preference for child protection and welfare work and a professional commitment to improving the lives of children and families facilitated them in reducing the impact of stressful issues such as a lack of resources and high caseloads. Fifth, the variety in the work was highly valued as it provided opportunities for professional growth, was intellectually challenging, and made for a stimulating job which was not 'boring'. Sixth, for those who received it, the quality of social supports from managers and supervision was important and helped workers to feel that the organisation was supportive and helped them to process the stresses and anxieties of the work. Seventh, some of the social workers stayed, not because of professional or organisational issues, but because of a tight labour market where job alternatives were few. Others stayed because of life choices: for example, living in a particular geographical area was more important than commuting to a preferable job. Lastly, employment terms such as salary and other benefits such as 'time off in lieu', and arrangements and opportunities to take career breaks were highly valued and kept some social workers in the job. This summary list should not be construed as one in order of importance, as for each social worker there was a different confluence of factors which were important for their decisions at that time.

5.5.2 Factors that influence social workers' decisions to leave

Of the 35 social workers/senior social work practitioners in direct service provision in child protection and welfare in the HSE 'Area A' on the day of their interview, one third had decided that they wanted to leave their job and were about to, or had already begun, to search for other jobs. There were seven main factors contributing to these decisions. Firstly, the most persistent theme in their transcripts was their dissatisfaction with the quality and frequency of supervision. This lack of supervision contributed to social workers feeling unsupported by managers and by extension, unsupported by the HSE 'Area A'. Secondly, these social workers generally felt that they made little or no difference in the lives of children and families. Contributing factors to this feeling were the crisis nature of the work, working with involuntary clients and difficulties accessing essential resources for children and families. Thirdly, social workers felt that their high caseloads and specifically the impact of these high caseloads on service users and social workers was a cause for dissatisfaction, and this enhanced the perception that they were unsupported by the organisation. Fourthly, social workers that had decided they wanted to leave were less able to reconcile themselves with what they perceived to be a lack of 'basic' resources to support them in their jobs, such as alternative care placements, therapeutic and mental health services. Fifth, these social workers found that the work left them physically exhausted and 'drained'. Sixth, the level of administration and bureaucracy involved in the work contributed to social workers feeling more like 'case-managers' than social workers. They had decided to seek other jobs which they perceived as more likely to provide them with more time to do face-to-face work with clients and therefore with opportunities to use their skills. Lastly, team atmosphere was perceived by these social workers as insufficiently supportive, particularly as a result of poor quality relationships with managers. Nonetheless, even though these social workers had decided that they wanted to leave, a lack of alternative employment options may result in them staying in the sector for longer than they wished:

... it's just the fact that there are no more jobs available to social workers or we are kind of stuck where we are (Holly).

This is an undesirable situation for both the social workers and the organisation. For some of the social workers, the work was clearly impacting upon their health and it would be in their interests, the interests of their clients and also the organisation to be able to leave. For Deborah, her decision to leave was expressed as follows:

I do not want to be that person standing on the doorstep knocking on the door (Deborah)

For many years, Deborah had been happy to be that person 'knocking on the door', but over time the factors identified above contributed to a decision to leave. The organisation is avoidably losing some social workers that want to stay but feel that they cannot do so due to organisational conditions. For example, Erin said:

I still enjoy the work. And I wouldn't have changed it. And I would love to stay in it. But the impact that the restrictions and the caseloads were having on my personal life had to take priority ... I would love to stay in child protection. But because of the impact I...I need to leave (Erin).

The HSE should examine how it could develop strategies to retain social workers who want to work in child protection and welfare and to provide pathways out for those who don't, even if this is internally within the HSE. For some of the social workers who wanted to leave, their decisions had little to do with their experience of the work or the factors described in this chapter, but were linked to their motivation to enter child protection and welfare in the first place. This theme is central to the analysis contained in Chapter Seven. When I analysed decisions to leave by team, on *a pro-rata* basis, more social workers wanted to leave Team 4 than any other team. This finding fits with the qualitative data presented in this chapter, which outlined serious human resources issues on that team. Relationships with social work managers were described by social workers as poor, and to a greater degree than on other teams, social workers in Team 4 perceived that the employing organisation was unsupportive. Subsequent to the conclusion of the fieldwork for this study, quite a number of social workers had left this team.

5.6 Concluding comments

In her study of child welfare workers in Sweden, Tham (2007) found that slightly under half intended to leave their jobs, despite being there for less than two years. My research found that two thirds of the social workers interviewed for this chapter had decided that they wanted to stay working in this practice setting. This finding is contrary to some of the views expressed by social workers outlined earlier in the book, which indicated that most social workers wanted to leave child protection and welfare in the HSE 'Area A'. It is also contrary to what might have been expected taking into account the studies examined in the literature review. This chapter sought to illuminate, beyond the anecdotal, what social workers thought about staying and leaving their jobs and to explore what they understood to be the factors that most influenced these decisions. This book suggests that anecdotal accounts within the profession may portray a view of child protection and welfare that does not correspond with the experiences of individual social workers in this study. Social workers leave for many reasons besides being dissatisfied with the job, as Jessica explains:

> It's probably something we would have gotten in college it was a high turnover, and that wouldn't have come from lecturer that would have come from placements as well and meeting other people and I don't know if that's true, yeah in [name of child protection and welfare team] there is loads of staff leaving and coming in and, but that's not because they are not happy there, people take career breaks or you know they do move on maybe to team leader positions and stuff, it's not always because they are unsatisfied (Jessica).

In this chapter, I have argued that we need to expand our analysis of why social workers stay or leave child protection and welfare beyond job dissatisfaction to take into account complex interactions between a variety of organisational, supervisory, social supports and personal factors. The chapter has challenged the view that all social workers want to leave, while acknowledging that there are a group of social workers who want to leave but are constrained from doing so by economic and other factors. The chapter contains data to suggest that while social workers make decisions to stay, they are sometimes staying in jobs where organisational conditions are challenging. They sometimes receive less than optimal levels of organisational support in terms of inadequate resources, insufficient structured supports such as supervision, and they practise under unrealistic organisational expectations regarding caseloads/workloads. Some of the social workers who wanted to stay

172

were staying, not because of their commitment to service users and job satisfaction, but because of more instrumental reasons to do with tenure/contract conditions, and family/life style factors. The chapter also presented data to suggest that this work may negatively affect the health of some social workers more than others.

A limitation of this study was that health as a theme required greater attention and resources than this study could offer and there is a clear need for further research in this area. Given the pervasive nature of problems with the supply of alternative care placements as an issue for social workers in the data, there appears to be an avenue for further research to examine the extent of children being left in unsafe environments and being 'supervised' by social workers at home due to an inadequate supply of alternative care placements. Research could examine the following areas: the views of senior managers in the HSE 'Area A' on this issue; the numbers of children at home that should be in care; families' experiences of coping with these children who need care; the impact on children's health and welfare, and social workers' views about 'supervising' these children in the community. The chapter also identified other avenues for further research in the area of retention and turnover and I will examine these research opportunities further in Chapter Eight.

In analysing the data in this chapter and the wide variety of factors implicated in the retention and turnover of child protection and welfare social workers, a number of theoretical models were used to analyse the data. Within these models, some social workers 'fitted' the models and factors and some did not. However, job characteristics theory, social exchange theory and perceived organisational support theory were helpful in identifying overlapping and significant themes to structure the data collection and analysis. Data collected using job characteristics theory on social workers' skills variety, autonomy and task significance particularly fitted the study and generated important data related to social workers' retention. Social exchange theory facilitated the collection of data on social and economic exchange resources which the theory suggested may influence social workers' retention. Supervision, affirmation/praise, salary, and social supports from colleagues as exchange resources were particular influential in social workers' accounts of the factors that influence their retention.

Deciding to stay in or leave a job is a very individual process, and while there were key factors that were particularly important, I do not believe that hierarchical models can capture the qualitative complexity of the personal and professional lives of these social workers. Far from arguing for the rejection of theory, the chapter merely suggests that current theoretical models are limited, particularly when used on their own.For example,similar to Mor Barak's *et al.*'s (2006) finding regarding the limited applicability of organisational support theory to examining social workers' retention in child protection (published towards the end of the data collection phase), my research also found that social workers generally perceived the HSE 'Area A' as an unsupportive organisation that did not care for their well-being and value their contribution, which resulted in a low level of commitment by social workers to the HSE 'Area A' as an organisation. Rather than a large number of social workers wanting to leave as suggested by this model, two out of every three expressed a desire to stay. Similar to the Mor Barak *et al.* study, there was a considerable level of commitment by social workers to service users and colleagues/team, which social workers described as being more important for their retention, rather than an attachment to the organisation. Social exchanges between social workers and their colleagues, and social workers and their supervisors, were most important in terms of social workers' retention as predicted by social exchange theory and the research. As part of these exchanges, the research confirmed the importance of supervision in retaining social workers, and the Hawkins and Shohet's (1989) model of supervision greatly assisted in structuring the collection and analysis of data on this topic. A range of other factors examined in the previous section account for the other reasons why social workers stay.

This chapter highlighted the merits of employing qualitative research methods in this area of study. One example which underlined this point was when the very low turnover data from one team was juxtaposed with the qualitative data from social workers on this team - it became clear that quite a few wanted to leave, but were unable to do so because of economic conditions. The qualitative data rendered the initial statistical figure of 5%, which is an exceptionally low turnover rate, meaningless.

Beyond the specific factors identified in the two findings chapters thus far, a further analysis of the data appeared to suggest that there were different 'types' of social workers in child protection and welfare in the HSE 'Area A'. This analysis suggested that a theme not presented in the book thus far appeared to provide another layer to our understanding of how social workers make decisions to stay or leave. Social workers' understanding of a career in social work appeared to play a role in their decisions to stay in or leave this work, and my analysis of this theme led to the construction of a typology with three 'types' of social worker, each with a specific approach to making decisions regarding their employment and retention in this practice setting. In the next chapter, I examine this theme in greater depth to further develop an understanding of how social workers make decisions to stay or leave child protection and welfare in the HSE 'Area A'.

Chapter 6
Social workers' understandings of a career in social work and the implications for their retention

6.1 Introduction

In the previous chapter, I examined how personal, supervisory, social support and organisational factors are implicated in the retention of child protection and welfare social workers in the HSE 'Area A'. In this chapter, I expand this analysis by exploring social workers' understandings of a career in social work and the links between these understandings and their decisions to stay in or leave child protection and welfare. The literature reviewed in Chapter Two indicated a disproportionate number of newly-qualified and young social workers are employed in child protection and welfare (Gibbs and Keating, 1999; Healy *et al.*, 2009). In a critical commentary on Irish child protection and welfare social work, McGrath (2001) highlights how employers in social work settings other than child protection and welfare were less likely to employ newly-qualified social workers. This apparent imbalance in the distribution of newly-qualified social workers across all social practice settings in Ireland, he argued, results in a disproportionate number of newly-qualified graduates beginning their social work careers in child protection and welfare. This observation was subsequently supported by data from the most recent social work labour force report (National Social Work Qualifications Board, 2006). Table 6.1 summarises information on the 'top' four sectors identified in this report employing newly-qualified social work graduates in 2005:

Table 6.1: Recently qualified practitioners by social work practice setting

Social work practice setting	% of newly-qualified practitioners employed	Total posts by practice setting
Child protection and family support (statutory)	58.8%	33%
Medical social work	16%	13%
Fostering	4.7%	8%
Probation service	2.7%	13%
Other social work settings combined	17.8%	33%
	100%	100%

The National Social Work Qualifications Board study reported that 72% of all newly-qualified social workers started their social work career in the Health Service Executive, and approximately 60% of all newly-qualified social workers began their professional career in the area of 'child protection and family support (statutory)'. This practice setting took nearly double the number of newly-qualified social work graduates *pro rata* to its size by total number of social work posts. The next two largest employment sectors combined – probation (13%) and medical social work (13%) – employed 19% of newly-qualified social workers[50]. As previously outlined in Chapters Two and Four, the expansion of Whole Time Equivalent (WTE) posts in child protection and welfare social work ended in 2003 and the numbers of WTEs in 2008 for this sector is virtually identical to the 2003 figure (National Social Work Qualifications Board, 2006; RTÉ, 2008b). It is therefore unlikely that the expansionary period at the end of the last, and the beginning of this decade, explains why nearly two out of three newly-qualified workers began their social work career in child protection and welfare in 2005.

Of the 44 social workers who participated in this study, four out of five participants obtained their first social work job post-qualification in statutory child protection and welfare. Of those interviewed who trained in Ireland, nine out of ten started their social work career in child protection and welfare. Why do a disproportionately large number of

---

[50] In 2005, 736.9 out of a total of 2,236.4 posts (33%) were in 'Child and Family Work (Statutory)' (sic. child protection and welfare). Medical social work (281.1 - 13%) and probation (285.7 – 13%) were the next largest employers (National Social Work Qualifications Board, 2006).

social workers begin their career in child protection and welfare and what are the implications, if any, for social workers' retention in this practice setting? Is child protection and welfare the preferred career choice of social workers, or are there other factors that influenced their decision to work in this job? In this chapter, I explore data from the study that examined social workers' understandings of career pathways in social work, and how their understandings influenced their motivations to work in child protection and welfare, and subsequent decisions to stay or leave. This focus, in addition to the factors examined in the previous chapter, provides additional insights into how social workers make decisions to stay in or leave child protection and welfare. I then move on to analyse the metaphors used by social workers in describing their career choices and time spent doing social work in child protection and welfare. The findings raise questions about social workers' perceptions of employment options in social work; their perceptions of social work employers' expectations of prospective staff members; where newly-qualified graduates get their practice experience and first job in social work, and whether this practice setting plays a role in 'proving' newly-qualified social work graduates. The chapter concludes with an examination of the implications of the chapter's findings for retaining social workers in child protection and welfare.

6.2 Career pathways in social work

Social workers' motivations for entering employment in child protection and welfare were not present in the literature reviewed in Chapter Two as a factor in determining whether social workers would stay or leave. However, interviewees made links between their decision to want to stay or leave their post in child protection and welfare with their perceptions of career pathways in social work, which contributed to their initial decision to work in child protection and welfare. Some of the interviewees stated that before they started work as a child protection and welfare social worker, they understood that this job would be a 'stepping stone' to a job in a preferred area of social work. A job in child protection and welfare for some social workers is a transitory stop - a stop that some social workers suggested was 'obligatory' - before leaving for a preferred career in another social work setting. For other social workers, working in child protection and welfare was their first choice career preference.

It is challenging to try and encapsulate social workers' motivations for staying and leaving child protection and welfare social work, as these motivations may have varied at different points during their time in the sector. For example, a social worker may have entered child protection and welfare because it was their first choice career preference with an expectation to stay long-term, but following some exposure, they may have become disillusioned with the work and decided they want to leave. Nonetheless, despite the diverse range of pathways, it was possible to identify three archetypical career social work 'types' within child protection and welfare: 'career preference', 'transient' and 'convert'. The social work career typology emerged by using grounded theory: *nVivo* codes were developed during the data analysis and memos were written and refinedwhich helped to refine the typology and to keep it anchored in the emerging data analysis. Each iteration of the typology was tested against the data to ensure it was sufficiently comprehensive and representative of all research participants' experiences (Ritchie and Lewis, 2003). This chapter explores how each of these three groups' understandings of a career in social work influenced their employment decisions and retention within child protection and welfare, and how these may change over time. In undertaking this analysis, the chapter examines their career expectations, questions the 'choice' made by each of these social workers to enter this work, and explores the likelihood of their retention.

6.2.1 Child protection and welfare as a 'career preference'

Twenty two of the forty three social workers interviewed indicated that child protection and welfare was their preferred career choice in social work and that they did not see employment in this area as a first step towards another type of social work. These decisions and career pathways are presented in a diagram that will be developed throughout this chapter:

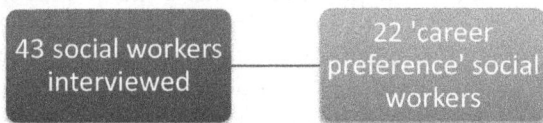

The following quotes show that these social workers made very deliberate decisions to enter child protection and welfare: this work was their career preference. Jessica and Claire emphasised their commitment to children and their protection, and the excitement associated with this type of work and its working conditions were significant in their career preference for child protection and welfare:

Child protection social work was my first job after graduation with an MSW. I purposefully pursued a post in child protection and welfare as it was of most interest to me, it can be exciting as a child protection social worker. I believed in the importance and necessity of good child protection social work, as I believe it can protect children from terrible abuse and hurt (Jessica).

My commitment is to look after children. That's the area that interests me most ... kind of more excited about the bit...the variety that was in the work...the idea of being out in the community and kind of meeting families and working with families and that kind of thing, as opposed to being office-based. So that....that appealed to me. (Claire).

Lucy, Erin and Grace further emphasised the unequivocal character of their decision to enter child protection and welfare. Grace had other social work practice experiences, but child protection and welfare was the career she chose to pursue, and Lucy clarified that the availability, or lack of other job alternatives, did not influence her decision. As examples of the 'career preference' cohort, all five of these social workers challenged stereotypical views, and also the view expressed by Rycraft (2000) in her study, that some social workers enter child protection and welfare without much thought:

It was nothing to do with the lack of jobs or anything like that. It was my main area of interest really to be honest (Lucy).

I suppose I never thought of going any place else ... I had done three placements; one was in [name of organisation removed], one was in the [name of organisation removed], and the other was in community care [child protection and welfare social work] and I never even considered a job in either of the other two [social worker laughs] (Grace).

Less equivocal amongst the group who identified that child protection and welfare was their career preference, was a group of social workers who identified additional factors in their decision to enter. These social workers were aware that statutory child protection and welfare in the HSE was the largest employer of social workers and suggested that there was a perception within the profession that child protection and welfare was where one had to start one's professional social work career. Denise suggested that for some, it is a career preference only due to the large size of the sector, and therefore it is more likely to be a pragmatic 'choice':

... it was the biggest employer [statutory child protection and welfare]. So the chances were you were going to end up there whether you had aspirations...you might as well just get used to it from the outset, like it or not (Denise).

I always felt that child protection was kind of your starting off point and then you kind of climbed. But, I couldn't see myself as doing anything else in [name of geographical area] within social work, except child protection. I find other areas as quite unchallenging (Laura).

These are interesting points: if for some social workers child protection and welfare is seen as a 'starting off point' in one's professional career, as Laura described, they may have already decided that they will eventually leave the practice setting to 'climb' to a post in another social work setting. Laura's suggestion that child protection and welfare is a 'lower' status career choice, where the newly-qualified begin their career, was also identified by Ciara when describing how some social workers saw that other social work jobs were 'better' than child protection and welfare:

They do their time and then they move onto better jobs (Ciara).

Ciara's use of the metaphor 'do their time' - a metaphor used to describe being in prison - is interesting as it may suggest that social workers perceive that they have to work in this area for a limited period before they work in another social work setting. Of the 22 social workers who described child protection and welfare work as their first career preference, by the end of the study four had left their post in the HSE 'Area A', but continued to work in child protection and welfare elsewhere. The factors which were significant in these social workers' decisions to leave will be examined in Chapter Seven. In summary, table 6.2 combines the key factors which influenced 'career preference' social workers' retention:

Table 6.2: Key retention factors for 'career preference' social workers

Typology descriptor	Key factors identified
'Career Preference'	These were social workers whose first preference was to work in child protection and welfare. They • feel that they have good to high levels of job satisfaction, • perceive that they are making a difference, • feel a strong commitment to child protection work and its service users, and • are not thinking about leaving. These social workers may identify aspects of the organisational conditions that they are unhappy with and want to change, but they are likely to have good peer supports and/or experience their supervisor as supportive, which ameliorates the negative aspects of the organisational conditions. If alternative employment opportunities are available, they are described as somehow less 'attractive' or do not conform to these social workers' expectations of professional growth and/or need for a challenge.

Of these twenty two social workers, ten wanted to continue to work in child protection and welfare, four had left by the end of the study, and eight indicated that they wanted to leave. Within the eight who wanted to leave, there was a discernible group who were disillusioned with their professional experience in child protection and welfare. As outlined in Chapter Five, these social workers may have good peer supports, but experience supervisor support as low and do not perceive the organisation as supportive. Organisational conditions are perceived to be poor and they express disillusionment at the impact they are making as professionals. Should this group eventually leave, their turnover should be considered as potentially 'avoidable': this work is their career preference and the employing organisation (HSE) could have considered the possibility of developing mechanisms to address their concerns and thus help them to stay. Some of these social workers were actively seeking ways of improving their working conditions in order to try and stay – they were seeking ways of lessening the impact of the work (for example going part-time), or were active within their teams, either through the union or team fora, advocating the improvement of organisational conditions. Those who were intent on leaving described themselves as 'stuck' if alternative employment opportunities were perceived to be unavailable to them.

It should not be assumed that the 'career preference' social workers are guaranteed to stay or that those who want to leave will actually leave. Some social workers stay not because they like or dislike the job/organisation, but their decision is based on the degree of their embeddedness within the organisation and/or the community (Holtom *et al.*, 2006), aspects of which are often external to, and outside the control of, the employing organisation. As outlined in Chapter Five, a range of factors may contribute to social workers' retention besides their level of job satisfaction. Even if they are disillusioned, some of these social workers are likely to be retained, at least in the short to medium-term, because employment contract conditions are perceived to be better than non-HSE jobs, they want to stay living in a particular geographical area (family or life-style), or other life choices are more important that work environment and/or professional considerations at this time.

Even though working in child protection and welfare is a preferred career choice for this group of social workers a theme arose in the data-analysis where social workers indicated that there may be a 'shelf-life' for social workers in child protection and welfare, and I will return to this theme later in the chapter after exploring the data relating to the 'transient' and 'convert' groups.

The second group of social workers identified in the data-analysis were the 'transients', whose motivations for entering child protection and welfare suggested that their decision to leave child protection may have been made even before they entered and this group is examined more closely in the following section.

6.2.2 Child protection and welfare as a career 'stepping-stone'
('transients')

Within the study, there was a discernible group of social workers who also 'chose' to enter child protection and welfare, but their reasons were different to the 'career preference' group. The other half of the social workers (21) in the study initially entered the sector for instrumental reasons or because they had no 'choice' due to a lack of alternative employment options, and they had a clear expectation of a short-term career in child protection and welfare ('transients'):

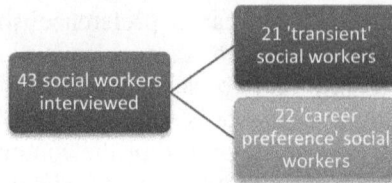

```
43 social workers
interviewed
    ├── 21 'transient'
    │    social workers
    └── 22 'career
         preference' social
         workers
```

Following a period of employment in this setting, two thirds of the transient group revised their career plan and expectations regarding their tenure length in the sector, and these social workers ('converts') are discussed in the next section (6.2.3). However, for one third of the transient group who entered for instrumental reasons, their experience in the setting did not contribute to a revision of their career plan and their career in child protection and welfare continues to be 'transient'. Therefore, it is unlikely that the sector will retain this group of social workers, irrespective of organisational conditions. One example of the instrumental reasons highlighted by social workers for entering the sector was to get additional practice experience. This instrumental use of the sector is illustrated by Sophia, Isabelle and Holly who pointed out:

> It's like having a third placement. I am going to use this and get out (Sophia).

> I didn't have any preference really, except to kind of gain as much kind of knowledge and information and experience that I could do. I very much saw the social work side of things as a period before I would move into the whole [identifying information removed] area. I went into social work and I went back into college to do the social work as kind of a stepping stone to …just gaining experience in that area and that I would move on into the [identifying information removed] area (Isabelle).

> I certainly didn't think, I certainly didn't think it was a job for life to be honest. Again what I, what I would hear from a lot of people is that most people would start off in child protection but it's not an area that one would want to stay in for, for life (Holly).

In her quotation, Holly once again raises the issue of child protection and welfare being a job that one undertakes for a particular length of time, rather than as a career for life. Furthermore, the availability of posts in child protection and welfare, compared to other sectors, was highlighted by social workers whose preference was to work in another practice setting. Simon explained how child protection and welfare for him was a place to learn until the opportunity arose to move to his preferred area of social practice:

184

It was where the jobs were ... That's the bottom line ... Here to learn ... the job that I hope to get into is in [area of social work practice – identifying information removed] (Simon).

Roisin, a social worker who left child protection and welfare and is now working in her preferred area of social work practice, points to the role of her college classmates in forming her opinion that child protection and welfare is where you started your career. A move to your preferred area of practice is perceived to be unavailable upon graduation until you first get experience in child protection and welfare:

> ... when we were in college the whole two years of the Master's course revolved around child protection ... But I always got the impression from...and I wouldn't even say lecturers, you receive it from other students, that it was the place to go to serve your time and that eventually then you would get something that you actually wanted to do. But that child protection was always going to be something that you just....it filled the gap, it gave you experience. It was your two years experience....two years experience that you needed to move on to something else ...I am doing [current area of social work practice – identifying information removed] and I always had an interest in working [in this area]. But again it was the same thing. There was an idea that no-one is going to walk in off the...off....after just being newly-qualified into a job in [current area of social work practice – identifying information removed]. You are going to have to work your way up to that. And to get that....that would follow child protection (Roisin).

Roisin's quotation underscores a perception held by many social workers in the study that you need to 'serve your time' in child protection and welfare, in her opinion for two years, before you 'work your way up' to your preferred career interest. Roisin's use of language is of note: 'serve your time' is both a penal and apprenticeship metaphor, and was also used by other social workers. She described other careers in social work as 'up' from child protection and welfare and she also understood that employers in other practice settings would not employ graduates who had not first served apprenticeship/time in child protection and welfare.

The 'transient' social workers entered child protection and welfare for instrumental reasons and are unlikely to be retained as they are only moving through. They were unlikely to have taken a job in child protection and welfare if they could have secured a job in their preferred career setting direct from college. Some of this group were experienced social workers, and for this group, wanting to work in a particular geographical area was more important than working in their preferred area of social work. For example, in smaller towns, child protection and welfare posts may be the only available social work posts. The key factors which influenced 'transient' social worker in their decision to stay or leave this work are summarised below:

Table 6.3: Key retention factors for 'transient' social workers

Typology descriptor	Key factors identified
'Transient'	Social workers who took a job in child protection and welfare as they felt it was necessary for their *curriculum vitae*, felt it was a good place to develop skills and/or they were unable to access their chosen employment direct from college or in a particular geographical area of the country. These social workers do not intend to stay beyond the short/medium term and will leave once the opportunity arises to work in their preferred social work practice setting. While they may enjoy aspects of the work and the working conditions may be perceived as satisfactory, the experience of doing the job has not changed their intentions to leave the sector.

The use of child protection and welfare as a place to build one's experience and learn is interesting: it can be beneficial to the sector also as it assists in the recruitment of staff, but a disadvantage is that these social workers are never going to be retained in the long-term as their career preference is for a different practice setting. It would be interesting to examine in a further study whether the orientation of these 'transients' towards their employment in child protection and welfare 'insulates' them from some of the job stresses that others experience.

The study also identified a group related to the 'transients' and their data is presented separately in the next section. These social workers may have had initial motivations and reasons for entering child protection and welfare which were similar to those of 'transients', but differ in terms of their retention in one very important way.

6.2.3 Child protection and welfare as a career surprise ('converts')

While these social workers are part of a group who initially entered the sector for instrumental reasons or because they had no 'choice' due to a lack of alternative employment options ('transients'), the experience of doing child protection and welfare work led them to revise their decision to leave in the short-term ('converts'). Nearly two-thirds of the 'transients' subsequently changed their decision to leave as a result of their experience of doing the work:

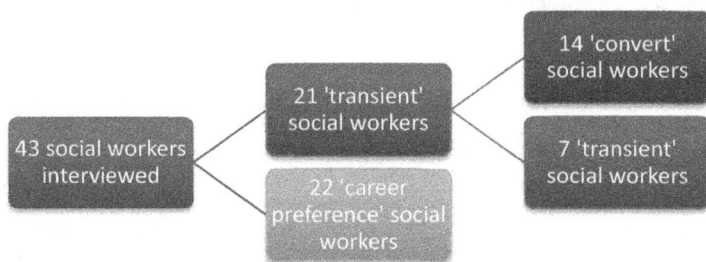

Caoimhe, a social worker with a career preference to work in another practice setting but who took a job in child protection and welfare as a 'stop-gap', described how her initial negative or ambivalent feelings about the work changed as a result of doing the work:

KB: Was it your preference to take up a post in child protection?

Caoimhe: No, not child protection! ... when I was in college studying to become a social worker, it was probably the area that I would have avoided, at all costs. But, again, monetary motivated that I am, it was the only post that became available to me in the [geographical – identifying information removed] area. So that's why I took it. In hindsight, it's probably fate dealing me a blow, because, I think it was actually meant for me ... I just took the child protection one as a stop-gap, basically. It was never my intention to become a child protection social worker, but I think it was probably meant for me, for whatever reason. I didn't like the job at all [child protection and welfare]. I didn't want the job; I was just doing it from day to day and from week to week, seeing how I was getting on, seeing if there was anything else out there. I think, once I realised actually, that the crux of the job was protecting children, vulnerable children, then it's like - right yeah - I am in this job for a different reason.

Caoimhe's engagement with the political and professional goals of the work contributed to her revised decision to stay. Similarly, Clodagh described her initial instrumental reason for taking a post - to gain experience and to stay short-term - and how doing the job changed her career plans. While Clodagh grew to like the work, in another part of the interview she described how she found the organisation unsupportive and was struggling with a decision to leave or stay. She wants to stay and is actively engaging with the HSE to improve working conditions, but feels that she may have to leave, not because of the work, but due to unsatisfactory organisational factors. Should Clodagh leave, her turnover should be considered avoidable. Similarly, Thomas, a social worker who said that child protection and welfare was a career option at the bottom of his list, grew to like and enjoy the work, and wanted to stay. Thomas entered child protection and welfare as there were no other available social work jobs in the geographical area in which he wanted to work:

> ... my motivation for going into child welfare and child protection was that I felt it would be a good basis for practising in social work. My initial commitment was for a year. I suppose after a year I felt I needed another maybe two years. And I stayed ...I grew to like it, even though I never thought I would say that. I thought it would be kind of...you know, me doing something for x amount of time in order to achieve an objective (Clodagh).

> Child protection would have been pretty much at the bottom of my choices, my dream was always [area of social work practice – identifying information removed]. Where incidentally I never worked, but that's how it goes, but I am very happy in my job, I am really interested in what I am doing and I really enjoy it (Thomas).

Hannah described how she 'fell into' child protection and welfare social work. While it was not her career preference initially, after some exposure to the work, it has now become her preference:

> Hannah: Yeah, I did the [name] for two years, I only fell into child protection because that was all there was in [name] at the time in [place name], and then here for the next.

> *KB: So you took up a post in child protection and welfare because that was the only post in social work?*

> Hannah: Yes. My background before that, the two years between the psychology degree and social work was with learning disabilities, adult learning disabilities and, I really felt that's where I wanted to go, but, when I was looking for a job, with [identifying family information], all they had in the [name] was with, now where I was, was child protection, so, that's how I fell into it.

> *KB: Would you have described it as your preference?*

> Hannah: Not then, but, once I was into it, definitely.

Charlotte, a 'convert' social worker who worked in child protection and welfare, but had no initial preference for this work, raised another theme which I will examine in greater depth in section 6.3. Like other social workers, she highlighted the perception that child protection and welfare social work is a good place to learn and develop one's skills, but also to the fact that there is an element of 'proving' oneself in what she alluded to as a challenging work context. If one can do and cope with this work, one can 'manage anything':

> I fell into it really. And I....I did enjoy doing it. And I suppose I would have heard that it's the best experience that you will get. And if you can ... you know you learn so much there and you can manage ... if you can manage to stay there you will manage anything. So I suppose that was at the back of my mind (Charlotte).

This perception that child protection and social work is a challenging and demanding workplace was acknowledged by the Government in a report by the Office of the Minister for Children and Youth Affairs (2008).

In summary, the key factors which influenced 'converts' in their decision to stay in or leave this work include:

Table 6.4: Key retention factors for 'convert' social workers

Typology descriptor	Key factors identified
'Converts'	Social workers who entered the sector for one or more of these reasons: they initially had no interest in child protection and welfare citing the negative image of the area, had ambivalent feelings about working in the sector, they took the job as they were unable to access other social work posts, the area offered a good foundation in practice and skills development and/or the social workers were simply willing to try the job. These social workers were likely to have intentions to leave in the short to medium-term or were ambivalent about their retention in the sector.
	Following a period of employment in the sector, they developed a different outlook: they began to enjoy the work, feel that they were making enough of a difference, had good peer supports and/or experienced their supervisor as supportive and intended to stay in the job. A decision to leave is now less straightforward and a matter of weighing up the pull factors (team atmosphere, job satisfaction, stimulation, making a difference, growth opportunities, employment conditions, and so on) which for the moment outweighs the push factors (job stress, availability of resources, job security, and so on).

The next section examines in greater depth a question identified in this section, namely whether child protection and welfare serves as a 'proving ground' for newly-qualified social workers in Ireland, and the potential implications for retaining social workers.

6.3 A 'proving ground' for newly-qualified social workers?

Coding in the grounded theory tradition emphasises the importance of analysing research participants' use of language as 'specific use of language reflects views and values ... and coding should inspire us to examine hidden assumptions in our own use of language as well as that of our participant' (Charmaz, 2006, p. 47). The analysis of emerging data (Glaser, 1978) in the early part of the coding process focused on the language used by social workers to describe the time they spent in child protection and welfare. Most of the social workers interviewed in the study expressed the view that all social workers were expected to spend time in child protection and welfare and that this time would range from somewhere between 2-5 years. An analysis of the language used by social workers in these parts of the transcripts identified how social workers employed 'military' and 'prison' metaphors to emphasise their perceptions of child protection and welfare as an employment 'choice', particularly for newly-qualified graduates. Metaphors used to highlight this point illustrate the transient nature of social workers' employment in this sector, in addition to the possible prison/apprenticeship characteristics of 'time' spent there:

> do your time (Kelly)
>
> serve your time (Roisin)
>
> your stint (Tara/Charlotte/Nicole/Claire)
>
> do your dues (Jenna)
>
> under my belt (Nicole)
>
> I never saw myself as a life timer in child protection (Abbey)
>
> earn your stripes (Mya)
>
> a stepping stone (Isabelle)

Nicole and Kelly underlined the perception that employment options are limited for newly-qualified graduates and that child protection and welfare is the only 'choice'. Caitlin was looking for other work as she felt she had done her time:

> I think child protection is perceived as the shitty end of the stick, where you start off, do your time and get out (Kelly).

... it's basically your only option anyway starting off ... I wanted to do a few years of this, just to have it under my belt. But then, you know, I would be hoping to move on further (Nicole).

I have been looking around ... I just feel I have kind of done my time you know within that area [child protection and welfare]. It seemed to be the only area really that was recruiting straight, do you know, people straight out of college. And that other areas were looking for people with maybe more experience or whatever (Caitlin).

Mya, a social worker who wanted to stay in the sector, described how she was told that child protection and welfare was where you went to 'earn your stripes'. Significantly, the message also indicated that your length of tenure was short-term; you left before something negative happened to your health, again suggesting that it is a challenging practice environment:

I'd heard you know from various sources [fellow social work students and from probation workers while on a placement] that child protection was where you go in to, you earn your stripes, so to speak, and then you leave before it burns you out [social worker laughs] (Mya).

As highlighted in earlier chapters, social work is considered to be one of the occupations with the highest risk of stress (European Foundation for the Improvement of Living and Working Conditions, 2005; Millet et al., 2005), 'with large caseloads, intense responsibility and heavy administration work' (Mor Barak et al., 2006, p. 566). This view of the sector was reflected in a Government review of compliance with the national child abuse guidelines, in which it was acknowledged that:

... the work is complex, difficult and emotionally demanding - particularly for front-line staff delivering child welfare and protection services ... (Office of the Minister for Children and Youth Affairs, 2008, p. 19).

In the interviews, perceptions that child protection and welfare is 'tough' work and a good place to learn and to 'prove' oneself were raised by Abbey, Leah, Caitlin and Charlotte. They suggested that there is a perceived expectation that child protection and welfare is where you start your career: you 'did your time'/'stint', developed your skills, and then you leave the work:

There is a perception that …I suppose that child protection is tough and that you do your experience there. You do about your two years and then you go on to something else. I think there is….certainly when I was qualifying there was that….you know, you did your…..your time and went somewhere else, do you know….it's like that's….that's where you started….child protection, and went on to something else (Abbey).

I think if you can do child protection you can do anything to be honest. I think it's…it's the hardest social work job out there. There is not a shadow of a doubt about it (Leah).

I think it's a very good grounding. And I think…you know, and I think realistically no other area of social work could be as crisis-driven or as tough or as high case loads or….but certainly no other area that I have…you know, spoken to people that they work in or whatever. So I think it is definitely….right, it is kind of throwing you into the deep end … generally people need to kind of do their time in child protection to get the background, to get the experience, and that that's…kind of I suppose it would have been seen as the toughest area (Caitlin).

I definitely recommend that every social worker does a stint in child protection. But as a career…I mean if…if it's for you, yes, go with it. But I don't think…I think….five years…I think and you need to be getting out (Charlotte).

These social workers share a view that child protection and welfare is the hardest social work setting and that an employment period in this setting is short-term. If Charlotte's thinking represents that of a significant number of social workers, and as child protection and welfare social work is the largest employment setting, one must ask what are the jobs to which all these social workers are going to move to. It may also mean that child protection and welfare could be left with a cohort of dissatisfied social workers who cannot leave, as the wider labour market for social workers is unable to accommodate them due to its relative size. Some social workers sought to challenge the normative expectation that one should move on after one's time is served, thus challenging one of the dominant views held by the previous social workers that everyone wants to, or should, leave child protection and welfare:

That we can move away from I have done my stint now, four or five years and it is time to move on. Why can't we stay there [child protection and welfare]? (Jane).

I know they say that two years is your stint and you can move on but I
wouldn't see that because I still enjoy, I would say, I enjoy 90% of
aspects of the work (Tara).

In addition to social workers entering the profession to do their time, they
also explained their entry motivation in terms of 'proving' themselves as
professionals. Tara, a career preference social worker that wanted to stay,
identified that a perceived function of entering child protection and
welfare was to 'prove' oneself: one could show one's ability of working
in a demanding practice setting without breaking down. Also of note
again is the short-term nature of the expected tenure – one proves oneself
and then one leaves:

> People kind of say - I have done that, ticked the box, proved yourself to
> be able to be in child protection, without completely breaking down,
> two years tick the box and off you go (Tara).

Isabelle explicitly described how a social worker who has not 'proved'
themselves in child protection may feel inadequate before his/her peers
and employers: in some way, they would be 'less' of a social worker if
they had not done child protection and welfare:

> I felt I had to have child protection experience. I felt on a level I
> couldn't take myself seriously, nor would other colleagues take [you]…
> seriously, if you hadn't done child protection (Isabelle).

This point was also stressed by Hannah who employed a military
reference, a tour of duty to a conflict zone, to highlight the unspoken
expectation that an employment period in child protection is crucial to
prove one's *bone fides* as a social worker, and by Jessica who
reemphasises its importance to employers. Again, we note the transient
and short-term employment choices of social workers, and the suggestion
from Hannah that newly-qualified social workers may reluctantly decide
to enter because of expectations created by others while at college that
working in child protection and welfare is a prerequisite for professional
social work practice:

> … you were very much told that [while at university] it was like
> Beirut[51], you do a year in child protection and then you get out and you
> need to do it because no one will take you seriously and really you
> were kind of frightened into it (Hannah).

---

[51] Irish defence force soldiers were key participants in the United Nations
(UNIFIL) peacekeeping force in Beirut, Lebanon, between 1978 and 2001.

> ... when you go [to] apply for other jobs they [employers] look for experience in child protection (Jessica).

Another factor which appeared significant in social workers' motivations to enter child protection and welfare was the perception that it provided the best grounding, training and exposure to a wide range of practice issues (for example, addiction, mental health, child abuse, domestic violence, working with involuntary clients, and so on). An employment period in child protection and welfare is an opportunity to develop skills and competence, which are both a continuing professional development opportunity and a way of improving attractiveness to future employers:

> I would like to do maybe a five year stint here, just to get all my experience and you know feel more comfortable in the job. And I would feel more competent ... I would like to kind of have other experiences of working in social work. College kind of focuses in on as well, you know. So...that's kind of...you know, I had an idea, and they kind of drum it into you anyway that it's...kind of, you should do a few years of this, before you do anything else, for the experience (Nicole).

> ... you have to go in and do your time in this and then...then you have options (Roisin).

Nicole and Hannah, identify the role of their university training in setting the expectation to work in child protection for a couple of years for the 'experience'. For Jane, her decision to stay was influenced by the fact that she felt she had more to learn and that HSE training opportunities were good:

> *KB: Are you actively looking to leave?*

> Jane: No. No. I would love to develop my skills more. I have recently applied to do ... training ... in the risk assessment around perpetrators of sexual abuse.

In summary, social workers in this study may be suggesting that child protection and welfare is used as the 'proving ground' in social work. A 'proving ground' is a military term used to describe a place where machinery and weapons are tested/proved prior to general use. This definition has widened with usage to incorporate an area or situation where a person is tested or proved. By describing child protection and welfare as a 'proving ground', social workers are suggesting that there are implicit assumptions about career paths for newly-qualified social workers in Ireland, the implications of which are examined in the next section.

6.4 Implications for employers seeking to retain social workers

Social workers in this study described how their understanding of a career in social work influenced their employment choices and their decisions to stay in or leave child protection and welfare. The previous chapter examined the factors that were significant in retaining child protection and welfare social workers, but the data in this chapter suggests that in addition to examining personal, supervisory, social support and organisational factors, social workers' understandings of a career in social work are also crucial to understanding social workers' retention in child protection and welfare. For analytical purposes, social workers were categorized into three broad groups based upon their career pathways in social work: 'career preference', 'transients' and 'converts'. Figure 6.1 provides a graphical view of how these social workers' understandings of a career in social work influenced their decisions to stay or leave:

Figure 6.1: Social workers' career decisions flow chart

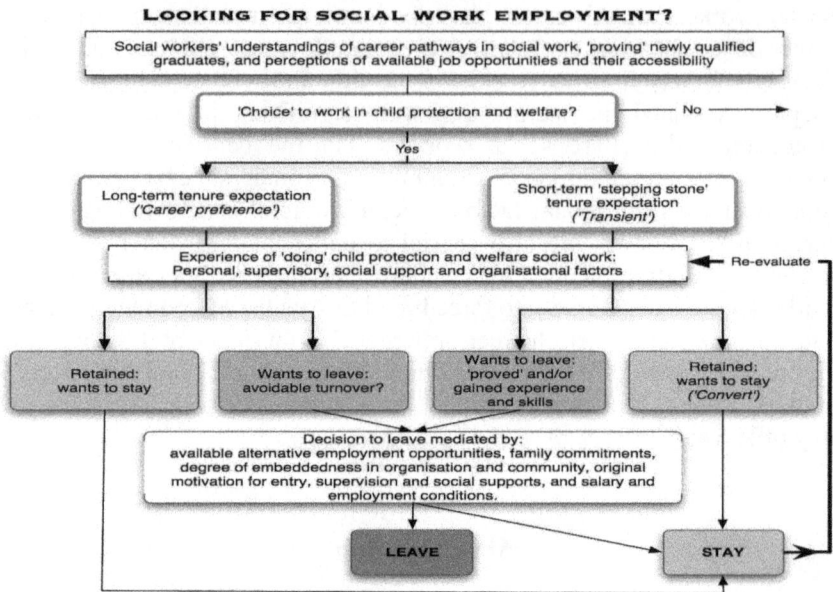

LOOKING FOR SOCIAL WORK EMPLOYMENT?

Social workers' understandings of career pathways in social work, 'proving' newly qualified graduates, and perceptions of available job opportunities and their accessibility

'Choice' to work in child protection and welfare? — No →

Yes

Long-term tenure expectation ('Career preference')

Short-term 'stepping stone' tenure expectation ('Transient')

Experience of 'doing' child protection and welfare social work: Personal, supervisory, social support and organisational factors ← Re-evaluate

Retained: wants to stay

Wants to leave: avoidable turnover?

Wants to leave: 'proved' and/or gained experience and skills

Retained: wants to stay ('Convert')

Decision to leave mediated by: available alternative employment opportunities, family commitments, degree of embeddedness in organisation and community, original motivation for entry, supervision and social supports, and salary and employment conditions.

LEAVE

STAY →

While all of the social workers in the study 'chose' to enter child protection and welfare, the analysis in this chapter highlighted that there are differing motivations for entry, which in turn, influence the length of their tenure expectations. Firstly, if newly-qualified social workers perceived that their preferred career in social work (for example, older adults, mental health) was accessible directly following college, it is unlikely that they would have 'chosen' to enter child protection and welfare. Secondly, some social workers indicated that they 'chose' to enter for pragmatic reasons: it was the sector recruiting, but also there was a perception of it being a good place to develop one's skills. Thirdly, social workers in the interviews highlighted the fact that they understood there was an expectation within the profession that newly-qualified social workers should first 'prove' themselves in child protection and welfare before they moved on to work in their preferred area of social work practice, therefore they did not feel that they had any choice but to enter to 'earn their stripes'. However, social workers re-evaluated their initial decisions to enter and career plan in light of their experience in the organisation, which impacted on the likelihood of their retention, as illustrated in Figure 6.1.

Within these groups, of particular concern for employee retention are those social workers whose career preference was to work in child protection and welfare or who have grown to like it with some exposure, but who are becoming disillusioned and are thinking about leaving (further examples of potentially avoidable turnover). An analysis of the data from these social workers highlighted how the factors which contributed to these social workers' dissatisfactions were mainly organisational and were potentially within the control of the HSE. As outlined in Chapter Five, social workers highlighted the poor quality of professional supervision, support from managers, and the under-resourcing of child protection teams (staffing, caseloads and essential support services such as foster-care placements) as the most significant factors that led to their disillusionment, factors which have subsequently been acknowledged as problematic by the HSE (Health Service Executive, 2008a). However, the HSE may not be able to influence the retention of some social workers as they have made pragmatic choices to view child protection and welfare as a 'stepping stone' to working with service user groups in other employment settings.

Social workers' motivations for entering employment in child protection and welfare and their subsequent decisions to stay or leave appear to be influenced by five key perceptions. Firstly, social workers perceived that a period of employment in child protection and welfare was expected of newly-qualified social workers, views that were generated from their placement experiences and practice teachers, conversations with peers, university courses and from social work employers. Secondly, statutory child protection and welfare is one of the few sectors that social workers believed will employ newly-qualified graduates. Thirdly, social workers believed that social work employers preferred applicants with child protection and welfare experience on their *curriculum vitae*. Fourthly, child protection and welfare was considered a good place to hone post-qualification skills as it provides a good 'grounding' in professional practice. Fifth, by working in what social workers describe as a challenging and 'tough' area of social work practice, one 'proves' to oneself, employers and the profession that one is competent and able to 'cope', thereby becoming 'eligible' for one's preferred area of social work practice.

While the international literature references a range of factors which are closely linked to social workers' decisions to stay or leave (see, for example, Smith, 2005; Tham, 2007; Healy *et al.*, 2009), social workers' understandings of career paths for newly-qualified social workers and the

197

related perception that child protection and welfare is 'used' both by social workers and employers as a 'proving ground', was not apparent in the literature. It is possible that social workers in Ireland describe the area in this manner as child protection and welfare is the largest area in which social workers are employed, and therefore is also the area that employs most newly-qualified social workers. There are relatively few mental health, adoption, or disability posts, and it is unrealistic that everyone would get their first choice in employment directly from college. Nonetheless, the data does suggest that social workers perceived that employers view child protection and welfare as essential training for all social workers and a 'proving ground' for newly-qualified graduates.

Whether this 'proving ground' phenomenon is specific to Ireland is unclear, although two non-Irish born and trained social workers interviewed in the research also identified similar messages in their home countries[52]. The data suggests that social workers' entry motivations shape their decisions to stay or leave. If they entered for instrumental reasons (training, 'earning stripes', no other posts) they are only likely to be retained in the short to medium-term: these social workers had decided to leave before they even began working in this practice setting. On the other hand, child protection and welfare may have benefited from recruiting staff who were initially uninterested or ambivalent, but were retained as they came to appreciate the work and its challenges and opportunities ('converts'). Since 2010 and the completion of the filling of the new Ryan report posts, many newly-qualified graduates are unable to start their career in social work in Ireland and emigration for graduates is now a real prospect.

For some social workers in the study there may have been no decision to make as a job in child protection and welfare was their only 'choice', either because there were few other sectors recruiting, they wanted to live in a particular geographical area or because they perceived that employers in other social work settings expected prospective staff to have first done their time in child protection and welfare. It is possible that the generic method of training in Ireland contributes to this issue by not producing graduates with a specialism that would facilitate graduates to access non-child protection and welfare posts straight from university. The interviews also raised some interesting questions regarding the

---

[52] Countries are not identified as it would compromise the anonymity of these social workers.

messages conveyed about child protection and welfare as a social work practice setting within university training courses.

While it is unclear from the findings of this study whether child protection and welfare is actually used within the profession as a 'proving ground' for newly-qualified social workers, social workers' assumptions affected their behaviour, their decisions to stay in or leave the sector and the length of time they expect to practise there. This data suggests that further research is required to explore these assumptions with social workers, social work students, employers of social workers and university staff.

6.5 Concluding comments

In this chapter, I argued that a focus on social workers' understandings of a career in social work contributes to the analysis of how social workers make decisions to stay in or leave child protection and welfare. The three findings chapters so far have presented statistical and qualitative data which examined the issue of job retention and turnover for social workers in statutory child protection and welfare in the HSE 'Area A'. The findings contained in these chapters challenge some of the prevailing views held by social workers concerning job retention and turnover in child protection and welfare and contribute to a small but growing body of research in this area of social work. The analytical typology and career decisions flow chart presented in this chapter suggest that during the period of the study and beforehand, there were particular assumptions about career pathways for newly-qualified social workers in Ireland, assumptions which impact upon social workers' retention in child protection and welfare. This analysis makes an original contribution to the research in this area and furthers our understanding of the importance of 'career' in social workers' decisions to stay or leave this work.

In her research on why 'caseworkers' stay in child protection and welfare, Rycraft (2000, p. 227) noted that a limitation of her study was that she had not interviewed some of those that 'terminated their employment'. She described how data from staff that had actually left the work could be used in a comparative way to deepen understanding of why some decide to stay and why others terminate their employment. In the next and final findings chapter, I present data from interviews with social workers that had left their employment as child protection and welfare social workers in the HSE 'Area A' and I examine the factors that influenced their decisions to leave.

Chapter 7
Analysis of social workers' decisions to leave child protection and welfare social work in the HSE 'Area A'

7.1 Introduction

To explore why social workers left their employment, a supplementary sample of social workers who terminated their employment in child protection and welfare in the HSE 'Area A' during the fieldwork period was created. This second sample population of ten social workers who had been working in child protection and welfare in the HSE 'Area A' and left, was created by analysing changes in the HSE 'Area A' staff lists (see figure 4.1 in Chapter Four). Social workers[53] with whom the researcher could make contact and who were not living an impractical distance from Cork were selected for interview. These social workers were contacted through the use of peer and professional networks and all ten social workers who were contacted consented to participate in the study.

All of the ten social workers interviewed were still working in social work. Three of the ten were working within statutory child protection and welfare social work (outside of the HSE 'Area A') and seven were working with other service user groups (for example, disability and hospitals). In the interviews presented in earlier findings chapters, there were a range of opinions presented about why social workers leave. In this chapter, I present data from interviews with these ten social workers in which they discussed their recollections of having 'done' child protection and welfare work in the HSE 'Area A'; their reasons for leaving this employment; whether they or family members noticed any discernible changes in their quality of life since leaving; and whether they would consider returning to work in child protection and welfare at some point in the future.

7.2 Factors that influenced social workers' decisions to leave

In this section, I will introduce and analyse quotations and data from these interviews. Key themes emerged from the data and are used to explore why these social workers decided to leave child protection and welfare social work in the HSE 'Area A'. These themes include: making

---

[53] Two of the ten were senior social work practitioners, but they are not identified by their grade to preserve their anonymity.

career choices in social work; balancing work/family life, and leaving due to a 'shock' event.

7.2.1 Making career choices in social work

Similar to the data presented from social workers still working in the HSE presented in Chapter Six, these social workers' understandings of a career in social work were also important in their decisions to leave. Leah, Vicky, and Roisin described how some social workers see child protection and welfare as a short-term career option. They start in child protection and welfare social work because these jobs are available to newly–qualified workers and it is viewed as an area that provides a good grounding in social work practice. Another reason for social workers suggesting that a career in this practice setting is short-term is connected with their view that child protection and welfare is physically and emotionally demanding work. Roisin, an example of a 'transient' as described in section 6.2.2 in Chapter Six, describes in other parts of her interview how she entered child protection and welfare social work for pragmatic reasons, and in the following quote she describes how she had decided to leave before she even started:

> At the end I had my mind made up that I was going anyway. So....I don't think...I suppose again it's likely that I had my mind made up before I ever went into it, that I just wasn't going to be here (Roisin).

She went on to describe how child protection and welfare was a place to 'serve your time' - a stop-gap until she accrued enough experience to get a job in her preferred area of social work practice:

> You just had the impression that you were going to go in, serve your time there [name of child protection and welfare team] and then move on ... I am doing [another type of social work[54]] and I always had an interest in working with [clients of new area of social work]. But again it was the same thing. There was an idea that no-one is going to walk in off the...off....after just being newly qualified into a job in [social worker's preferred area of practice]. You are going to have to work your way up to that and to get that ... that would follow child protection ... it just was a thing that you kind of had to go and do your time in child protection (Roisin).

---

[54] Including details on the new area of social work employment may have led to the interviewee's identity being revealed.

The choice of language in the next quotation, for example use of the word 'stint' which is also used by other participants in the study presented in Chapter Six, further highlights the fact that social workers saw employment in this practice setting as time-limited. Here, Claire suggested five years as the maximum:

> I definitely recommend that every social worker does a stint in child protection. But as a career...I mean if...if it's for you, yes, go with it. But I don't think...I think....five years...I think and you need to be getting out ... not even just five years....but I just don't think you could do a lifetime of it....for the reasons I stated I suppose (Claire).

Like Roisin, social workers suggested that there is a hierarchy of posts within social work, where most other jobs are described as 'up'/higher than child protection and welfare. Both Roisin and Claire, like other participants in the sample presented in Chapter Six, used the metaphors of 'do your time', 'serve your time' and 'stint' to describe their period of employment in the sector. A career in social work begins with a period where you 'serve your time', you 'prove' yourself in child protection and welfare, and then you move on to your preferred career option. Like Roisin, Leah described how she wanted to work in another area of social work when she left college, but that child protection and welfare was where most newly qualified graduates get their experience before they 'move on' to work in their preferred area of social work:

> That was the only place [child protection and welfare] I could get a job. So you are very...where you work is to a large extent, initially anyway, until you get some experience under your belt, it's dictated by what is available. And I think that is probably one of the reasons that child protection social workers have such a hard time as well ... I think kind of the more experienced people move on and they move into, you know, different areas. And it tends to be newly qualified social workers who go into child protection and they get the hardest cases and you know it's not really a solution (Leah).

Leah left her post in child protection and welfare in the HSE 'Area A' when she secured a job in her preferred area of social work in another county. These changes were part of her original career plan when she left college. If Leah had not got the job in her preferred area of practice, she would have continued to work in child protection and welfare in the HSE 'Area A', but she was clear that it was not a long-term career option (irrespective of the geographical location) and that she would have only been biding her time until an opportunity arose in her preferred area of social work.

Vicky, a social worker who initially had no professional interest in child protection and welfare, took up employment there as felt that it would give her the 'best' experience. At the time, she thought that it would be relatively easy to leave child protection and welfare for a job in another area of social work practice:

> I wasn't sure where I wanted to go. But I thought that I would get the most experience in child protection initially. So I went there, even though I was offered a job somewhere else as well. I thought I could get the best experience [in child protection and welfare]. And at the time you could go from one area to the other very quickly anyway (Vicky).

Vicky has since left the HSE 'Area A' and now works as a social worker in the voluntary sector. Five of the ten social workers primarily took a job in child protection as they felt that it would be a good professional experience or grounding and they were always intending to leave ('transients'). Of these five, two became 'converts' (see section 6.2.3 in previous chapter) and now describe child protection and welfare work as their first choice career preference in social work. The other five social workers were 'career preference' social workers (see section 6.2.1 in previous chapter) who took a post in child protection and welfare because it was their first choice. The experience of doing this work, balancing work and family life, and the impact of 'shock' events led some of these social workers to reconsider these decisions.

7.2.2 Balancing work/family life and leaving due to a 'shock' event

In her interview, Vicky described how she had enjoyed child protection and welfare, that she had excellent support from her peers and that it was worthwhile work where she felt she made a difference. Lee and Mitchell's unfolding model of turnover suggests that employees start thinking about leaving organisations due to a 'shock' event inside or outside the organisation[55], rather than a result of job dissatisfaction as suggested by earlier models of turnover. Data to support this model is best collected using retrospective interviews (Hom and Griffeth, 1995; Holtom et al., 2002). In Vicky's case, a 'shock' event associated with her health, which she felt may have been related to work stress, contributed to her decision to leave, as she wanted to have another child. Contributing factors to this decision to leave the work were that it was

---

[55] Examples of 'shocks' include: industrial dispute, birth of a child, death or loss, being head-hunted, or a dispute with manager/colleague (Holtom et al., 2006).

leading to friction with her home life relating to having energy for her role as a mother and partner, and because she felt that the resources available to support her in doing the work were deteriorating:

> I suppose really I think [I left] probably for family reasons, you know. I wanted another child as well, you know. So I think…you know, for those reasons I kind of thought … I can't stay in this long term. And I also felt that some of the services were getting worse and the system was getting a little bit worse, and I found that very difficult to deal with as well … to be honest with you we were probably talking about health (personal health details removed)[56]. But you know I would have been quite stressed as well at the time. Now as I say really…I couldn't…like if somebody said that to me now I wouldn't say, oh yes, it was the stress of the job, I really wouldn't, you know what I mean. But I think…you know, all those kind of things you kind of start reanalysing your own life as well … (Vicky).

In the preceding quotation, we again see another social worker describe a mixture of personal reasons, ill-health and stress which combine to influence social workers' career choices. The question of doing child protection and welfare work and having children was also influenced Charlotte's decision to leave. This could also be partly explained by a 'shock' event. Charlotte felt unsupported by management and by the organisation after an incident at work, which prompted her to start thinking about leaving:

> I just thought it was very heavy duty stuff. And I wanted to get more into …you know, my own…my own life and whatever and possibly having kids in the future or whatever. And I thought it wouldn't be something I would stay in for the rest of my life, and particularly if I had kids or a family, to be facing that level all the time and then to just go home and be your person again. So I suppose I never thought I would stay in it fully. I think that…yes, I think that incident [unsupported by management following a serious event in a case – details removed to protect anonymity] did have a big…a big impact. I suppose I had expectations around being looked after by my manager which aren't fully…you know her responsibility. I mean it's my responsibility. But there is an element that needs to exist for me …being clinically supervised, or being managed, that they will look after you. And I just felt it was completely unmet then (Charlotte).

In this quotation, two significant themes arose which also occurred in data presented from social workers still working in child protection and

---

[56] Including personal health details may have led to the interviewee's identity being revealed.

welfare in earlier chapters. These were the importance of professional supervision in supporting social workers, and a long-term career in child protection and welfare not being part of the plan. Charlotte's use of language ('heavy duty stuff') - which in her interview referred to high work demands, having responsibility for children, the emotional labour of child protection and dealing with child abuse - reemphasises the view often expressed by the social workers that the work was difficult.

The impact of child protection and welfare work on a worker's personal and family life identified in Vicky's text earlier, was also a concern for Erin and Charlotte:

> Difficult in that I felt my job was impacting on my personal life. And I suppose, when the job came up in (identifying information – practice area) would have been where I did my first year placement. I would have been interested in it so went for it but the location was a huge factor. I don't think I would have gone for the same post if it was in (name of HSE 'Area A' geographical area). I suppose, it was always a desire that I would return home anyway (Erin).

Erin moved to a job in another area of social work practice, primarily for its proximity to her home. Charlotte felt that the demands of doing this work necessitated that one's home life be uncomplicated and content, and she used the metaphor of a 'picket fence'[57] to accentuate this point:

> I just think that anyone that works in child protection needs…this is my view and I know it's probably wrong, but that you need to have your big house and your picket fence and….you know, that life is pretty calm … and OK. But I don't think you can afford to have any drama in your own life (Charlotte).

In discussing this further with Charlotte, she explained that 'picket fence' meant that one's life is preferably uncomplicated as child protection and welfare work takes a lot of energy.

In another part of her interview, Erin described the 'fear' that she was not adequately dealing with her caseload due to time pressures. Consequently, she felt she was not building satisfactory quality relationships with children. This anxiety, associated with social workers' awareness of managing 'risk' in child protection and welfare (Morrison,

---

[57] The reference to a picket fence (sometimes white) symbolises the 'ideal' middle class suburban life where a person has a good home in suburbia with a picket fence in front, family life is uncomplicated and one is content with one's life.

1996; Ferguson, 2004), articulated here as a pressure and responsibility not to miss 'things', weighed upon her:

> The fear that I was sort of just touching on things and maybe missing things ... Well I suppose, just the, the fact that you know, I, I, I felt that your planning, planning a child's life because you are planning for a care plan for a child's life. And I just felt that how well do I as a social worker get to know this child so I can know what his or her wants and needs? Like have I such, have I got the time to develop a relationship with them so they can tell me what they want you know? So that they feel, feel included in it (Erin).

When asked to describe what she meant by 'fear', Erin described how she felt under-resourced to do the quality of work she felt these children required, hence the fundamental work of relationship-building could not be adequately undertaken. Data presented from Erin and Vicky in this chapter on the under-resourcing of child protection and welfare - which also mirrors the experiences of the other eight social workers that left - parallel the experiences of social workers still working in child protection and welfare presented in earlier chapters. Erin's concern regarding children's assessment of the quality of her work suggests some unease with her professional work standards:

> The fear is I suppose, those children growing up and looking back and thinking about the social workers that worked with them through the year. And some of them not getting like, what, what would their opinion [be]? ... [when] compiling a care plan I know you're doing it with other agencies but you know, you're meant to be the social worker, you're meant to be the child's voice and you need that input from the child and a child isn't going to tell a stranger what they really think you know (Erin).

Of the seven social workers now working in social work settings other than child protection and welfare, one social worker (Hannah), described herself as an 'avoidable' leaver who reluctantly left the work due to the poor working conditions on her team. Earlier in her interview, Hannah, an experienced practitioner, described her commitment to this work and her high level of job satisfaction, but she also flagged significant tension in relationships between social workers and team management over working conditions. While she acknowledged that it was her decision to leave, she also felt that these factors contributed to her being avoidably 'pushed' out of the organisation (Hannah presently works in another social work setting). Caringi et al.(2008) highlight how such 'push out' factors contribute to workers' decisions, even those workers like Hannah who have a commitment to this work, to leave the sector. Hannah expressed anger at having to leave a job she loved, which, she felt, led to a loss of her identity and powerlessness:

> I still feel the pull you know. And I also still feel a lot of anger, because I loved my job so much … (identifying information removed) I loved what I did and I have lost my identity. I was very well known and you know I was good at what I did. But there is a bit of anger in the back of me that feels….I know I made the decision, but at the same time, there is a bit of anger that says, God, do you know, I was pushed out … I think there are a good few experienced practitioners in my position who feel that way, who feel that….that they are not…they are not within a management structure that works for them. And that was…would be certainly a significant part of me wanting to get out as well (Hannah).

In summary, prominent factors in these seven social workers' decisions to leave their employment were work-life balance issues, critiques of an unsupportive organisation, and social workers' perceptions of career pathways for newly qualified graduates. Some of the social workers that left the work were 'transients' and were always unlikely to be retained in this work. Some of the factors which contributed to social workers leaving were unavoidable, such as moving closer to home or family, and there is little an organisation can do to retain these workers. However, factors within the control of the organisation and which social workers directly related to their decisions to leave were the low levels of support and supervision experienced by some of them, but it is important to note that this was not the universal experience of all workers. Of particular note was that Hannah's departure in particular could have been avoided and that the two 'converts' were also not retained. Three of the career preference social workers were retained in child protection and welfare, but they moved to work in other HSE areas.

The next section explores why these three social workers who are still working in child protection and welfare in locations outside of the HSE 'Area A' decided to leave. The section also explores whether the other seven social workers would consider returning at some point in the future to work in child protection and welfare.

7.3 Returning to work in child protection and welfare in the future

The seven social workers who were no longer working in child protection and welfare were asked if they would consider returning to work in this practice setting. Only Hannah was certain that she wanted to return to this work citing her love of, and preference for, this work:

> There is a high likelihood that I would go back ... I wouldn't go back to (child protection and welfare department she just left). But I would be interested in (another child protection and welfare team in the HSE 'Area A') or something like that ... I do want a few years out. But I can't see myself not going back, because it is still something that...that I love and I have a huge interest in (Hannah).

Claire was certain that she would not work in direct service provision in child protection and welfare again as it would be too stressful. Earlier in her interview, Claire described the negative impact of this work on her health and professional identity when she had to go out on extended stress leave because of the strain of doing the work:

> KB: Would you come back to child protection in the HSE 'Area A'?

> Claire: No. I couldn't really. I loved it in lots of ways you know but I, I think it wouldn't be long before I was back ... the, the type of person that I am, I'm, I'm very hard on myself and so I don't think, I don't think it would be long before I'd be stressed again (Claire).

Leah and Vicky both expressed an interest in returning only if organisational issues which they identified in their interviews were resolved. In the following quotation, Leah additionally highlights commuting as an issue:

> I wouldn't say, no ... I went with here because again you are back into commuting, you are back into...you know, everything that we spoke about. So...I suppose that's...I would never say never. But it would...they would have to change an awful lot I would say (Leah).

> Not as a worker on the ground, no, no. Just because I feel I have done it. I have done it for a number of years. And unless there was significant changes made ....like you know unless the [under] resourc[ing] issue. And the [high] case loads ... I wouldn't, no (Vicky).

Erin and Roisin emphasised 'the buzz', stimulation and variety of the work as being positive factors which they enjoyed about child protection and welfare, which were in direct contrast to their current jobs which do not contain these features. Yet, for Erin, the quality of her home life since she left is presently more important, yet she also expressed the possibility, although not very definitively, of going back to this work at some point in the future. Similar to Charlotte and Vicky earlier, planning for children is also a component of Erin's decision-making process, amongst a range of other factors:

> Erin: I still I see people and they're just getting the buzz you know. I've no buzz now. So they're getting you know, the something in it that they're really enjoying and that some of them would openly say that you know … I miss that.

> *KB: Is it enough for you to go back for that?*

> Erin: No … because there has been so much improvements I suppose, in my personal life you know. I'm now working only Monday to Friday. I'm enjoying myself. I'm sleeping better. And I feel myself you know, I've got more time for like my you know, for my brothers and my sisters you know … and like I wouldn't, I don't think I would have done that as much. I would have met them at home at the weekend and that would have been it. Whereas, now I've, I've more I feel I have more time to, and I'm more interested actually … I wouldn't be surprised if I went back in a number of years. Not maybe, not now you know I suppose, and that again is personal reasoning reasons you know - (identifying personal information). Maybe starting a family, that kind of thing, but I wouldn't be surprised in a few years time if I were to go back.

Roisin also identified the 'buzz', variety and stimulation associated with child protection and welfare work compared to her current job, but these positives were juxtaposed with her disappointment at not being able to make a difference:

> Just even talking about it there now, I was thinking back, well it's not all bad … I did enjoy certain aspects of it … I think there is…there is an awful lot of good in there as well. There is an awful lot of…you know there is great buzz and it's good and it's…but….. Well I mean it's good that I suppose it's…it's challenging and it's interesting and there is so many different …I mean maybe in a way the job that I have at the moment could be…and I don't really mean mundane, but it…maybe child protection is, because it's that fast…you know it's fast paced and it's interesting and that…you know, that it's…every week is different, every day is different. I think that maybe I was a bit naïve as well in there kind of….that you do think everything is going to be all wonderful and that you are going to make such a difference. And it's a bit… whatever…a bit of a shock when you realise that you are not going to…you know what I mean, you are not doing anything (Roisin).

Finally, Charlotte, like other social workers in the study who described their employment period in child protection and welfare as short-term, may consider returning to do a 'stint', but a long-term career in the sector was not part of her career planning:

> I may at some stage return to it. I don't know....for a short stint. I don't know (unclear) I couldn't see myself you know doing it for 30 years or whatever. But then again, things change ... I don't miss it. I mean I like it and it really did an awful lot for me and gave me lots of experience and.....But it's not a great place for building your confidence ... Yes, I suppose I would consider it (Charlotte).

These social workers shared similar issues with the social workers from previous chapters who are still doing the work. In their interviews (data not presented here due to space considerations) the level of under-resourcing of this work, the quality of supervision and supports, and feeling like you are making a difference are significant. Despite these factors, for many of these social workers it was the 'unavoidable' turnover factors such as a geographical move and having children (Hom and Griffeth, 1995), and the social worker's 'type' (mainly transient), which were the key factors in social workers' final decisions to leave the work. Two social workers clearly indicated that they wanted to return to child protection and welfare work at some point in the future, and one may return for a short-term 'stint'. Three continued to work in child protection and welfare and seven worked with other service user groups. From the data it appears that social workers have more difficulty with the HSE as an organisation than child protection and welfare work.

Three of the ten social workers left child protection and welfare in the HSE 'Area A' to do the same work closer to their family home. Amy, Claire and Danielle's (all 'career preference' social workers) commitment to this work was strong and in their interviews they explained that they had made a deliberate choice to continue to work in child protection and welfare work. Despite leaving, all three expressed reservations about leaving the HSE 'Area A', citing high-quality supports and friendships with peers as being retention factors. For example, Claire and Amy said:

> The group of friends (referring to colleagues) that, that I acquired, that acquired me were were fabulous. I really, I still really miss them and I don't think I'll get that again. Because, because everybody made me feel warm and welcoming and yeah real ... I wouldn't have survived if it wasn't for them ... in that environment the, the newness of it and the difficulties that are involved, difficulties that are involved with the high numbers, with a different legislation, with different services that are not available in (name of team), I don't think I would have lasted at all (Claire).

> Managers and colleagues were very supportive. Team atmosphere is most important for me. Would have stayed in (name of child protection and welfare team) for this (Amy).

While friends were important, the desire to move geographically closer to family, (and in Amy's case, the additional factor of seeking promotion), was a core factor in some social workers' decisions to leave, as expressed in the following quotations:

> I wanted a managerial post and was from (name of home geographical area) originally and wanted to return home (Amy).

> I suppose, it was a personal, for personal reasons not much more than the actual job ... we decided that because of the limitations for his career [partner], he wanted to come back to the (name of country). And, and family connections you know and friends that, that we missed. I didn't really choose to leave. I didn't particularly want to leave. I just being, I got the post of Senior Social Work Practitioner and I was quite pleased about that and excited about you know, what that would entail. But obviously you know, I needed to come back. Between myself and my husband. It was a joint decision (Claire).

> Danielle: I think I would have taken a job in anything really within kind of social work field, just to position myself in (geographical area). But my intention would have been to go back and do child protection. So I would have taken work until something came up in child protection in (name of home geographical area). So the way it happened is that, I landed like a job here in (child protection and welfare in another HSE), because it was the nearest to (name of home geographical area) that I could get.

> *KB: Was it always your intention to leave child protection and welfare in the HSE 'Area A' and come back to (name of home geographical area)?*

> Danielle: Oh yes, it would have been. Like the plan was eventually like but maybe not when it happened. But it just...it's just the way things worked out. I could have stayed longer in Cork. I wasn't leaving for....it's just the way life like happened.

To expand upon the themes of health and work-life balance examined in earlier chapters, these social workers were asked if they noticed changes in their quality of life since leaving the HSE 'Area A', and their responses are analysed in the next section.

7.4 Quality of life after leaving the HSE 'Area A'

The ten social workers were asked if they or family members noticed a difference in their quality of life since leaving child protection and welfare work in the HSE 'Area A'. Hannah described how there is now a better balance between her home and work life, she is calmer at home and has more energy for activities, family and friends and is home earlier as her new job does not require working late:

> There was this whole discussion going on about how much more relaxed things are at home since I have changed jobs … a lot of that is around the hours and stuff. I am no longer rocking in at 7 o'clock…8 o'clock at night, you know. I am in by 6 o'clock…and, you know, so things are a bit more calm. For the first month to six weeks I dreamt about (Name of Social Work Department). It was the weirdest thing. I used to dream about the clients. I used to dream about the team. And ….almost like my subconscious was getting rid of it. That is gone now. I don't like hearing from them anymore, which sounds awful. I just want them to go away. Definitely more relaxed, definitely more energy and more interest in things outside of work.

Vicky described how not working in child protection and welfare has improved her home life. Not working in child protection and welfare, she felt, is also better for her child as she was conscious of the impact of work stress on the relationship with her child:

> I have a small child now as well and I think for him as well it's much better … But then I was watching a particular programme on the television, it was talking about stress and parents and it just interviewed way older children now ….seven, eight, nine, ten or whatever. And they…how aware they were of their parents when they were stressed and things like that. And I think that's what got me thinking because even though I was…you know, at home and you know as I say a demanding child, it's…it was still going on in my head. You know…so I kind of thought, God, that's not good, I don't want that, you know what I mean (Vicky).

Social workers were also aware of their partner's and friends' views of changes since they moved jobs: social workers felt they were more relaxed and their home/family life had improved. Vicky's partner was happy that she had changed jobs and felt she was more relaxed, and Erin's friends also noted significant changes in her:

> My partner definitely … [is happy] That I left, yes … I would be more relaxed (Vicky).

I mean, friends have sat me down seriously have sat me down and … friends have said God like you're so relaxed now. You're [a] completely different person. That might be a bit exaggerating but you know, they, they would comment on that. I feel much more relaxed you know. I can now have conversations about like you know, silly things not silly things but unimportant things and I'm not thinking about something else you know. Even though my work now is, is, is almost more emotionally draining now because I'm getting to know people better and I'm empathising with people more do you know … But at five o'clock I'm out the door. I'm winding down the, I'm winding down in the car and that's it. That's work. So I feel, I feel much better (Erin).

Erin also noted that her health had improved since she left child protection and welfare:

Well, my mental health. And my (medical condition) is now maybe once a year instead of three or four times a year, which is quite interesting.

Now that she has stopped working in child protection and welfare altogether, Leah feels she has a better quality of life, and would find it difficult to go back:

It's a tough job, Kenneth, you know. And as I said, I would…I could do it, but I couldn't do it forever. I definitely couldn't do it for kind of ten years or fifteen years, you know. I just…and having such a good quality of life now, and knowing the way that…how difficult things were before, it would be very hard to go back into that, you know. You know….other things take over, don't they, you know. And it's nice to have…to leave work at…work at 5 o'clock in evening (Leah).

Similar to data presented on social workers' health in previous chapters, the ten social workers that left, particularly the seven that were not working in child protection and welfare, noted how they felt that their general quality of life had improved. In Erin's case, she directly linked her move to a new social work job with a reduction in health-related illness. The most significant features for social workers were an improved level of energy and quality of relationships with family and friends. The interviews were unable to dedicate sufficient time to explore this theme in further depth, and there may be some merit in undertaking further research on the issue of social workers' health and quality of life, particularly the strength of a more detailed comparative study between those who left this work and those still working in child protection and welfare.

7.5 Discussion and analysis

Factors which contributed to social workers' decisions to leave included: work-family life conflicts; moving home, where home is defined as outside of the HSE 'Area A's' geographical boundaries; social workers' understanding of a career in social work; newly qualified social workers' perceptions of employment opportunities in the social work labour market post-qualification; the demanding nature of the work; not being valued and taken care of by managers, and 'shocks' that stimulated social workers to start thinking about leaving. There was some evidence of social workers 'avoidably' leaving as a result of factors that may be within the control of the HSE, but the turnover decisions were attributed mainly to 'unavoidable' personal factors such as having children and wanting to move closer to home and family. Rycraft (2000, p. 211) noted that many of her study's participants became child protection workers 'without prior thought or an original intent'. The findings presented in this and previous chapters provide another perspective on this issue; social workers made clear decisions to enter and leave child protection and welfare social work.

Social workers who left their employment as child protection and welfare workers in the HSE 'Area A' had a clear view of their career path within social work, and their understanding of a career pathway influenced their employment decisions, both about their entry and exit from child protection and welfare. Social workers perceive that child protection and welfare is a necessary first step on their career and for many it was the only work available to them. Contrary to Rycraft's (2000) finding, social workers in this study who had left their employment as child protection and welfare social workers in the HSE 'Area A' had made careful career decisions and were clear on why they entered the sector. Firstly, social workers' believed that child protection and welfare was the sector most likely to employ newly qualified graduates. Secondly, social workers with an interest in other areas of professional social work practice felt that they should first gain experience in child protection and welfare social work to get a good practice grounding which would subsequently help them gain access to their preferred choice of employment. Thirdly, some social workers have a preference for this work: they make informed decisions to enter the sector and stay in this work even if they move geographical areas, despite the challenges associated with 'doing this work' and the reported issues with working conditions in child protection and welfare teams.

Some social workers reported that child protection and welfare was a difficult practice context in which to have a long-term career and that one's time in this setting is limited. This is an interesting theme which was also expressed by social workers in earlier chapters and raises important policy and practice implications that are discussed in the next chapter.

There was some evidence to support Lee and Mitchell's (1994) theory that employees start thinking about leaving as a result of a 'shock', in that two of the social workers' accounts fit with this model (Vicky and Charlotte). While this theoretical model of turnover was not explicitly used in the data collection, a further study which specifically examines this model may have some merit, although researchers should note the methodological complexity and difficulty of designing a study using this model, as noted by Holtom and colleagues (2002).

Three of the ten social workers interviewed remained in the child protection and welfare system, although they were all working outside of the HSE 'Area A'. These social workers' decided to stay working in child protection and welfare because of their preference for child protection and welfare work, they felt that they made a difference with families, they experienced job satisfaction, and had a commitment to working with children and families.

The more nuanced classification of turnover outlined by Phillips and O'Connell (2003) in Chapter Three suggests that organisations should seek to classify turnover beyond a straight numerical calculation to one which estimates if employees' resignations are 'avoidable' or 'unavoidable'. Two of social workers' departures could be classified as 'avoidable' and appeared to be directly related to problems with managers and organisational factors. For example, Hannah's account suggests that her resignation might have been avoidable and represents a human resource loss to the sector as she was an experienced practitioner who was committed to the work and wanted to stay. The data presented in this chapter suggests that eight of the ten social workers' departures were 'unavoidable' due to geographical moves closer to family and friends, and decisions to have children.

While social workers' views on returning to the sector were not overtly negative, the likelihood of the sector reemploying this cohort appears small. While social workers clearly missed certain aspects of child protection and welfare work, namely working in a team, support and friendships, the 'buzz' and the variety of the work, other positive factors such as reduced stress, improved health, work-life balance, and improved quality of relationships with family and friends outweigh aspects of the work that they miss. These factors influenced their decisions to leave their employment in child protection and welfare, their future career pathway in social work and whether they would work in child protection and welfare social work again.

Exit interviews are often suggested as an important tool for organisations to examine causes of turnover, although there has been some doubt cast on their reliability and accuracy as staff participation can be low, staff may not accurately report their true feelings due to fears of retaliation or getting a poor reference, and the quality of data collected can be short and incomplete (Phillips and O'Connell, 2003). Therefore, exit interview were not part of the research design of this study. Of the social workers who discussed exit interviews, none had been invited to an exit interview and some indicated that they may not have been too forthcoming or critical if they had had one.

7.6 Concluding comments

In this chapter, I presented findings from qualitative interviews with ten social workers that had left their posts in child protection and welfare in the HSE 'Area A'. The primary benefit of interviewing these social workers was the ability to compare themes between the two samples of social workers. The data collected and findings confirm the validity of the decision to interview these social workers. The findings presented in this chapter should be considered in more tentative terms than the findings from earlier chapters, due to the relatively small sample size. However, the important themes raised in this chapter confirm the need to undertake further research with social workers who resign from this work. The data presented in this chapter facilitated a development of the analysis of how social workers make decisions to stay or leave child protection and welfare work.

This exploratory study raises additional questions and avenues for further research. In the next and final chapter, I will summarise the book and examine the implications of the research findings for users of child protection and welfare services, social work practitioners, the social work profession, social work employers and social work education.

Chapter 8
Developing a retention policy for child protection and welfare social workers

8.1 Introduction

This study examines the factors that influence the retention of statutory child protection and welfare social workers. The main goals of the study were to explore the professional experiences of a group of child protection and welfare social workers in the HSE 'Area A', to establish the levels of turnover and employment mobility, to explore the factors that influenced their decisions to want to stay in or leave this work, and to highlight significant factors for the development of a retention policy for social workers in child protection and welfare. Many of the issues outlined in the political and social context described in Chapter One remain unresolved and are discussed throughout this chapter. This study's findings illustrate the far from optimal practice conditions in child protection and welfare social work in the HSE 'Area A' during the period of the fieldwork.

This research makes a significant contribution to the knowledge on child protection and welfare social workers' retention by undertaking an in-depth analysis of this issue in one Health Service Executive area. This study challenges the prevailing orthodox that the turnover of child protection and welfare social workers is high and in doing so charts the complex nature of social workers' movements within and out of child protection and welfare. By employing both qualitative and quantitative methods, but primarily a qualitative research design, this study highlights the factors which social workers identify as influencing their decisions to stay or leave child protection and welfare. Data collected in the semi-structured interviews also shed light on social workers' experiences of 'doing' child protection and welfare work and their understandings of the complex nature of this area of social work. In undertaking this research I examined the applicability of three organisational theories to examine social workers' retention: perceived organisational support theory, social exchange theory and job characteristics theory. Questions were raised regarding perceived organisational support theory where I argued that this theory has limited applicability for researching social workers' retention. One of the main findings was that social workers' commitment to co-workers and service users is more important in explaining their retention. This study makes an original contribution through the development of a typology that focuses on social workers' perceptions of a career in social work and how five key perceptions influence their subsequent decisions to stay or leave (Chapter Six). A further original contribution is the retention framework for child protection and welfare social workers presented in section 8.2 of this chapter. This typology and the findings of this study are likely to have broader implications and relevance for the employers of social workers in Ireland outside of the HSE and employers of social workers in other countries.

This study addresses a significant gap in the Irish research by making a contribution to the long-running and under-researched debate on social workers' retention in child protection and welfare in Ireland. The research findings do not support the view, at least in the HSE 'Area A' during the fieldwork period, of there being high turnover for child protection and welfare social workers. However, I also argue that this does not mean that there are not important issues to be addressed regarding social workers' retention. The study highlights specific areas that require attention and investment by the government, which in addition to addressing social workers' retention would also enhance the development of child protection and welfare social work services. The study also discovered a majority of social workers who want to continue working in child protection and welfare: these social workers' experiences provide important insights into how retention issues can be addressed, and challenges the dominant assumptions that social workers want to leave this area of professional practice. The study extends our understanding of social workers' retention by arguing that future research in this area should consider social workers' perceptions of career pathways in social work, and a social work career typology was developed to structure such an analysis. The implications of such a focus for employers will be discussed in section 8.3.1 below. The study also makes a contribution by demonstrating how qualitative research that draws on the experiences of social workers can contribute to research in this area.

Contrary to expectations, the findings suggest that two thirds of social workers interviewed wanted to continue working in child protection and welfare. The quality of social workers' supervision, social exchanges between social workers and their co-workers, high levels of autonomy in their work practices, a career preference for this work, wide variety in the work, social workers' commitment to co-workers and service users, and a perception that they were making a difference, emerged as important themes in social workers' decisions to stay. However, certain social workers were staying not because they enjoyed the work or because it is their preference, but for more pragmatic reasons that include the quality of public service employment contracts and personal, including family, commitments. Social workers' perceptions of being unsupported by the organisation, which usually meant poor quality and infrequent supervision, high caseloads and demanding workloads, a lack of resources, working with involuntary clients and perceptions that they were not making a difference were most significant in social workers' decisions to want to leave. Of those who want to leave, some describe themselves as stuck and may have to stay due to a 'tight' labour market connected to deteriorating economic conditions and the HSE's policy of limited recruitment.

In this study, social workers had very high average caseloads of 41.3 children each. The social workers reported that the size of their caseloads resulted in some of these children being rarely seen; that there was serious under-resourcing of services for children and families in the areas of alternative care, mental health/therapeutic and family supports and that the quality and frequency of their professional supervision was less than adequate, all of which led to a perception that the HSE 'Area A' was not sufficiently supportive of their work. Since the completion of the fieldwork, the deteriorating economic conditions of the country has contributed to further cutbacks in health and social services where vacant posts are left unfilled, and it is now even more difficult for social workers to access essential resources for children and families.

In this concluding chapter, based on the study's findings, I summarise key areas of development that could form the basis of a retention policy for social workers in child protection and welfare. The implications of the research findings for child protection and welfare policy, social work employers, social work practice and education, and the users of child protection and welfare services are also outlined. The chapter identifies opportunities for further research, and some of the limitations of the study are discussed.

8.2 Developing a 'retention' policy for social workers in child protection and welfare

Some degree of turnover should be considered normal in all organisations, and the goal of social work organisations should not be to try and retain all social workers. Nonetheless, it is important to retain skilled and experienced social workers in child protection and welfare and it is recommended that the HSE should regularly generate data on social workers' turnover and employment mobility. As argued in Chapter Four, employment mobility changes such as maternity leave and secondments should not be considered in turnover calculations, but should be factored into the general analysis of staff mobility and requirements for temporary 'replacement' staff. Future analyses of social workers' retention should seek to look beyond blunt statistical turnover rates towards identifying and preventing avoidable turnover, which should include the views of current staff and staff who moved within and left the organisation. To this end, the following framework presented in figure 8.1, developed from the research findings outlined in previous chapters, indicates the key areas that need to be considered in developing a strategy to retain skilled, experienced and committed social workers that want to stay.

Figure 8.1: Retention framework for social workers in child protection and welfare

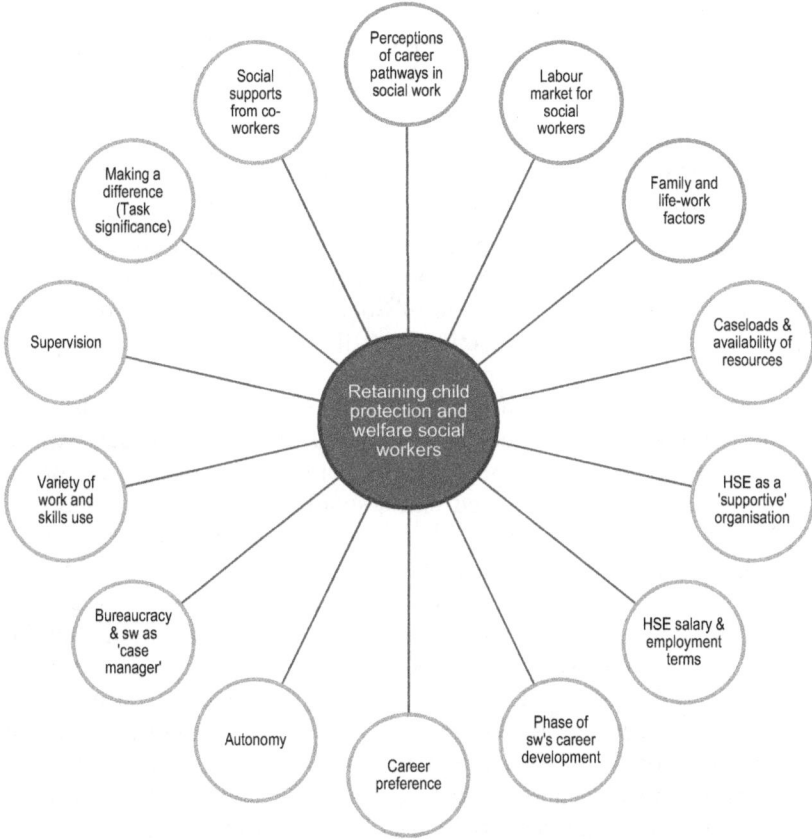

The framework draws together the key factors which social workers in this study described as influencing their decisions to stay or leave. Rather than present a hierarchical or causal model, the framework is presented as an inter-related matrix of factors, the mix of which will be different for each social worker. This framework reflects the methodological approach of the study, which sought to represent the voices of social workers - to acknowledge their diversity and the differing meanings and constructions which they ascribe to their work in this setting. While these social workers were working for the one organisation, their understandings of this work and the organisation influenced how they talked about their experiences, leading to multiple and sometimes conflicting stories of social workers' retention in the HSE 'Area A'. The diversity of experiences, shaped by all of the factors identified in the framework, suggest that more causal models, popular in this type of research, are too simplistic and do not adequately capture the rich complexities of these professionals' experiences. To this end, the framework should be used as a basis for further research and conversations on this issue within the profession and the HSE, rather than as a predictive model.

The framework is colour-coded to highlight the factors which the interviewed social workers considered were largely within the control of the HSE to address (green), those to which other parties (for example, trade unions, the Irish Association of Social Workers, and so on) could make a contribution in conjunction with the HSE (orange), and factors that are largely outside of the HSE's control (blue). The findings from this study lend weight to Caringi *et al's.*(2008)opinion that organisations that do not attempt to address what they describe as 'push out' factors within their control, will contribute to committed workers avoidably leaving. The study data revealed that a small but significant number of social workers presently employed in child protection and welfare who enjoy the work and would like to stay ('career preference'), had decided that they would leave because of their frustrations with the HSE not supporting social workers in their role of protecting and promoting the welfare of children. Yet these social workers felt that their departure could be avoided if the HSE made certain organisational changes, for example in the areas of supervision, caseloads and administration. The finding that not all factors are within the control of the employing organisation and the value of seeking to identity which factors can be addressed or which partners could assist in addressing factors outside of the employer's direct control, is relevant for all employers who are seeking to address the retention of workers.

However, while the research originally focused on the changes the HSE could make to influence social workers' retention, the study data also points out the contributions that the educators of social workers, social workers themselves, and the wider profession of social work could make in addressing this issue. One example would be the role that the wider social work profession and the educators of social workers could play in addressing the issue of career pathways for newly-qualified social workers (see Chapter Six), a finding which also has relevance for child protection and welfare services in other countries. By highlighting the factors that are within the control of the HSE, the framework provides a mechanism to focus resources towards areas that this and other research studies have shown can influence social workers' retention. Should the HSE develop a strategy to address some of these issues, the dividend for service users, the HSE, social workers and the profession overall would be greater than simply the retention of social workers: it would, I argue, alsoimprove the quality of service provision in child protection and welfare, and social workers' morale. The data presented in sections 5.4.1, 5.4.3 and 7.3 suggest that social workers' retention and the factors that influence it are inextricably linked with the quality of service provision to, and the safety of, children at risk, the implications of which are also relevant to child protection and welfare services in other countries. Some of the social workers in the study were critical of the levels of resources provided to support their work, and the study highlights many gaps in service provision. The next sections explore some of these issues in greater depth and examine the implications of the study's main research findings, and the key elements of the retention framework, for improving social workers' retention.

8.2.1 Labour market for social workers and HSE salary/employment terms

This study revealed a relatively low turnover rate for social workers in the HSE 'Area A' during the fieldwork period. This raised the question as to why so many social workers were staying, when the literature indicated that the turnover rate of child protection and welfare social workers was relatively high. It is likely that the specific economic and political context at the time of the fieldwork contributed to the low turnover rate. There were few available job alternatives within the wider Health Service Executive, within the social work profession, and more generally in Ireland. Other non-pay/benefit factors that influence social workers' retention are discussed in sections 8.2.2 – 8.2.8.

In some instances employees often have a greater need for benefits than pay which contribute to creating an appropriate work environment that influences their retention (Phillips and O'Connell, 2003). Employment benefits available to social workers in the HSE, in addition to social workers' pay which is quite high relative to other public sector workers (see tables 5.2 and 5.3), include: 27 annual leave days a year, a defined benefit pension scheme, *force majeure* leave, a time off *in lieu* system which social workers in the study described as valuable, maternity leave benefits and terms in the public sector that are better than the private sector, job-share possibilities, sabbaticals, unpaid leave, and job security (public sector workers are unlikely to be made redundant). Since the study was completed public sector staff now pay a new pension levy and a Universal Social Charge from their salary to help address the substantial deficit in the public sector finances. These new charges have greatly reduced public sector workers' take home pay, but the benefits listed above have remained largely intact.

The implications of the study's findings are that in the worsening domestic and global economic climate, it is likely that the conditions of the labour market and social workers' conditions of employment are likely to encourage high levels of social work staff retention. However, in this climate, there may be little incentive for the HSE to address some of the issues identified in this research because of low turnover, an 'over-supply' of social workers, a lack of resources to implement recommendations, and a minimum amount of staff recruitment. A further possible implication for the universities of the 'over-supply' of social workers is that it may be necessary to reconsider graduate numbers in the coming years should the demand for social work courses reduce in line with the reduction in employment opportunities.

8.2.2 Caseloads and resources to support children at risk

The study discovered that each social worker in the HSE 'Area A' is responsible for an average of 41.3 children (see table 5.1), which represents between three to four times the numbers of children in Haringey council's (UK) maximum caseload guidelines[58]. These high caseloads impact on social workers' perceptions of, and ability to make a difference, contributes to their 'stress of conscience' (see section 5.2.1), and impacts upon their ability to provide protective and supportive services to children (see section 5.4.1). The introduction by the HSE of a maximum caseload policy is likely to be viewed by social workers as supportive and could promote their retention. To avoid waiting lists, such a policy would require at least a doubling of the workforce. Lower caseloads could have both positive and negative implications for service users. Lower caseloads should significantly increase the frequency of face-to-face contact with children and reduce the work which social workers 'farm out' or delegate to other workers (see section 5.4.2),

---

[58] In the reporting of the 'Baby P' child death case in the UK, it was reported that Haringey has an upper caseload limit of 12 children per social worker (Rayner and Allen, 2008). See Chapters Two and Five for maximum caseload limits in other HSE areas and data from the USA.

thereby using more of their own skills and talents which job characteristics theory recommends as a positive (Oldham, 1996). However, in the current economic climate, the government is more likely to reduce staff numbers than increase them. Thus, the only options would be to introduce waiting lists and/or change the entry criteria for the provision of child protection and welfare services to very high levels. Both of these options would have serious negative implications for the protection and welfare of children, and opportunities for social workers to be involved in welfare or preventative type work would be minimised.

8.2.3 Variety of work, autonomy and skills use: incentivising social workers to stay longer or rotate into child protection and welfare

Similar to Woodcock and Dixon's (2005) findings, social workers in the study wanted to have their skills valued and utilised. While social workers felt their work was varied and they generally had high levels of autonomy, which are important factors in job characteristics theory leading to job satisfaction (Oldham, 1996), these were under threat as social workers were increasingly involved in bureaucratic tasks and mainly high-end crisis cases. Social work in child protection and welfare is more conflict-laden and usually has fewer possibilities to see positive change (low task significance in job characteristics theory) than work in other social work settings. Moreover, the supportive and therapeutic face-to-face work with service users is, in some teams, increasingly contracted out to other professionals. As other studies have also recommended (Reagh, 1994; Westbrook et al., 2006; Healy et al., 2009), a rotation policy could give social workers time away from the type of crisis work found in child protection and welfare and this is under active consideration by the HSE.

Social workers in Team 1 said that its internal rotation practice kept them longer in child protection and welfare (see section 5.4.6); however, such a practice has limited relevance to some of the other child protection and welfare teams as they are significantly smaller in size. Finding ways for social workers to rotate out of child protection and welfare for a period may give them more opportunities to feel that they make a difference, and to get a sense of achievement and success in work that is more supportive, less crisis-driven, and with less conflict. Social workers could develop their skills in this other work and experience a variety of work tasks, all of which would benefit child protection and welfare when they rotate back. The HSE could also consider addressing the experience and skills needs of social work in child protection and welfare by developing flexibility between work settings, possibly by introducing incentives at all grade levels to move/rotate between other social work settings in the HSE and child protection and welfare, a strategy that would need to be negotiated with labour unions but is common practice in the probation service in Ireland. Another possibility for the HSE could be to consider structuring social workers' career development and/or their continuing professional development in a way that benefits social workers who work for longer in and/or work regular blocks of time in child protection and welfare. A further option could be the introduction of a retention bonus where social workers are given financial bonuses or increased benefits for staying beyond a set period of time in child protection and welfare. Career progression options such as the senior social work practitioner grade in child protection and welfare could also be expanded. Additionally, finding ways to provide more 'balanced' workloads for social workers where they are facilitated to do some supportive and preventative work along with the more child-protection-type cases (see section 5.4.2), could also aid their retention.

Despite the potential benefits of a rotation policy for retaining social workers, it must be acknowledged that such a policy may contribute to further issues for service users who may have an even greater frequency of change in their allocated social worker.

8.2.4 Making a difference

The concept of task significance from job characteristics theory (Oldham, 1996), otherwise described in some of the research as making a difference (see Samantrai, 1992; Ellet et al., 2006), was found in this study to be amongst the most important for social workers' retention. The data showed that doing social work with children at risk was meaningful for social workers, but a range of organisational factors were identified (for example, workloads and involuntary clients) as impacting upon their ability to improve and protect children's welfare, and to feel like they were making a difference. For example, a particular implication of the finding of working with involuntary clients and its impact on social workers' task significance (see section 5.2.1), similar to Ferguson's (2005) recommendation, is that professional and in-service training needs to equip social workers with better skills and theoretical frameworks for working with involuntary clients. A further implication for the HSE is that the limited quality and frequency of supervision, where supervision is regularly described by social workers as an 'add-on', may also be affecting social workers' perceptions of making a difference, particularly when working with involuntary clients.

Social workers described how their ability to make a difference is also under threat from the bureaucratisation of their work. In the study data, social workers described themselves as 'case-managers' and bureaucrats, 'farming out' the work to others (see section 5.4.2). This is compounded by the impact of managerialism on practice, whereby as Buckley (2008, p. 23) points out, there is a:

> danger that an over-concentration on simplistic organizationally-centred auditing processes and performance measures will stifle the continued development of child protection work. This places a high priority on tangible outputs and ignores the crucial elements of relationship and principle-based work.

Social workers' responses to children and families in need may become even more bureaucratised with the deployment of the 'standard business model' although the implementation is currently mid-cycle and it is difficult to assess its impact. This model may provide a further challenge to social workers in the HSE hoping to reshape social work practice towards the 'crucial elements of relationship and principle-based work' (*ibid*). Rather than moving towards professional practice based upon supervision (Gilligan, 2004), this development may lead towards an increasingly proceduralised form of social work practice.

However, workers in general may need to moderate their expectations of the degree to which work enables them to feel that they make a difference, and the extent to which work will provide meaning in their lives. For example, Svendsen, commenting on work in general, argues that (2008, p. 127):

> ... [we] expect too much from work these days, more specifically that it should be able to bring us so much of the meaning we need in our lives. Those expectations will probably not be met, and we become nomads at work, going from one job to another, never finding what we are looking for.

Further research could be located in debates on the importance placed on work in the formation of our identities and how increased individualisation [re]shapes our orientation towards work.

8.2.5 Perceptions of career pathways in social work and implications for retention

This study points out the importance of expanding our understanding of social workers' retention to include how social workers' understanding of a career in social work influences their employment decisions and retention. This insight came from the use of a grounded theory approach to the data analysis which examined the metaphors used by social workers in their interviews. The learning from this process is that a strict focus on codes solely derived from theory and research findings can limit one's analysis of the data, and there is much to be gained from developing other ways to analyse and understand qualitative data (see sections 3.5.1, 6.2, 6.3 and 7.2.1). This new understanding makes an original contribution to knowledge in this area and may also have relevance for employers of social workers other than the HSE in Ireland and employers of social workers in children's services in other countries. It may also have some relevance to the experiences of other front-line professionals in health and social services (for example, occupational therapy, nursing, physiotherapy, and social care), but this would need to be examined in further studies.

The career social work analytical typology developed in section 6.2 facilitated an examination of the career expectations for each social work archetype – 'career preference', 'transient', and 'convert' – by categorising their entry motivations for working in child protection and welfare. While all of the social workers in the study 'chose' to enter child protection and welfare, there are differing motivations for entry, which in turn influence the length of their 'time' in this setting. The data presented in section 6.3 built on the career social work typology and explored data which suggested that child protection and welfare may be used by employers and newly-qualified graduates as a 'proving ground', which is a place to first test people or machinery before general release. These analyses suggest that during the period of the study and beforehand, there were particular assumptions about career pathways for newly-qualified social workers in Ireland, assumptions which impact upon social workers' retention in child protection and welfare.

The data suggests that employers should not alter their recruitment processes to not select 'transients'. Data presented in section 6.2.3 showed that some of these 'transients' may become 'converts' - a group whose career pathway has altered and whose subsequent retention is likely. However, the typology suggests a group of social workers - the 'transients' - that the HSE could seek to retain by providing opportunities to enhance their retention. The HSE already has a large cohort employed that want to stay – 'career preference' and 'converts'; however, it should not be assumed these groups will stay regardless of the quality of their working conditions. For example, the data presented in section 6.2.1 from 'career preference' social workers who have decided to leave because of what they described as poor working conditions suggests that the HSE 'Area A' needs to be proactive in working towards retaining these groups.

Due to its position as the largest employer, many social workers start their career in child protection and welfare in the HSE. The implications for social work education are that courses may need to evaluate whether they are giving explicit or implicit negative messages about students 'earning their stripes' in child protection and welfare, and perpetuating the view that turnover is high and that there is a 'shelf-life' on one's time in child protection and welfare. A question raised by this research for other social work employers is whether they are taking their 'share' of responsibility for the induction of newly-qualified graduates into the workforce. If this is not the case, service users in child protection and welfare will continue to receive services from a higher portion of social workers who are at the 'novice professional' phase of their development (Rønnestad and Skovholt, 2003). These findings indicate the need to explore whether there are similar processes in other professions and to examine how this study can contribute to these literatures.

A further implication of the findings presented in sections 5.3.1 and 5.4.4 for the HSE is that it needs to implement and resource an induction programme for new staff, particularly for newly-qualified graduates who are not ready at their stage of professional development to take on full caseloads with complex cases. This is a core recommendation of the Ryan implementation plan, but it may be 2014 before a concrete policy is published and implemented to address this issue. According to social workers, the absence of such a programme has a serious impact on the quality of service provision, on social workers' health, and on their perceptions of the HSE as a supportive employer - primary reasons given by social workers in the study who had decided they wanted to leave. In doing so, the HSE needs to address the perception, expressed by some social workers in the study, that newly-qualified staff are treated as 'fodder' and 'expendable' by the HSE because they are easily replaced by newly-qualified social workers who are available for work. Regarding these perceptions, and specifically those perceptions of the HSE as a supportive employer, perceived organisational support theory

(Eisenberger *et al.*, 2004) attempts to explain retention in terms of an employee's increased commitment to an employer (increasing the likelihood of their retention) when they perceive that the organisation 'takes care of them' and values their contribution. This theory helped to explain why social workers in this study who did not see the HSE as 'taking care of them' or valuing their contribution wanted to leave. However, those that wanted to stay also described the HSE in this way. Therefore, this study supports Mor Barak *et al.* 's(2006) finding that this theory has limited applicability for researching social workers' retention, and that social workers' commitment to co-workers and service users is more important in explaining their retention.

8.2.6 Social exchanges with colleagues

This study found that social exchanges such as supports, mentoring and friendships with colleagues were amongst the most important factors that helped social workers to stay. Social supports from colleagues play a large part in reducing and buffering social workers from work stresses (Thompson *et al.*, 1996; Collins, 2008). Therefore, a policy that promotes team development through team meetings, team days and other fora that promote team cohesion and peer-supports, which were in operation before and during the period of the study, may return dividends in enhancing social exchanges between co-workers. In the current climate of cutbacks, this study's findings suggest that it will be important for the HSE 'Area A' to protect these spaces.

Current developments in Team 1 and Team 3 to establish peer-support groups, and the established peer supervision group in Team 2, are practices that may further promote social supports within child protection and welfare teams. However, current financial cutbacks may threaten such practices and may have costly long-term implications in terms of social workers' retention. The HSE 'Area A' should actively seek to establish and promote such practices, which are relatively inexpensive to set up and maintain, and have a great potential to influence social workers' retention. These practices have been shown to be more effective supports than other types of interventions such as Employee Assistance Programmes (EAP) which 'teach' coping and stress management skills (Um and Harrison, 1998).

8.2.7 Social exchanges with managers and the quality and frequency of supervision

Social exchange theory emphasises the importance of the exchange of resources between employees and the organisation, and employees and their supervisors. Some of the social exchange resources which social workers in the study described as important, but for the most part lacking, included: praise from supervisors, feedback on their work, an induction programme for new staff, and regular and comprehensive supervision from managers.

Of significant concern to the HSE 'Area A' should be the findings contained in the literature and child abuse inquiries which highlight the link between the quality of social workers' supervision and the care and protection of children at risk (see, for example, Ferguson, 1993; Western Health Board, 1996; Lord Laming, 2003). Social workers in the study highlighted supervision practices which were too administrative in focus, with little emphasis on the supportive and educative functions (Hawkins and Shohet, 1989) and 'formal' supervision was often infrequent and short. There was also with little evidence of supervision practices containing the anxieties of workers (Ruch, 2007) or acknowledging and processing the emotions generated from child protection and welfare work (Morrison, 1990; Harlow, 2004). The study found that the HSE 'Area A' has no formal induction system for new workers, which is concerning given the sizeable number of newly-qualified and younger workers doing this work. Social workers recounted, when they first started working in child protection and welfare, that they were thrown in at the 'deep end' by the HSE 'Area A' - the 'sink or swim' model outlined by Mya and others in section 5.3.1 - with a full caseload and little supervision when they first started working in child protection and welfare. This situation was exacerbated by workers having little practice experience as this was often their first job after qualifying (see section 3.4.1). This practice is at variance with the National Social Work Qualification Board (2004b)*Induction Framework for Newly Qualified and Non-Nationally Qualified Social Workers*and a specific recommendation of the *Kilkenny Incest Investigation* report, which stated:

Regular professional consultation and supervision are also essential for those working in child abuse. Supervision facilitates learning, provides an opportunity to plan and evaluate and support workers. Supervision also promotes good standards of practice to the benefit of the public. *We recommend that newly qualified staff should have additional support and supervision when working in this area*(McGuinness, 1993, p. 113. Emphasis in original).

This research supports the overwhelming thrust of the literature which states that if child protection workers receive regular supportive supervision, which addresses all of the functions of supervision (administration, support and education), from a supervisor whom they perceive to be competent and supportive, that workers are less likely to express intention to leave or actually leave their job (Smith, 2005). The findings of this study also emphasise the importance of supervision as a concept in this literature and its relevance for researching social workers' retention. The decision to use Hawkins and Shohet's (1989) supervision model and the applicability of social exchange theory (Cropanzano and Mitchell, 2005), and supervisor support as concepts for researching social workers' retention, were shown to be beneficial in this study. This Irish study's findings on the importance of social workers' inter-personal relationships with managers and co-workers supports Tham's (2006) conclusion in a Swedish regarding their significance for the retention of social workers. Tham also argued that inter-personal relationships with managers and co-workers are of greater importance for social workers' retention than workloads or job demands.

It is, therefore, unsurprising that some social workers perceived that the HSE 'Area A' was unsupportive in certain areas, particularly in the areas of staff induction (see section 5.4.4), the provision of adequate resources to support practice (see section 5.4.4), and supervision (see section 5.3.1). Social workers did acknowledge that the HSE 'Area A' did provide high salaries, very good employment benefits and job security, and that social work managers were available for consultation and advice. However, social workers' perceived that the HSE 'Area A' as an organisation was more concerned with the successful completion of managerial and bureaucratic tasks (see sections 5.4.1, 5.4.2, and 5.4.4). When these findings are set against a literature which repeatedly highlights the importance of employers supporting employees to cope with the emotional demands of this work, particularly through the provision of nurturing, supportive and regular supervision (Rushton and Nathan, 1996; Gibbs, 2001), it is unsurprising that those who want to leave, in particular, were frustrated with the HSE as an employer in the areas identified above. This data suggests that the HSE 'Area A' may need to review whether it is in compliance with national and organisational supervision policies, and recommendations on supervision from child abuse inquiries (McGuinness, 1993). This study's findings indicate that investment by the HSE 'Area A' in quality and frequent professional supervision should be a core part of its retention policy. Social workers in the study were often critical of their supervisors' managerial and supervisory skills and leadership qualities (see section 5.3.1). Therefore, the HSE should consider the development of training and leadership skills training and mentoring systems for its managers and supervisors. Investment in supervision is likely to result in the improvement of the quality of service provision to children and families, social workers' morale, and social workers' perceptions of the HSE 'Area A' as a supportive employer and the culture of the organisation.

8.2.8 Family and life-work factors

Finally, for social workers that had left child protection and welfare in the HSE 'Area A', most of the factors that influenced their decisions were 'unavoidable', usually relating to personal factors such as moving closer to family home and/or having children. For social workers that were still employed in child protection and welfare in the HSE 'Area A', life-work factors were also a crucial part of the decision-making process, particularly in some of the more rural teams in terms of social workers' decisions to stay. Working in a particular geographical area and the degree of their embeddedness within their organisation and the local community as defined by job embeddedness theory (Holtom *et al.*, 2006), contributed to some social workers' decisions to stay.

8.3 Limitations of the study

A strength of the study was the specific focus on the experiences of social workers and senior social work practitioners directly involved in child protection and welfare social work in one HSE area. However, this in-depth and comprehensive analysis of one HSE area somewhat limits the generalisability of the findings to other HSE areas. Despite this, when contrasted with recent publications and an investigative documentary concerning issues at a national level in child protection and welfare (Buckley *et al.*, 2008; Burns and Lynch, 2008; RTÉ, 2008c; Lynch and Burns, 2012), there are many themes and issues raised in this study of the HSE 'Area A' that are also shared by other HSE areas (quality of supervision, administrative burdens, high caseloads, and so on). Also, service users, managers and other key stakeholders were not interviewed in the study (see section 3.4.1 for rationale behind these decisions).

The study adopted two methods of data collection: semi-structured interviews and the collection of statistical data to establish turnover rates. My use of semi-structured interviews was productive in that I was able to access the type of data that addressed the research questions, and they afforded participants privacy and a space to discuss personal and sensitive data in a 'safe' environment. On reflection, while I had a clear rationale for excluding focus groups, if I were to repeat the study, I would consider the use of focus groups as a supplementary data collection method. Focus groups could offer a better understanding of how the process of interaction between social workers produces or [re]produces professional identity and influences their retention.

The sampling strategy and characteristics of interview participants may have led to some limitations. The size of the 'leavers' sample was small and as a result the conclusions from this chapter are tentative. However, this data contributes to our understanding of how social workers make decisions to leave and affirms the need for further research in this area with a bigger sample of social workers. The decision not to specifically sample for participants from minority ethnic communities, gay and lesbian workers, and social workers with disabilities, may have limited the diversity of experiences within the sample. However, the literature review did not indicate that such a revised sample would have contributed further to the study. The sampling strategy also meant that comparisons could not be made with other professionals and social work managers in child protection and welfare, nor with social workers in other practice settings.

Finally, by basing the study in one period of time, albeit over a 22-month duration, certain factors were present that may have influenced the findings. For example, the HSE employment recruitment practices during this period appear to have limited social workers' turnover. However, studies are inevitably set within a specific temporal context with a particular set of political, social and economic factors, and where appropriate, the study indicated how specific contextual factors impacted on the interpretation of the findings.

8.4 Concluding comments

Since the publication of the *Kilkenny Incest Investigation* report (McGuinness, 1993),significant progress has been made by the Irish government in developing services and addressing the systemic, procedural and policy developments that were required to improve the State's response to children in need. Some near recent Irish research has argued that four out of five children in Ireland are now safer, healthier, happier and educated to a higher standard than in previous decades (Office of the Minister for Children, 2006; Nolan, 2008). However, despite these improvements, there is much that needs to be done to adequately protect and enhance the welfare of *all* children. The ability of the State to develop and resource social policies to address the pressing needs of children at the margins of society is, in the present deteriorating economic climate, hampered by the government's low-tax/low-spend model of economic development. This model, combined with the current cuts to spending and staffing levels in the public sector may place these children at increased risk due to reductions in service delivery in the areas of health, social services, and education. This is despite the findings of a report by the Organisation for Economic Co-operation and Development (OECD) on the public service which found that 'public spending is lower in proportion to the size of the economy than it was a decade ago' (O'Toole, 2008, p. 1).

For those that provide these services, the *Kilkenny Incest Investigation* report provides a salutary reminder of the potential negative impact on those who undertake this work, and argues for the need to support and protect these employees:

> The nature of intervention in these cases is such that it often causes workers to become isolated, vulnerable and stressed. Employing agencies need to have an understanding of the on-going complexities of the work and should provide appropriate support systems and structures to ensure that both clients' needs are met and that workers do not become casualties (McGuinness, 1993, pp. 113-114).

The nature of this work, as outlined in the McGuinness quotation, suggests a need for supports for child protection and welfare social workers over and above what the HSE provides for its general workforce. This is not to say that social workers practising in other settings don't require additional supports; however, the absence or low quality of such supports places child protection and welfare social workers at an unnecessarily increased risk of stress and isolation, and they continue to be left in professionally vulnerable positions. Further inaction by the HSE 'Area A' may mean that social workers who do child protection and welfare work will continue to be at risk of becoming 'casualties' and it may become harder to retain them and/or for them to view being a child protection and welfare social worker as a positive career choice.

On a positive note, in November 2008, government policy in this area took a strategic change of direction when the Health and Safety Authority announced that in addition to the usual focus on the safety elements of health and safety organisations are now advised to give 'equal focus to worker health and well-being' (Health and Safety Authority, 2008a, p. 1). One aspect of this new strategy highlights how workers' mental health can be affected by workplace stress. This strategy could inform HSE practice in meeting its responsibilities to employees, including the development of guidance and codes of practice on managing stress, initiatives in the area of bullying, minimising the risk of violence to staff, amongst other recommendations (Health and Safety Authority, 2008b). A further positive development has been the addition of 270 extra social work posts in child protection and welfare; however, the number of posts in child protection and welfare in Ireland by population is low compared to some other countries (Healy and Oltedal, 2010).

The 'story' of social workers' retention is a complicated one and approaches to address it, in addition to specific factors highlighted in this and previous chapters should be developed within the broader context of social work careers. High levels of retention of social workers may not indicate that social workers are satisfied with their conditions of employment and/or working to their full potential. This research highlights the many organisational issues in child protection and welfare in need of attention, but it also highlights the many positive aspects of social workers' satisfaction in their work and the relatively high levels of their retention in this area of work.

This book has argued that retaining social workers in child protection and welfare posts is an important goal in itself, but one which also has a direct impact on the quality of social work services provided to children and their families, and the morale of those who do this work. Organisational and government policies, in particular, need to develop to support and resource those who undertake this valuable work so that skilled and experienced workers can be retained to continue to make a positive difference in the lives of children and families. This research found that the situation in the HSE 'Area A' is not as negative as is

236

suggested in the literature: many social workers enjoyed this work, a good proportion wanted to stay, those who left did so for largely unavoidable reasons, and recent or near recent initiatives by the HSE and Government highlight differences between Ireland and other countries where in Ireland the salary of social workers' has improved, public sector employment conditions are still relatively strong, a career progression option called the senior social work practitioner post has been introduced and team development initiatives are still supported by the HSE 'Area A'. Another positive from this study is that it found that it is possible to improve the retention of social workers through some relatively straightforward organisational changes, in particular the provision of regular and supportive supervision and mechanisms to foster social exchanges and contact between co-workers. It is hoped that this research provides sufficient evidence to encourage the new Child and Families Support Services Agency to implement changes that will improve the current unsatisfactory employment conditions of many child protection and welfare social workers, and to give greater priority to retaining social workers within child protection and welfare.

References

All Party Oireachtas Committee on the Constitution (1996) *Report of the Constitution Review Group* [Online], Dublin, Stationery Office, Available from: http://www.constitution.ie/reports/crg.pdf [Accessed: 1st February 2005].

Allen, D. G. (2004) 'Explaining the Link Between Turnover Intentions and turnover: The Roles of Risk, Personality, and Intentions-Behaviour Linkages', in Griffeth, R. and Hom, P. (eds.), *Innovative Theory and Empirical Research in Employee Turnover*, Connecticut, Information Age Publishing.

American Public Human Services Association (2001) *Report from the Child Welfare Workforce Survey: State and County Data and Findings*, Washington, American Public Human Services Association.

American Public Human Services Association (2005) *Report From The 2004 Child Welfare Workforce Survey*, Washington, American Public Human Services Association.

Andalo, D. (2006) *What can a newly qualified social worker do?* [Online], The Guardian, Available from:
http://www.guardian.co.uk/society/2006/jul/26/guardiansocietysupplement4 [Accessed: 30th May 2008].

Anderson, D. G. (2000) 'Coping Strategies and Burnout Among Veteran Child Protection Workers', *Child Abuse and Neglect*, 24(6), pp. 839-848.

Audit Commission (2002) *Recruitment and Retention: A Public Service Workforce for the twenty-first century*, London, Audit Commission.

Balfour, D. L. and Neff, D. M. (1993) 'Predicting and Managing Humans in Human Service Agencies: A Case Study of an Organisation in Crisis', *Public-Personnel Management*, 22(3), pp. 63-75.

Barber, J. E. (1991) *Beyond Casework*, Basingstoke, Macmillan Press.

BBC (2008) *What happened to Baby P?* [Online], London, BBC, Available from: http://www.bbc.co.uk/programmes/b00fw6s6 [Accessed: 17th November 2008].

Beck, U. (1992) *Risk society: towards a new modernity*, Sheffield, Sheffield Region Centre for Science and Technology.

Beck, U. (2000) *The Brave New World of Work*, Cambridge, Polity Press.

Begg, D. (2005) *Statement from Congress General Secretary David Begg, on Irish Ferries demonstration: Displacement of Jobs in the Irish Economy* [Online], Irish Congress of Trade Unions, Available from:
http://www.ictu.ie/html/news/releases/p031105.htm
[Accessed: 12th November 2005].

Blanchflower, D. G. and Oswald, A. (1999) *Well-being, Insecurity and the Decline of American Job Satisfaction* [Online], Available from:
http://www.dartmouth.edu/~blnchflr/papers/jobsat.pdf [Accessed: 15/1/'04].

Bourdieu, P. (1998) *Acts of Resistance: Against the New Myths of Our Time*, Oxford, Polity Press and the New Press.

Bowling, A. (2005) *Measuring Health: A Review of Quality of Life Measurement Scales(3rd edition)*, Milton Keynes, Open University Press.

Bryman, A. (2001) *Social research Methods*, Oxford, Oxford University Press.

Bryman, A. (2004) *Social research Methods(2nd Edition)*, Oxford, Oxford University Press.

Bryman, A. and Burgess, R. G. (eds) (1999) *Qualitative Research - Volume II*, London, Sage.

Buckley, H. (2002) *Child Protection and Welfare: Innovations and Interventions*, Dublin, IPA.

Buckley, H. (2005) 'Reviewing children first: some considerations', *Irish Journal of Family Law*, 3, pp. 2-8.

Buckley, H. (2008) 'Heading for collision? Managerialism, social science, and the Irish child protection system', in Burns, K. and Lynch, D. (eds.), *Child Protection and Welfare Social Work: Contemporary Themes and Practice Perspectives*, Dublin, A. & A. Farmar.

Buckley, H., Skehill, C. and O'Sullivan, E. (1997) *Child Protection Practices in Ireland: A Case Study*, Dublin, Oak Tree Press.

Buckley, H., Whelan, S., Carr, N. and Murphy, C. (2008) *Service users' perceptions of the Irish Child Protection System*, Dublin, The Stationery Office.

Burns, K. and Lynch, D. (eds) (2008) *Child Protection and Welfare Social Work: Contemporary Themes and Practice Perspectives*, Dublin, A. & A. Farmar.

Burns, K. and Lynch, D. (2012) 'Politics, democracy and protecting children', in Lynch, D. and Burns, K. (eds.), *Children's Rights and Child Protection: Critical Times, Critical Issues in Ireland*, Manchester, Manchester University Press.

Burns, K. and Murray, B. (2003) 'Child protection in crisis: growing pains from a rapid period of expansion or back pain from the increased burden?', *Irish Social Worker*, 21(1-2), pp. 13-16.

Campion, M. A., Mumford, T. V., Morgeson, F. P. and Nahrgang, J. D. (2005) 'Work redesign: eight obstacles and opportunities', *Human Resource Management*, 44(4), pp. 367-390.

Caringi, J. C., Strolin-Goltzman, J., Lawson, H. A., McCarthy, M., Briar-Lawson, K. and Claiborne, N. (2008) 'Child Welfare Design Teams: An Intervention to Improve Workforce Retention and Facilitate Organizational Development', *Research on Social Work Practice*, Advance Online Copy.

Carpenter, J., Schneider, J., Brandon, T. and Wooff, D. (2003) 'Working in multidisciplinary community mental health teams: the impact on social workers and health professionals of integrated mental health care', *British Journal of Social Work*, 33, pp. 1081-1103.

Cassell, C. and Symon, G. (eds) (1994) *Qualitative methods in Organizational Research*, London, Sage.

Central Statistics Office (2008) *Vital Statistics: Third Quarter 2007*, Dublin, Stationery Office.

Charmaz, K. (2006) *Constructing Grounded Theory: A Practical Guide Through Qualitative Analysis*, London, Sage.

Child Care Information Unit (2007) *HSE South 2006 Datasets Final - Personal Communication*, Skibbereen, Health Service Executive South.

Child Welfare League of America (2008) *Children's Legislative Agenda* [Online], CWLA, Available from: http://www.cwla.org/advocacy/2008legagenda.pdf [Accessed: 14th March 2008].

Collins, S. (2008) 'Statutory social workers: stress, job satisfaction, coping, social support and individual differences', *British Journal of Social Work*, 38, pp. 1173-1193.

Colton, M. and Roberts, S. (2007) 'Factors that contribute to high turnover among residential child care staff', *Child and Family Social Work*, 12, pp. 133-142.

Committee on the Rights of the Child (1998) *Consideration of Reports Submitted by States Parties Under Article 44 of the Convention. Concluding observations of the committee on the rights of the child* [Online], United Nations, Available from: http://www.hri.ca/fortherecord1998/documentation/tbodies/crc-c-15-add85.htm [Accessed: 15th July 2005].

Committee on the Rights of the Child (2006) *Consideration of Reports Submitted by States Parties Under Article 44 of the Convention on the Rights of the Child. Concluding Observations: Ireland* [Online], Geneva, United Nations, Available from: http://www.childrensrights.ie/pubs/IRLCONCOBS.pdf [Accessed: 17th February 2008].

Cropanzano, R. and Mitchell, M. S. (2005) 'Social exchange theory: An interdisciplinary review', *Journal of Management*, 31(6), pp. 874-900.

Daly, M. (2004) *Families and Family Life in Ireland: Challenges for the Future*, Dublin, Department of Social & Family Affairs.

Davies, R. (1998) *Stress in Social Work*, London, Jessica Kingsley Publishers.

Department of Children and Youth Affairs (2011) *Children First: National Guidance for the Protection and Welfare of Children*, Dublin, Department of Children and Youth Affairs.

Department of Education and Science (2008) *Schedule to Circular letter: - Pay 0011/2008 (Revised Salary Scales)* [Online], Available from: http://www.education.ie/servlet/blobservlet/cl0011_2008_scales.doc [Accessed: 30th May 2008].

240

Department of Finance (2008) *Circular 5/2008: Revision of pay of Civil Servants. Application of increases under Section 27.17 of Towards 2016* [Online], Dublin, Department of Finance, Available from: http://www.finance.gov.ie/documents/circulars/circulars2008/circ5of2008.pdf [Accessed: 16th June 2008].

Department of Health (1996) *Report of the inquiry into the operation of Madonna House*, Dublin, Government Publications.

Department of Health and Children (1999) *Children First: National Guidelines for the Protection and Welfare of Children*, Dublin, Stationery Office.

Department of Health and Children (2001) *Report of the Working Group on Foster Care. Foster Care - A Child Centred Partnership*, Dublin, Stationery Office.

Department of Health and Children (2008) *Department of Health and Children Consolidated Salary Scales effective from 1st March, 2008* [Online], Dublin, Department of Health and Children, Available from: http://www.dohc.ie/publications/pdf/salary_scale_dec06.pdf?direct=1 [Accessed: 30th May 2008].

Department of Justice Equality and Law Reform (2008) *Human Resources and Industrial Relations: Pay* [Online], Available from: http://www.justice.ie/en/JELR/Pay Rates 2008.xls/Files/Pay Rates 2008.xls [Accessed: 30th May 2008].

Dickinson, N. S. and Perry, R. (2002) 'Factors Influencing the Retention of Specially Educated Public Child Welfare Workers', *The Journal of Health and Social Policy*, 15(3/4), pp. 89-103.

Dill, K. (2007) 'Impact of stressors on front-line child welfare supervisors', *The Clinical Supervisor*, 26(1/2), pp. 177-193.

Dollard, M. F., Winefield, H. R. and Winefield, A. H. (2001) *Occupational Strain and Efficacy in Human Service Workers*, Norwell, Kluwer Academic Publishers.

Donnelly, D. P. and Quirin, J. J. (2006) 'An extension of Lee and Mitchell's unfolding model of voluntary turnover', *Journal of Organizational behaviour*, 27, pp. 59-77.

Drake, B. and Yadama, G. N. (1996) 'A structural equation model of burnout and job exit among child protection services workers', *Social Work Research*, 20(3), pp. 179-187.

Dressel, P. (1984) *The Service Trap: From Altruism to Dirty Work*, Charles C Thomas.

Eborall, C. and Garmeson, K. (2001) *Desk research on Recruitment and Retention in Social Care and Social Work*, London, Business and Industrial Market Research.

Eisenberger, R., Jones, J. R., Aselage, J. and Sucharski, I. L. (2004) 'Perceived organizational support', in Coyle-Shapiro, J. A. M., Shore, L. M. and Taylor, M. S. (eds.), *The Employment Relationship*, Oxford, Oxford University Press.

Eisenberger, R., Stinglhamber, F., Vandenberghe, C., Sucharski, I. L. and Rhoades, L. (2002) 'Perceived Supervisor Support: Contributions to Perceived Organizational Support and Employee Retention', *Journal of Applied Psychology*, 87(3), pp. 565-573.

Ellet, A. J. (2007) 'Linking Self-Efficacy Beliefs to Employee Retention in Child Welfare: Implications for Practice, Theory and Research', *Journal of Evidence Based Social Work*, 4(3/4), pp. 39-68.

Ellet, A. J. and Ellet, C. D. (2003) 'A study of personal and organizational factors contributing to employee retention and turnover in child welfare in Georgia. Presentation to Georgia DHR/DFCS', 2008(1st February 2008).

Ellet, A. J., Ellis, J. I., Westbrook, T. M. and Dews, D. (2006) 'A qualitative study of 369 child welfare professionals' perspectives about factors contributing to employee retention and turnover', *Children and Youth Services Review*, 29(2), pp. 264-281.

European Foundation for the Improvement of Living and Working Conditions (2005) *Work-related stress*, Dublin, European Foundation for the Improvement of Living and Working Conditions.

Ferguson, H. (1993) 'Child Abuse Inquiries and the Report of the Kilkenny Incest Investigation: A Critical Analysis', *Administration*, 41(4), pp. 385-410.

Ferguson, H. (2001) 'Promoting child protection, welfare and healing: the case for developing best practice', *Child and Family Social Work*, 6, pp. 1-12.

Ferguson, H. (2003) *Time to focus on public relations* [Online], Society Guardian, Available from: http://societyguardian.co.uk [Accessed: 12/9/03].

Ferguson, H. (2004) *Protecting Children in Time: Child Abuse, Child Protection and the Consequences of Modernity*, London, Palgrave Macmillan.

Ferguson, H. (2005) 'Working with violence, the emotions and the Psycho-social dynamics of child protection: reflections on the Victoria Climbié case', *Social Work Education*, 24(7), pp. 781-795.

Ferguson, H. and O'Reilly, M. (2001) *Keeping Children Safe: Child Abuse, Child Protection and the Promotion of Welfare*, Dublin, A. & A. Farmar.

Figley, C. R. (1995) *Compassion Fatigue: Coping with secondary traumatic stress disorder in those who treat the traumatized*, New York, Brunner-Routledge.

Figley, C. R. (2002) *Treating Compassion Fatigue*, New York, Brunner-Routledge.

Fitzgerald, F. (2011) *Keynote Conference Paper (28th October)*, Univeristy College Cork, Biennial Child Protection and Welfare Social Work Conference.

Flick, U. (2006) *An Introduction to Qualitative Research(3rd Edition)*, London, Sage.

Freund, A. (2005) 'Commitment and Job Satisfaction as Predictors of turnover Intentions Among Child Welfare Workers', *Administration in Social Work*, 29(2), pp. 5-21.

Gibbons, C. (2007) *Judiciary's ultimate duty to children* [Online], Dublin, The Irish Times, Available from: http://www.ireland.com/newspaper/opinion/2007/0710/1183751751071.htm [Accessed: 9th June 2008].

Gibbs, J. A. (2001) 'Maintaining front-line workers in child protection: A case for refocusing supervision', *Child Abuse Review*, 10, pp. 323-335.

Gibbs, J. A. and Keating, T. P. (1999) *Recruitment and Retention of Child Protection Workers in Rural Victoria*, Albury/Wodonga, La Trobe University.

Gibson, F., McGrath, A. and Reid, N. (1989) 'Occupational stress in social work', *British Journal of Social Work*, 19(1), pp. 1-18.

Gilligan, R. (2000) 'The key role of social workers in promoting the well-being of children in state care - a neglected dimension of reforming policies', *Children and Society*, 14, pp. 267-276.

Gilligan, R. (2004) 'Promoting resilience in child and family social work: Issues for social work practice, education and policy', *Social Work Education*, 23(1), pp. 93-104.

Glasberg, A. L., Eriksson, S. and Norberg, A. (2007) 'Burnout and 'stress of conscience' among healthcare personnel', *Journal of Advanced Nursing*, 57(4), pp. 392-403.

Glaser, B. G. (1978) *Theoretical sensitivity*, Mill Valley, CA, The Sociology Press.

Glaser, B. G. and Strauss, A. L. (1967) *The Discovery of Grounded Theory: Strategies for Qualitative Research*, Chicago, Aldine de Gruyter.

Government of Ireland (1970) *Reformatory and industrial schools systems report (The Kennedy Report)*, Dublin, Stationery Office.

Government of Ireland (2000) *The National Children's Strategy. Our Children - Their Lives*, Dublin, Stationery Office.

Hackman, J. R., Wageman, R., Ruddy, T. M. and Ray, C. L. (2000) 'Team Effectiveness in Theory and Practice', in Cooper, C. L. and Locke, E. A. (eds.), *Industrial and Organisational Psychology: Linking Theory and Practice*, Oxford, Blackwell.

Hackman, R. J. and Oldham, G. R. (1980) *Work redesign*, London, Addison-Wesley.

Harlow, E. (2003) 'New Managerialism, Social Service Departments and Social Work Practice Today', *Practice*, 15(2), pp. 29-44.

Harlow, E. (2004) 'Why don't women want to be social workers anymore? New managerialism, postfeminism and the shortage of social workers in social services departments in England and Wales', *European Journal of Social Work*, 7(2), pp. 167-179.

Hawkins, P. and Shohet, R. (1989) *Supervision in the Helping Professions: An Individual, Group and Organizational Approach*, Milton Keynes, Open University Press.

Health and Safety Authority (2008a) *Minister Kelleher calls for greater focus on occupational illness* [Online], Dublin, Health and Safety Authority, Available from:
http://www.hsa.ie/eng/News_and_Events/Press_Releases_2008/Minister_Kelle her_calls_for_greater_focus_on_occupational_illness.html [Accessed: 5th November 2008].

Health and Safety Authority (2008b) *Workplace health and well-being strategy: report of expert group*, Dublin, Health and Safety Authority.

Health Service Executive (2003) *Southern Health Board Annual Report 2003* [Online], Southern Health Board, Available from: http://www.shb.ie [Accessed: 7th July 2005].

Health Service Executive (2006a) *Corporate Safety Statement - October 2006*, Dublin, Health Service Executive.

Health Service Executive (2006b) *Transformation Programme 2007-2010* [Online], Dublin, Health Service Executive, Available from:
http://www.hse.ie/eng/Publications/Hospitals/HSE_Publications/Transformatio n_Programme_2007_-_2010.pdf [Accessed: 2nd July 2008].

Health Service Executive (2007a) *An Introduction to the HSE* [Online], Dublin, Health Service Executive, Available from: http://www.hse.ie/eng/Publications/corporate/An_Introduction_to_the_HSE.pd f [Accessed: 16th June 2008].

Health Service Executive (2007b) *Parents Who Listen, Protect* [Online], Dublin, Health Service Executive, Available from: http://www.hse.ie/eng/publications/Children_and_young_people/parents_who_ listen_protect_English_.pdf [Accessed: 16th June 2008].

Health Service Executive (2008a) *HSE South Review of Adequacy of Child And Family Services 2005* [Online], Dublin, Health Service Executive, Available from:
http://www.hse.ie/eng/Publications/Children_and_Young_People/Review_of_ Adequacy_of_Child_and_Family_Services_2005.html [Accessed: 21st April 2008].

Health Service Executive (2008b) *HSE staff figures and information* [Online], Dublin, Health Service Executive, Available from:
http://www.hse.ie/eng/Factfile/HSE_Facts/HSE_Staff_Figures_and_informatio n/ [Accessed: 23rd December 2008].

Health Service Executive (2008c) *Map of Local Health Offices and HSE Areas* [Online], Dublin, Health Service Executive, Available from:
http://www.hse.ie/eng/About_the_HSE/Map_of_Local_Health_Offices_and_H SE_Areas.pdf [Accessed: 16th June 2008].

244

Health Service Executive (2008d) *Review of Adequacy of Child and Family Services 2005 Health Services Executive Dublin North East* [Online], Dublin, Health Service Executive, Available from:
http://www.hse.ie/eng/Publications/Children_and_Young_People/Review_of_Adequacy_of_Child_and_Family_Services_2005.html [Accessed: 21st April 2008].

Health Service Executive (2008e) *Review of Adequacy of Child Care and Family Support Services 2005 HSE West - Clare, Limerick and North Tipperary* [Online], Dublin, Health Service Executive, Available from:
http://www.hse.ie/eng/Publications/Children_and_Young_People/Review_of_Adequacy_of_Child_and_Family_Services_2005.html [Accessed: 21st April 2008].

Health Service Executive (2008f) *Review of Adequacy of Services for Children & Families HSE Dublin Mid Leinster* [Online], Dublin, Health Service Executive, Available from:
http://www.hse.ie/eng/Publications/Children_and_Young_People/Review_of_Adequacy_of_Child_and_Family_Services_2005.html [Accessed: 21st April 2008].

Health Service Executive (2009) *HSE Child Welfare and Protection Social Work Departments Business Processes. Report of the NCCIS Business Process Standardisation Project October 2009*, Dublin, Health Service Executive.

Health Service Executive (2012) *Review of Adequacy for HSE Children and Families Services 2010*, Dublin, Health Service Executive.

Health Service Executive South (2005) *Particulars of Office. Post of Senior Social Work Practitioner*, Cork, Health Service Executive South.

Health Service Executive South (2007) *Child Care Budget 2000-2007*, Cork, Health Service Executive.

Healy, K. and Meagher, G. (2007) 'Social Workers' Preparation for Child Protection: Revisiting the Question of Specialisation', *Australian Social Work*, 60(3), pp. 321-335.

Healy, K., Meagher, G. and Cullin, J. (2009) 'Retaining novices to become expert child protection practitioners: Creating career pathways in direct practice', *British Journal of Social Work*, 39(2), pp. 299-317.

Healy, K. and Oltedal, S. (2010) 'An Institutional Comparison of Child Protection Systems in Australia and Norway Focused on Workforce Retention', *Journal of Social Policy*(39), p. 2.

Hodgkin (2002) 'Competing demands, competing solutions, differing constructions of the problem of recruitment and retention of frontline rural child protection staff', *Australian Social Work*, 55(3), pp. 193-203.

Holtom, B. C., Lee, T. W. and Tidd, S. T. (2002) 'The Relationship Between Status Congruence and Work-Related Attitudes and Behaviours', *Journal of Applied Psychology*, 87(5), pp. 903-915.

Holtom, B. C., Mitchell, T. R. and Lee, T. W. (2006) 'Increasing human and social capital by applying job embeddedness theory', *Organizational Dynamics*, 35(5), pp. 316-331.

Hom, P. W. and Griffeth, R. W. (1995) *Employee Turnover*, Ohio, South-Western College Publishing.

Horwath, J. and Bishop, B. (2001) *Child Neglect Is my view your view? Working with cases of child neglect in the North Eastern Health Board*, Dunshaughlin, North Eastern Health Board and University of Sheffield.

Houses of the Oireachtas (1996) *Dáil Debates, Dáil Éireann - Volume 464 - 1st May 1996*, Dublin, Oireachtas.

Houses of the Oireachtas (2000) *Dáil Debates, Dáil Éireann - Volume 522 - 27th June 2000*, Dublin, Oireachtas.

Houses of the Oireachtas (2003a) *Dáil Debates, Dáil Éireann - Volume 563 - 11th March 2003*, Dublin, Oireachtas.

Houses of the Oireachtas (2003b) *Dáil Debates, Dáil Éireann - Volume 574 - 19th November 2003*, Dublin, Oireachtas.

Houses of the Oireachtas (2008) *Dáil Debates, Dáil Éireann - Volume 653 No. 2 - 29th April 2008* [Online], Dublin, Oireachtas, Available from: http://debates.oireachtas.ie/DDebate.aspx?F=DAL20080429.XML&Dail=30& Ex=All&Page=1 [Accessed: 23rd May 2008].

Houston, M. (2007) 'Psychological problems 'linked to boom'', *The Irish Times*, Dublin.

Howe, D. (1992) 'Child abuse and the bureaucratisation of social work', *The Sociological Review*, 14(3), pp. 491-508.

Hughes, L. and Pengelly, P. (1997) *Staff Supervision in a Turbulent Environment: Managing Process and Task in Front-Line Supervision*, London, Jessica Kingsley Publishers.

IMPACT (2006) *Discussion paper on social work structures July 2006*, Dublin, IMPACT - National Social Work and Community Workers Vocational Group.

Jacquet, S. E., Clark, S. J., Morazes, J. L. and Withers, R. (2007) 'The role of supervision in the retention of public child welfare workers', *Journal of Public Child Welfare*, 1(3), pp. 27-54.

Jayaratne, S. and Chess, W. A. (1984) 'Job satisfaction, burnout and turnover: a national study', *Social Work*, 29, pp. 448-453.

Jones, L. (2002) 'A follow-up of a title IV-E program's graduates' retention rates in a public child welfare agency', *Journal of Health & Social Policy*, 15(3/4), pp. 39-52.

Jordan, B. and Jordan, C. (2000) *Social Work and the Third Way: Tough Love as Social Policy*, London, Sage.

Judge, T. A. and Church, A. H. (2000) 'Job Satisfaction: Research and Practice', in Cooper, C. L. and Locke, E. A. (eds.), *Industrial and Organizational Psychology: Linking theory and practice*, Oxford, Blackwell.

Karasek, R. A. and Theorell, T. (1990) *Healthy Work: Stress, Productivity, and the Reconstruction of Working Life*, New York, Basic Books.

Kearney, N. and Skehill, C. (2005) *Social work in Ireland: historical perspectives*, Dublin, Institute of Public Administration.

Kemp, T. (2008) 'Questioning quality: a critical analysis of the development and implementation of the 'quality agenda' and its impact on child protection social work practice in Ireland', in Burns, K. and Lynch, D. (eds.), *Child Protection and Welfare Social Work: Contemporary Themes and Practice Perspectives*, Dublin, A. & A. Farmar.

Koeske, G. F. and Kirk, S. A. (1995) 'The effects of characteristics of human service workers on subsequent morale and turnover', *Administration in Social Work*, 19(1), pp. 15-31.

Koeske, G. F. and Koeske, R. D. (1989) 'Work Load and Burnout: Can Social Support and Perceived Accomplishment Help?', *Social Work*, pp. 243-248.

Kvale, S. (1996) *InterViews: An Introduction to Qualitative Research Interviewing*, California, Sage.

Landsman, M. J. (2001) 'Commitment in public child welfare', *Social Service Review*, 3, pp. 386-419.

Lavan, A. (1998) 'Social work in Ireland', in Shardlow, S. and Payne, M. (eds.), *Contemporary Issues in Social Work: Western Europe*, Hants, Arena.

Lawrence, A. (2004) *Principles of Child Protection: Management and Practice*, Milton Keynes, Open University Press.

Lee, J., Forster, M. and Rehner, T. (2011) 'The retention of public child welfare workers: The roles of professional organizational culture and coping strategies', *Children and Youth Services Review*, 33(1), pp. 102-109.

Lee, T. W. (1999) *Using qualitative methods in organizational research*, California, Sage.

Lee, T. W. and Mitchell, T. R. (1994) 'An alternative approach: the unfolding model of voluntary employee turnover', *Academy of Management Review*, 19, pp. 51-89.

Lewis, J. (2003) 'Design Issues', in Ritchie, J. and Lewis, J. (eds.), *Qualitative research Practice: A Guide for Social Science Students and Researchers*, London, Sage.

Local Authority Workforce Intelligence Group (2006) *Social Care Workforce Survey 2005 - Adult, Children and Young People* [Online], Local Government Analysis and Research, Available from: http://lgar.local.gov.uk/lgv/core/page.do?pageId=12015&path=10854.10759&activeId=30140 [Accessed: 13th February 2008].

Lonne, R. L. (2003) 'Social workers and human service professionals', in Dollard, M. F., Winefield, A. H. and Winefield, H. R. (eds.), *Occupational Stress in the Service Professions*, London, Taylor and Francis.

Lord Laming (2003) *The Victoria Climbié Inquiry*, London, Stationery Office.

Loughran, H. (2000) 'Social Work into the Future', *Irish Journal of Social Work Research*, 2(2), pp. 5-6.

Lynch, D. and Burns, K. (eds) (2012) *Children's Rights and Child Protection: Critical Times, Critical Issues in Ireland*, Manchester, Manchester University Press.

Maslach, C. (1982) *Burnout. The Cost of Caring*, New Jersey, Prentice-Hall.

Maslach, C. (1993) 'Burnout: A multidimensional perspective', in Schaufeli, W. B., Maslach, C. and Marek, T. (eds.), *Professional Burnout: Recent Developments in Theory and Research*, Washington, DC, Taylor and Francis.

Maslach, C., Schaufeli, W. B. and Leiter, M. P. (2001) 'Job Burnout', *Annual Review of Psychology*, 52, pp. 397-422.

Mason, J. (2002a) 'Qualitative Interviewing: Asking, listening and interpreting', in May, T. (ed.), *Qualitative Research in Action*, London, Sage.

Mason, J. (2002b) *Qualitative Researching(2nd Edition)*, London, Sage.

McEvoy, O. and Smith, M. (2011) *Listen to Our Voices! Hearing Children and Young People Living in the Care of the State. Report of a Consultation Process*, Dublin, Government Publications.

McGrath, K. (2001) 'Crisis in Health Board Child Protection Services - Time to tell the truth', *Irish Social Worker*, 19(2-3), p. 3.

McGuinness, C. (1993) *Kilkenny Incest Investigation: Report Presented to Mr. Brendan Howlin T.D. Minister for Health*, Dublin, Stationery Office.

Mental Health Commission (2004) *Mental Health Commission Strategic Plan 2004-2005*, Dublin, Mental Health Commission.

Miller, O. J. (1996) *Employee Turnover in the Public Sector*, New York and London, Garland.

Millet, C. T., Johnson, S. J., Cooper, C. L., Donald, I. J., Cartwright, S. and Taylor, P. J. (2005) 'Britain's most stressful occupations and the role of emotional labour', *BPS Occupational Psychology Conference*, Warwick.

Mobley, W. H. (1982) *Employee Turnover: Causes, Consequences, and Control*, Reading Mass., Addison-Wesley.

Moore, C. (1995) *Betrayal of Trust: The Father Brendan Smyth Affair and the Catholic Church*, Dublin, Marino Books.

Mor Barak, M. E., Levin, A., Nissly, J. A. and Lane, C. J. (2006) 'Why do they leave? Modelling child welfare workers' turnover intentions', *Children and Youth Services Review*, 28, pp. 548-577.

Mor Barak, M. E., Nissly, J. A. and Levin, A. (2001) 'Antecedents to retention and turnover among child welfare, social work, and other human service employees: What can we learn from past research? A review and metanalysis', *Social Service Review*, 75(4), pp. 625-661.

Morgeson, F. P. and Campion, M. A. (2003) 'Work Design', in Freedheim, D. K., Weiner, I. B., Velicer, W. F., Schinka, J. A. and Lerner, R. M. (eds.), *Handbook of Psychology*, New York, John Wiley and Sons.

Morrel, K., Loan-Clarke, J. and Wilkinson, A. (2001) 'Unweaving leaving: the use of models in the management of employee turnover', *International Journal of Management Reviews*, 3(3), pp. 219-244.

Morris, J. (2005) 'For the Children: Accounting for Careers in Child Protective Services', *Journal of Sociology and Social Welfare*, XXXII(2), pp. 131-145.

Morrison, T. (1990) 'The emotional effects of child protection on the worker', *Practice*, 4(4), pp. 253-271.

Morrison, T. (1993) *Staff Supervision in Social Care*, London, Longman.

Morrison, T. (1996) 'Partnership and collaboration: Rhetoric and reality', *Child Abuse and Neglect*, 20(2), pp. 127-140.

Murphy, F. D., Buckley, H. and Joyce, L. (2005) *The Ferns Report: Presented to the Minister for Health and Children*, Dublin, Stationery Office.

Murray, C. J. (2006) *The Supreme Court: In the Matter of the Constitution and in the Matter of N. between N. and N. and the Health Service Executive and an Bord Uchtala* [Online], Dublin, Courts, Available from: http://www.courts.ie/Judgments.nsf/597645521f07ac9a80256ef30048ca52/B43 E456D7A8EEA87802572250052B81B?opendocument [Accessed: 26th February 2008].

National Council on Crime and Delinquency (2006) *Relationship Between Staff Turnover, Child Welfare System Functioning and Recurrent Child Abuse*, Houston, Corner Stones for Kids.

National Social Work Qualifications Board (2000) *Social Work Posts in Ireland on 1 September 1999*, Dublin, National Social Work Qualifications Board.

National Social Work Qualifications Board (2002) *Social Work Posts in Ireland on 1 September 2001*, Dublin, National Social Work Qualifications Board.

National Social Work Qualifications Board (2004a) *Induction Framework for Newly Qualified and Non-Nationally Qualified Social Workers*, Dublin, National Social Work Qualifications Board.

National Social Work Qualifications Board (2004b) *Induction Framework for Newly Qualified and Non-Nationally Qualified Social Workers* [Online], Dublin, NSWQB, Available from: http://www.nswqb.ie/downl/nswqb_framework04.pdf [Accessed: 14th August 2007].

National Social Work Qualifications Board (2006) *Social Work Posts in Ireland on 1st September 2005*, Dublin, National Social Work Qualifications Board.

National Social Work Qualifications Board (2007) *e-mail correspondence - 2001 & 2005 Dataset Query*, Dublin, National Social Work Qualifications Board.

Nissly, J. A., Mor Barak, M. E. and Levin, A. (2005) 'Stress, Social Support, and Workers' Intention to Leave Their Jobs in Public Child Welfare', *Administration in Social Work*, 29(1), pp. 79-100.

Nolan, B. (2008) *Tomorrow's Child*, Dublin, Barnardos.

O'Brien, C. (2007) 'Children at risk of abuse 'not getting checked'', *Irish Times*, Dublin.

O'Brien, C. (2009a) 'Children at risk as poor resources hamper services', *The Irish Times*, Dublin, The Irish Times.

O'Brien, C. (2009b) 'Up to €420,000 spent on child placements a year', *The Irish Times*, Dublin, Irish Times.

O'Connell, P. J., Russell, H., Williams, J. and Blackwell, S. (2004) *The Changing Workplace: A Survey of Employees' Views and Experiences*, Dublin, Economic and Social Research Unit/National Centre for Partnership and Performance.

O'Mahony, C., Shore, C., Burns, K. and Parkes, A. (2012) 'Child Care Proceedings in the District Court: What do we Really Know?', *Irish Journal of Family Law* 49, 15(2), pp. 1-14.

O'Toole, F. (2008) *Half-truths about public service and pay serve us ill* [Online], Dublin, The Irish Times, Available from: http://www.irishtimes.com/newspaper/opinion/2008/0909/1220629652929.html [Accessed: 2nd January 2009].

Obholzer, A. (1994) 'Managing social anxieties in public sector organizations', in Obholzer, A. and Roberts, V. Z. (eds.), *The unconscious at work: Individual and organizational stress in human services*, London, Routledge.

OECD Observer (2005) *GDP and GNI* [Online], OECD Observer, Available from: http://www.oecdobserver.org/news/fullstory.php/aid/1507/GDP_and_GNI.html [Accessed: 12th November 2005].

Office of the Minister for Children (2006) *State of the Nation's Children*, Dublin, Stationery Office.

Office of the Minister for Children (2007) *The Agenda for Children's Service: Reflective Questions for Front-Line Service Managers and Practitioners*, Dublin, Stationery Office.

Office of the Minister for Children and Youth Affairs (2008) *National Review of Compliance with Children First: National Guidelines for the Protection and Welfare of Children*, Dublin, The Stationery Office.

Office of the Minister for Children and Youth Affairs (2009) *Report of the Commission to Inquire into Child Abuse, 2009. Implementation Plan*, Dublin, Department of Health and Children.

Ofsted (2008) *Joint area review Haringey children's services authority area. Review of services for children and young people, with particular reference to safeguarding*, United Kingdom, Ofsted, Healthcare Commission and HM Inspectorate of Constabulary.

Oireachtas (2006) *Joint Committee on Child Protection* [Online], Dublin, Office of the Houses of the Oireachtas, Available from:
http://www.oireachtas.ie/viewdoc.asp?fn=/documents/Committees29thDail/Child_Protection.htm [Accessed: 24th November 2006].

Oldham, G. R. (1996) 'Job Design', in Cooper, C. L. and Robertson, I. T. (eds.), *International Review of Industrial and Organizational Psychology - Volume 11*, West Sussex, John Wiley & Sons.

Ombudsman for Children (2006a) *Report of the Ombudsman for Children to The Oireachtas Joint Committee on Health and Child Protection on Complaints Received about child protection in Ireland* [Online], Dublin, Ombudsman for Children, Available from:
http://www.oco.ie/GetAttachment.aspx?id=76f1cb1d-1f31-4b1a-868c-3dcfc79fc46c [Accessed: 21st February 2008].

Ombudsman for Children (2006b) *Submission to the Joint Committee on Child Protection* [Online], Dublin, Ombudsman for Children, Available from:
http://www.oco.ie/GetAttachment.aspx?id=76f1cb1d-1f31-4b1a-868c-3dcfc79fc46c [Accessed: 21st February 2008].

Organisation for Economic Co-operation and Development (2005) *Economic Review of Sweden 2005: Best Practice for Reducing Sickness and Disability Absences* [Online], Organisation for Economic Co-operation and Development, Available from:
http://www.oecd.org/document/45/0,2340,en_2649_201185_34971821_1_1_1_1,00.html [Accessed: 28th June 2005].

Oswald, A. (2002) *Are You Happy at Work? Job Satisfaction and Work-Life Balance in the US and Europe* [Online], Available from:
http://www2.warwick.ac.uk/fac/soc/economics/staff/faculty/oswald/finalwarwickwbseventpapernov2002.pdf [Accessed: 15/1/'04].

Parent-Thirion, A., Fernández Macías, E., Hurley, J. and Vermeylen, G. (2007) *Fourth European Working Conditions Survey* [Online], Dublin, European Foundation for the Improvement of Living and Working Conditions, Available from: http://www.eurofound.europa.eu/publications/htmlfiles/ef0698.htm [Accessed: 16th June 2008].

Parker, S. and Wall, T. (1998) *Job and Work Design: Organizing Work to Promote Well-Being and Effectiveness*, Thousand Oaks, Sage.

Parker, S. K. (2002) 'Designing Jobs to Enhance Well-Being and Performance', in Warr, P. (ed.), *Psychology at Work*, London, Penguin Books.

Peach, J. and Horner, N. (2007) 'Using supervision: Support or surveillance?', in Lymbery, M. and Postle, K. (eds.), *Social Work: A Companion to Learning*, London, Sage.

Phillips, J. J. and O'Connell, A. O. (2003) *Managing Employee Retention: A Strategic Accountability Approach*, Burlington, Elsevier.

Powell, M. J. and York, R. O. (1992) 'Turnover in county public welfare agencies', *The Journal of Applied Social Sciences*, 16(2), pp. 111-127.

Prospects (2008) *Social worker: Salaries and Conditions* [Online], Available from: http://www.prospects.ac.uk/cms/ShowPage/Home_page/Explore_types_of_job s/Types_of_Job/p!eipaL?state=showocc&idno=88&pageno=2 [Accessed: 30th May 2008].

Pryce, J. G., Shackelford, K. K. and Pryce, D. H. (2007) *Secondary Traumatic Stress and the Child Welfare Professional*, Chicago, Lyceum.

Punch, K. F. (1998) *Introduction to Social Research: Quantitative and Qualitative Approaches*, London, Sage.

Raferty, M. and O'Sullivan, E. (1999) *States Of Fear*, Dublin, RTÉ.

Rayner, G. and Allen, N. (2008) *Baby P: Haringey Council 'broke its own rules on caseloads for social workers'* [Online], Telegraph, Available from: http://www.telegraph.co.uk/news/uknews/3473893/Baby-P-Haringey-Council-broke-its-own-rules-on-caseloads-for-social-workers.html [Accessed: 7th December 2008].

Reagh, R. (1994) 'Public Child Welfare Professionals-Those Who Stay', *Journal of Sociology and Social Welfare*, 21(3), pp. 69-78.

Reder, P., Duncan, S. and Gray, M. (1993) *Beyond Blame: Child Abuse Tragedies Revisited*, London, Routledge.

Richards, L. and Morse, J. M. (2007) *Readme First for a User's Guide to Qualitative Methods(2nd edition)*, London, Sage.

Richardson, V. (2004) 'Children and Social Policy', in Quin, S., Kennedy, P., Matthews, A. and Kiely, G. (eds.), *Contemporary Irish Social Policy* Dublin, UCD Press.

Ritchie, J. and Lewis, J. (eds) (2003) *Qualitative Research Practice: A Guide for Social Science Students and Researchers*, London, Sage.

Ritchie, J., Lewis, J. and Elam, G. (2003) 'Designing and selecting samples', in Ritchie, J. and Lewis, J. (eds.), *Qualitative Research Practice: A Guide for Social Science Students and Researchers*, London, Sage.

Robin, S. C. and Hollister, C. D. (2002) 'Career oaths and contributions of four cohorts of IV-E funded MSW child welfare graduates', *Journal of Health & Social Policy*, 15(3/4), pp. 53-68.

Rønnestad, M. H. and Skovholt, T. M. (2003) 'The Journey of the Counselor and Therapist: Research Findings and Perspectives on Professional Development', *Journal of Career Development*, 30(1), pp. 5-44.

Rose, M. (2003) 'Good deal, bad deal? job satisfaction in occupations', *Work, Employment and Society*, 17(3), pp. 503-530.

RTÉ (2006) *RTÉ News at one interview with Seamus Mannion (16th August 2006)* [Online], RTÉ Radio 1, Available from: http://www.rte.ie/radio1/newsatone/ [Accessed: 16th August 2006].

RTÉ (2008a) *Morning Ireland interview with Minister of State for Children and Youth Affairs Barry Andrews (13th May 2008)* [Online], Dublin, RTE, Available from: http://www.rte.ie/radio1/morningireland [Accessed: 20th May 2008].

RTÉ (2008b) *Prime Time (13th May 2008)* [Online], Dublin, RTÉ, Available from: http://www.rte.ie/news/2008/0513/primetime.html [Accessed: 14th May 2008].

RTÉ (2008c) *Prime Time Investigates: In Harms Way* [Online], Dublin, RTÉ, Available from: http://www.rte.ie/news/2008/0512/primetimeinvestigates.html [Accessed: 12th May 2008].

Ruch, G. (2007) 'Reflective practice in contemporary child care social work: The role of containment', *British Journal of Social Work*, 37(4), pp. 659-680.

Rushton, A. and Nathan, J. (1996) 'The supervision of child protection work', *British Journal of Social Work*, 26, pp. 357-374.

Ryan, S. (2009) *Commission to Inquire into Child Abuse Report (Volumes I - V)*, Dublin, Stationery Office.

Rycraft, J. R. (1994) 'The party isn't over: The agency role in the retention of public child welfare caseworkers', *Social Work*, 39(1), pp. 75-80.

Rycraft, J. R. (2000) *The Survivors: A qualitative study of the retention of public child welfare workers (PhD Thesis)*, Denver, UMI.

Samantrai, K. (1992) 'Factors in the decision to leave: Retaining social workers with MSWs in public child welfare', *Social Work*, 37(5), pp. 454-458.

Sarantakos, S. (2005) *Social Research(3rd Edition)*, Hampshire, Palgrave.

Seidman, I. E. (1991) *Interviewing as Qualitative Research: A Guide for Researchers in Education and the Social Sciences*, New York, Teachers College Press.

Shaw, I. and Gould, N. (2001) *Qualitative Research in Social Work*, London, Sage.

Silverman, D. (2004) *Interpreting Qualitative Data: Methods for Analysing Talk, Text and Interaction(2nd Edition)*, London, Sage.

Sinclair, I., Baker, C., Wilson, K. and Gibbs, I. (2005) *Foster Children: Where They Go and How They Get On*, London, Jessica Kingsley Publishers.

Sinclair, R., Bamsey, S. and Mainey, A. (2003) *Staff Qualifications, Retention and Morale in Residential Child Care* [Online], National Children's Bureau, Available from: [Accessed: 22nd February 2002].

Skehill, C. (1999) *The Nature of Social Work in Ireland: A Historical Perspective*, Ceredigion, Edwin Mellen Press.

Skehill, C. (2004) *History of the Present of Child Protection and Welfare Social Work in Ireland*, New York, Edwin Mellen Press.

Smith, B. D. (2005) 'Job retention in child welfare: Effects of perceived organizational support, supervisor support, and intrinsic job value', *Children and Youth Services Review*, 27, pp. 153-169.

Snape, D. and Spence, L. (2003) 'The Foundation of Qualitative Research', in Ritchie, J. and Lewis, J. (eds.), *Qualitative Research Practice: A Guide for Social Science Students and Researchers*, London, Sage.

Social Information Systems (2005) *National Workload Management Pilot data Analysis. Report 1: Data Analysis*, Social Information Systems Ltd.

Social Services Inspectorate (2001) *Annual Report: Social Services Inspectorate 2001*, Dublin, Social Services Inspectorate.

Social Services Inspectorate (2003) *Report on the Monitoring of the Implementation of Children First National Guidelines for the Protection and Welfare of Children* [Online], Dublin, Health Information Quality Authority, Available from: http://www.hiqa.ie/media/pdfs/ssi_inspection_reports/childrens_first.pdf [Accessed: 26th February 2008].

Social Services Inspectorate (2006) *The Management of Behaviour: Key Lessons from the Inspection of High Support Units* [Online], Dublin, HIQA, Available from: http://www.hiqa.ie/media/pdfs/ssi_inspection_reports/overviewhsu.pdf [Accessed: 26th February 2008].

Söderfeldt, M., Söderfelt, B. and Warg, L.-E. (1995) 'Burnout in Social Work', *Social Work*, 40(5), pp. 638-646.

Stalker, C. A., Harvey, C., Frensch, K., Mandell, D. and Adams, G. R. (2007a) 'Confirmatory Factor Analysis of the Maslach Burnout Inventory: A Replication with Canadian Child Welfare Workers', *Journal of Public Child Welfare*, 1(3), pp. 77-94.

Stalker, C. A., Mandell, D., Frensch, K. M., Harvey, C. and Wright, M. (2007b) 'Child welfare workers who are exhausted Yet satisfied with their jobs: how do they do it?', *Child and Family Social Work*, 12(2), pp. 182-191.

Stanley, J. and Goddard, C. (2002) *In the Firing Line: Violence and Power in Child Protection Work*, West Sussex, Wiley.

Stanley, L. and Wise, S. (1993) *Breaking Out Again: Feminist Ontology and Epistemology*, London, Routledge.

Steel, R. P. (2004) 'Job Markers and Turnover Decisions', in Griffeth, R. and Hom, P. (eds.), *Innovative theory and empirical research on employee turnover*, Connecticut, Information age publishing.

Stiglitz, J. (2003) *Globalisation and its Discontents*, London, Allen Lane.

Strolin, J. S., McCarthy, M. and Caringi, J. (2007) 'Causes and effects of child welfare workforce turnover: Current state of knowledge and future directions', *Journal of Public Child Welfare*, 1(2), pp. 29-52.

Svendsen, L. (2008) *Work*, Stocksfield, Acumen.

Swift, T. (2007) *Personal correspondence: State of Rhode Island Classified Annual Salaries Schedule A00 (Effective June 24, 2007.*

Tham, P. (2007) 'Why are they leaving? Factors affecting intention to leave among social workers in child welfare', *British Journal of Social Work*, 37(7), pp. 1225-1246.

The Scottish Parliament Information Centre (2002) *Social Care Workforce Development* [Online], The Scottish Parliament, Available from: http://www.scottish.parliament.uk/business/research/pdf_res_brief/sb02-38.pdf [Accessed: 1st April 2003].

Thomas, G. and James, D. (2006) 'Reinventing grounded theory: some questions about theory, ground and discovery', *British Educational Research Journal*, 32(6), pp. 767-795.

Thompson, N. (2000) *Understanding Social Work: Preparing for Practice*, Hampshire, Macmillan Press.

Thompson, N. (2002) *People Skills*, Basingstoke, Palgrave.

Thompson, N., Stradling, S., Murphy, M. and O'Neill, P. (1996) 'Stress and Organizational Culture', *British Journal of Social Work*, 26, pp. 647-665.

Turnbull, S. (2002) 'Social construction research and theory building', *Advances in Developing Human Resources*, 4(3), pp. 317-334.

Um, M. Y. and Harrison, D. F. (1998) 'Role stressors, burnout, mediators, and job satisfaction: A stress-strain-outcome model and an empirical test', *Social Work Research*, 22(2), pp. 100-115.

United Nations Development Programme (2005) *Human Development Report 2005: International Cooperation at a Crossroads. Aid, trade and security in an unequal world* [Online], United Nations Development Programme, Available from: http://hdr.undp.org/reports/global/2005/ [Accessed: 12th November 2005].

United States General Accounting Office (2003) *Child Welfare: HHS Could Play a Greater Role in Helping Child Welfare Agencies Recruit and Retain Staff* Washington, GAO.

Van Knippenberg, D. and Sleebos, E. (2006) 'Organizational identification versus organizational commitment: Self-definition, social exchange, and job attitudes', *Journal of Organizational Behavior*, 27, pp. 571-584.

Vandervort, F. E., Pott Gonzalez, R. and Coulborn Faller, K. (2007) 'Legal ethics and high child welfare worker turnover: An unexplored connection', *Children and Youth Services Review*, Advance Internet copy, pp. 1-18.

Warman, A. and Jackson, E. (2007) 'Recruiting and retaining children and families' social workers: The potential of work discussion groups', *Journal of Social Work Practice*, 21(1), pp. 35-48.

Waters, J. (2007) 'Unfettered power of a faceless few', *The Irish Times*, Dublin.

Watson, T. J. (2003) *Sociology, Work and Industry(4th edition)*, London, Routledge.

Wayman, S. (2008) 'Children grow best in families', *The Irish Times Health Plus*, Dublin.

Weaver, D. and Chang, J. (2004) 'The Retention of California's Public Child Welfare Workers', 2008(31st January 2008).

Westbrook, T. M., Ellis, J. and Ellet, A. J. (2006) 'Improving Retention Among Public Child Welfare Workers: What Can we learn from the insights and experiences of committed survivors?', *Administration in Social Work*, 30(4), pp. 37-62.

Western Health Board (1996) *Kelly: A Child is Dead. Interim Report of the Joint Committee on the Family*, Dublin, Government Publications Office.

White, V. and Harris, J. (2007) 'Management', in Lymbery, M. and Postle, K. (eds.), *Social Work: A Companion to Learning*, London, Sage.

Willot, S. and Griffin, C. (1999) 'Building your own lifeboat: Working-class male offenders talk about economic crime', *British Journal of Social Psychology*, 38, pp. 445-460.

Woodcock, J. and Dixon, J. (2005) 'Professional Ideologies and Preferences in Social Work: A British Study in Global Perspective', *British Journal of Social Work*, 35, pp. 953-973.

Yao, X., Lee, T. W., Mitchell, T. R., Burton, J. P. and Sablynski, C. J. (2004) 'Job embeddedness: current research and future directions', in Griffeth, R. and Hom, P. (eds.), *Innovative theory and empirical research on employee turnover*, Connecticut, Information age publishing.

www.ingramcontent.com/pod-product-compliance
Lightning Source LLC
Chambersburg PA
CBHW032123020426
42334CB00016B/1045